Drive or Die:
A true story of addiction, murder and hope

By Mark E. Tucker
With Dan Richman

On the cover: Portland, Oregon's Burnside Avenue

ISBN: 1511928263
ISBN-13: 978-1511928267
www.CreateSpace.com/5462362
Available from Amazon.com and other bookstores

To all victims of violent crimes,
to the addict who still suffers
and to the child who has no choice

1

Note to Readers

This is a true story. And not for the faint of heart. The things I've seen, the places I've been and the anomalies that surround these events are nothing short of bizarre.

Until December 28, 2012, when I quit using, I'd been a heroin addict for 22 years. I know that makes me a criminal in the eyes of the law and of many ordinary people. But I must make this crystal clear: even though I have had 40 misdemeanor convictions, none were violent in nature. They were moving violations, shopliftings, or possessions of paraphernalia. I've been convicted of 11 felonies, too. But again, none were violent: all were possession crimes, for drugs or property.

I'm not a violent person. Not now, not ever. I've done 12 years of jail and prison time in all, but the violence I'll be describing in this book shocked me, and still does, as much as anyone. I was just an addict, sick and miserable much of the time.

One day in 2005 I was praised nationwide as a hero for helping capture the eighth most wanted man in America. I thought I was eligible for a $100,000 reward, and I was put up in a plush suite at a Red Lion Hotel by U.S. Marshals. Literally the next day I was whisked away to a holding cell in Kennewick, Washington, charged with first-degree rendering criminal assistance in a double homicide. I served five years and paid a fine of $70,000 for a crime I didn't commit.

This book tells my story of the events between mid-July 2005 and the end of 2007, when the appeals of the length of my sentence and the amount of the fines against me were denied. For the most part, it was hand-written on random pieces of borrowed paper with a three-inch golf pencil. It has been through four county jails, four penitentiaries, multiple chain buses (transports), two states, work release and then to the streets, where it was subjected to a whole other battery of abuse. Its pages have been ripped into a hundred little pieces by an angry girlfriend, taped back together, lost in storage units and garages, and even thrown away.

Since the first page was written, I have been back to prison three times, detox, several clean-and-sober houses, treatments, tents, couches and multiple county jails. It took a mass of self-induced adversity to bring me to a point in my life where all my options were exhausted. To a point of defeat and utter hopelessness. To a point where I was literally on my knees, begging my Creator to give me an exit strategy.

Perhaps this book will serve as a wakeup call for addicts who still suffer. And more importantly, it can show that **recovery is possible**. That no matter how far down the scale of life you have dropped, as long as you are able to draw breath, there is still hope.

For reasons beyond my scope of understanding, I managed to live through the cataclysmic events I am about to share with you. So ride with me, if you will, on a journey into a wide-awake nightmare.

Some names have been changed to protect privacy. All dialogue is accurate to the best of my recollection. --*M.E.T*

Part 1
I meet Juan

Chapter 1

The police cars pulled up to Vancouver's Red Lion Hotel. The Red Lion sits on the Columbia River in that southwestern Washington city, and it's one of the best hotels there. *These guys are really going crazy being nice to us*, I thought as Carrie Anne Blackford and I got out of our respective police cars and entered the lobby. Carrie was a victim of circumstance who'd been traveling on a long, nightmare car ride with Juan pointing a gun at us while I drove.

"Juan." Ugh. I never wanted to hear that name again.

Detectives escorted us to our separate rooms. Mine had plush carpeting, a king-sized bed, a coffee maker, a PlayStation and a decent view of the river. My detective sat in a chair in the corner of the room and picked up a magazine. I was too tired to care that he was intruding on my privacy. My head hit the fluffy pillows, my body hit the firm, plush mattress, and out I went. I had craved sleep so badly. For the past 14 days, I had slept perhaps 20 hours total.

The next morning, I was escorted to a Sheriff's car in front of the hotel.

"I hear you're the one who called 9-1-1," said the blonde female sergeant driving. "You're pretty much a hero, then."

Many people agreed with that assessment. I'd been called a hero and congratulated by countless cops over the past few days. I expected "America's Most Wanted" would be eager to award me $100,000 for information leading to the capture of James T. Moran, also known as Juan Martinez, America's 8th most wanted criminal at the time. He was a notorious gangster, associated with the feared 18th Street Gang. His street name was "The Grizz," but for most of our acquaintance I knew him only as "Juan."

It was August 6, 2005. Just five days before, on August 1, 2005, Juan had apparently shot and killed 52-year-old Linda Moreno and her 17-year-old daughter, Danielle, in their Kennewick, Washington, home. It was a random home invasion, though he told me at the time that Linda Moreno was his aunt.

I'd been driving Juan around the Pacific Northwest for days. For most of that time, he was constantly threatening to kill both Carrie and me. I was sitting outside in a car when he allegedly committed the Moreno murders, and I drove him away after the incident. But I had no certain knowledge that Juan had committed the crime. And with his gun to my head, I wasn't going to quiz him too hard. Carrie and I were virtually his prisoners.

I didn't know it for sure until after I was arrested, weeks later, but Juan was also wanted for the July 9, 2004 murders of Glenn Dale Carr, 57, and his wife, Debra Jolene Carr, 50, at their home in Kennewick. The deceased couple were the parents of Juan's children's mom.

Within a few hours of sitting down to tell my story to the Kennewick homicide unit, I was being read my *Miranda* rights. As I started to withdraw from heroin, my nose and eyes began dripping. I told my story as briefly as I could, leaving out big chunks that might have made a huge difference in my future.

Within one hour more I was stripped of all my clothes and put into an ill-fitting blue two-piece outfit with the words "Clark Co. Jail" stenciled across the back of the shirt. I was charged with one count of rendering criminal assistance in the first degree -- helping Juan commit the murders, essentially.

I went from hero to zero -- or rather, to criminal -- in 24 hours. The next day, it was our pictures that were plastered all over the newspaper, the TV -- and, ironically, America's Most Wanted.

As I sat in my cell, there was a pounding in my chest. Now what? There was no one to talk to, no one to confide in. Loneliness pinched my throat. I was still trying to figure out why I was in jail.

Fear dripped from me like drops of sweat. I was saturated with it. Fear of retaliation from the notorious 18th Street Gang. Juan was well connected. LA's biggest criminal organization, the 18th Street Gang is renowned for its extreme violence, even toward its own members when they step out of line. And then there were the charges I was now faced with. But somehow I was still alive, if only for a short time.

In a haze I grabbed my little pencil, pulled my mattress back for a flat surface and positioned myself to write. Someday, somehow, someone was going to read my story.

I began to write . . .

Chapter 2

My name is Mark Evan Tucker. I was born May 14, 1974, in Seattle. I was one of 10 children, the youngest born to my parents. Both were divorced when they married each other. My mother, Linda, brought two boys into the marriage, and my father, Bill, brought two boys and a girl. When I was one year old, my mom went blind. When I was two years old, my family moved to Whidbey Island from Seattle. Whidbey is a 55-mile-long, skinny island in Puget Sound, about 35 miles northwest of Seattle. It's home to a naval base at its north end and countless cows, sheep and horses elsewhere.

My dad was a daily drinker and a workaholic, so he wasn't home much. He ruled his family with an iron fist, though he always meant well. My mom left the house one day when I was four years old, packing up the elephant cookie jar. As a kid, you know where the goodies are, and mom used to bake cookies and put them in the elephant. She moved to Seattle, and then to Tacoma, about 35 miles south of Seattle.

I deeply resented her departure and took out my hostility on the babysitters my dad hired to take care of us while he was at work every day. I broke windows and screamed at them. I think we went through all the babysitters on Whidbey Island.

My father would come home to get the news of my misbehavior. His punishments were always swift and severe.

When I was six, my father married for the third time. His latest wife was Janet , who was 24 -- a year younger than my sister. He and Janet had four more children together, bringing to 10 the total number of mouths to feed. Now the Tucker tribe consisted, from oldest to youngest, of Merrilyn, Mike, Matt, Mark, Megan, Molly, Marshall and Miles. My older brothers from my mom and a different dad were Allen and Keith Starkey. At one point, eight of us lived in a one-bedroom house.

I played every sport my school had to offer, including baseball, basketball, football and soccer, and excelled at all of them, always playing first-string. My dad, whom I call Pops, had been playing or coaching baseball for years. He was a Korean War vet who smoked Lucky Strikes, which I began stealing from him at age 12. My jock friends ostracized me for smoking, but that just drove me to a different crowd. I also started drinking about this age, though stealing one of Pop's beers would always bring a beating with the stick of my choice.

During my 14th winter, while in 8th grade, my best friend and I began breaking into the numerous unoccupied summer houses on Whidbey's shoreline, in search of booze. My first arrest, that same winter, was for breaking into a house, stealing the liquor and holding a raucous party there. I got sentenced to 500 hours of community services and paying $700 restitution. My community service was working with the school janitor, so all the students thought I was his assistant.

Eighth grade was also when I took my first hit of LSD. My father reacted predictably -- with his customary anger -- and I decided I would no longer be subject to his rule. I told him I wanted to move in with my mother, in Tacoma. Since she was blind, I knew I'd be able to get away with anything. Then I left Whidbey for Tacoma.

I fit right into Tacoma's "stoner" crowd. The streets were rife with gangs that had overflowed from California. Drugs and violence littered the streets. I was home.

My after-school activities usually included scoring a couple of 40-ounce bottles of Old English malt liquor, a bag of weed and a sheet of acid. On weekends my friends and I would get into the cocaine and crank. Money I made from selling acid paid for beer, other drugs, and tickets to punk-rock shows.

My poor mom. When she was gone, traveling throughout Washington State to help other blind people get rehabilitated and back to work, a friend and I would have out-of-control parties in her apartment. Bullet holes through the walls, kegs through the back door, broken clown collections meticulously glued together while on multiple hits of acid. Those clowns never looked the same.

At age 15 I was arrested again, this time for my first felony, a burglary. I was put under house arrest until my next court date. But a few days later I got arrested for drinking while under house arrest, and I spent four months in Tacoma's juvenile-detention center. I also underwent a 30-day detox treatment.

I shot up -- cocaine -- for the first time that year, at age 15. Because of my dedication to drugs, I had pretty much missed my entire sophomore year in high school. My mom also kicked me out of her house for breaking the house rules, so every day after attending alternative high school, I had to find a place to spend the night.

At 17, before the beginning of my senior year in high school, I moved in with my older brother Mike and his girlfriend, Beth. I spent the summer consuming sheets of acid, smoking sherm sticks (joints dipped in PCP), and drinking gallons of Old English. Everyone said I'd never graduate high school, but despite my drug-ridden lifestyle, I was determined to prove them wrong.

I had to find a ride 20 miles to school every day. To make up missing credits, I attended extra early-morning classes at my high school and evening classes at a community college. I was also working two jobs: at Radio Shack and at a Sheri's restaurant. I ended up graduating with a 3.9 GPA, much to my relief and happiness.

Not that that would save me from myself. I got my first DUI (driving under the influence) at 17. That's also when I started using heroin. I had this ego that wanted to be a connoisseur of all drugs, and heroin was no exception. I was all for it. All the cool people were doing it, and nobody smoked it. We went straight to the needle. Since I'd already shot drugs, shooting heroin sounded great to me.

Once I got a taste for heroin, all other drugs became secondary. Not that I didn't continue to use crack, crank and hallucinogens, but heroin was my new escape. I did it a few times a week. There was always a user worse-off than me to make me feel I was still in control. With friends who did heroin, it was like we had a secret society. We had an amazing escape. My whole family could have been killed and if my system was saturated with "the business," then there was no pain, no remorse, no guilt, no anger. I was no longer a hostage of my childhood. The feeling of being a failure and of not living up to my father's high expectations for me slipped away in an undertow of chemical bliss. I no longer felt like I was going to burst into flames and the earth would swallow me as I walked down the street.

Most of my friends were in bands, and I met a lot of influential musicians during this time. Among them were Curt Cobain (Nirvana); Courtney Love (hole); Layne Staley, Mike Star and Jerry Cantrell (all of Alice in Chains); and Chris Cornell (Soundgarden). Most of my interactions with these people were drug related. It was 1992 and the grunge scene was in full swing.

I moved back up to Whidbey Island after I graduated high school and began culinary school in the winter of 1992. I had a dream of traveling the world on a cruise ship and wowing people with my food presentations and ice sculptures.

For culinary school, I commuted to Capitol Hill, a neighborhood in Seattle, every morning from Whidbey Island. My first class was at 7:00 a.m. A lot of my friends lived on Capitol Hill, and they would meet me after school and want to help me spend my student loan. We would score some heroin and I would head back to the island.

I watched as my friends became homeless, strung out and "boosting" (stealing for dope) to feed their habit. I remember saying to myself, "Well, at least I'm not *that* bad."

I ran into a guy who sold dope on Capitol Hill, and he would meet me between classes to sell me my fix. He turned out to be Lane Staley's dad.

After a couple of quarters of culinary school, I was so strung out I couldn't make it through a day without leaving class to go "get well" (shoot up). Instead of getting a degree in culinary arts, I got a degree in heroin arts. Come to find out that didn't pay very well. Soon, I too, found myself living on the streets and stealing to supply my habit. This went on for years.

I lived on the streets of Tacoma and Seattle, Washington; and in Riverside, Pomona and Oceanside, California. I lived in hotels, under bridges, in cars and in abandoned buildings. During this time I did manage to have short intervals of stability. I worked at my dad's business building furniture, did a lot of construction and cooked at many different restaurants. I even got a job at UPS. Unfortunately, I had a hard time being a functional addict. Heroin always took me out of the game. Trying to work while dope-sick (withdrawing) is no easy task. My moral compass was starting to point south.

In 2004 I moved back to Whidbey and moved in with my dad. I got a job at a local restaurant and tried to manage my habit -- an impossible task. I started to sell heroin to pay for my addiction, and when summer came I started working with my dad refurbishing decks. By the end of that summer I had saved about $10,000. Things were looking up!

Chapter 3
Mid-July 2005
Portland, Oregon

Flash-forward about one year, to mid-July 2005 in Portland, Oregon.

9

The sun had given birth to a magnificently bright day in the City of Roses. I was broke, 32 years old and searching the streets of Portland for the temporary cure to the addictive disease that was stripping me of mind, body and spirit.

It was scorching out. But I was cold, shaking like a paint mixer. It had been more than 24 hours since I'd done any heroin. My nose dripped and my eyes watered as I gripped the steering wheel like I was wringing out a wet towel.

The MAX, Portland's light-rail system, rumbled by me, and the city was streaming with activity as I scanned the streets of Old Town. I was looking for someone who could remedy my sickness, but it had been some time since I'd lived in Portland. In the 1990s, I used to get stuff near the Burnside Bridge. Now all that had changed.

With me were my younger sister, Molly; my girlfriend, "Sara"; and Eric, a friend from Whidbey Island. I was driving a red BMW 325i two-door Molly had given me. We were all miserable. And looking for some action.

For some reason, I got an adrenaline rush when I got to a city's run-down areas, like I'm a tourist seeing the Grand Canyon for the first time. The mystery that lingered in the alleys and the danger that lurks there pumped up my endorphins.

"Babe, you don't know where to get anything, do you?" I asked Sara. I knew she didn't know, but I asked anyway. She really didn't fit into my street life, but I loved her.

I was strung out. Rotting from the inside, but so what? Fear, guilt and shame were just words. And anybody close to me was along for the ride, whether they knew it or not.

I drove up and down Burnside but saw nothing and no one who showed promise. A few more hours and I'd have to lie down somewhere and suffer it out. I had some money, but no connection to give it to. My mind was frazzled. I was ready to snap.

"Goddamn! Where is everybody?" I yelled.

The car thing wasn't working so I decided to hoof it. It had been years since I'd run on the streets and as I said, things were not as they were in the 90's. Then, only the Saturday market and a few tourists camouflaged the blatant drug deals that were going down.

The hot zones were the Skidmore fountain, under the Burnside Bridge, and the waterfront. You could hit the bridge, score, and be well away in a matter of minutes. After 9/11 it all changed.

I scanned every alley and walked all the areas I had once known. Nothing.

I was getting frantic. Finally I ran into an overweight man with a round pock-marked face.

"Hey, native!" I shouted to get his attention. "Man, I'm hurtin' bad. You know where I can get some dope?"

There comes a time when you gotta take drastic measures to get results. And when you're on the street, the results vary from getting robbed to getting busted -- or maybe getting what you need.

Either way, if you're a new face on the block you're going to get the run-around. On "the blade" (the area of a city where drugs, gang-bangers and prostitutes can most easily be found), you have to prove you're street savvy before you're removed from the suspect category and promoted to a regular. Usually you can display some track marks, spout some war stories or drop a few names.

I had peeled my shirt off while in mid conversation with the native, exposing my slender, sun-burnt frame.

"Whoa! You're really goin' through it, aren't you, brother?" the native said in a slow methodical drawl. I didn't mind the sympathy and hoped it would encourage him to try harder to find what I needed.

"Yeah, it's all bad. Listen, I'll hook you up with a beer if you can help me get on."

My movements had become sudden and jerky. "Your nose, brother." He pointed to the long drip of snot dangling from the tip of my beak. I quickly wiped it off with the back of my hand and gave a sniff.

"Thanks, bro. My nose is pretty long, so I never know what's goin' on out there."

He smiled. "Yeah. It is pretty long, white boy." We both laughed, and he agreed to help me.

"My cousin Flea has a habit. She knows where to get shit." he said, and slowly looked around as if she was close by. "She usually don't go far from Burnside."

Now that I had a target, I scanned the streets like a sniper. "Damn, where is everybody?" I said.

"Cops got 'em spooked," he replied. After a few spins around the block he noticed the track marks on my legs. I was sporting my standard uniform -- black Dickies shorts, with white socks pulled up as far as they would go to avoid questions -- but they had fallen down from all the walking, exposing the brown scars from blown-out veins that covered both legs from my ankles to my knees. I wore a chain that bounced from my wallet to my belt and some fresh black-and-white DC skate shoes.

"White boy, what happened to your legs?"

"Dog bites, my friend," I said confidently.

"Damn, brother! That was one angry dog." He shook his head.

"He didn't want to let go." We left it at that and continued our search.

After another stroll up Burnside he spotted his cousin. My sickness subsided slightly just knowing we were on the right track. His cousin was a skinny woman in her early 40's: long black hair, high cheek bones, dark brown skin and a frisky attitude. A few of her teeth were missing and the remaining ones were black with decay. You could see the toll the streets had exacted from the lines that cracked her face.

"Hey, girl!" I said with a nod of my head. "Your cousin said you might know where to get some dope."

"You know this motherfucka?" she said, looking at her relative.

"Chill, Flea. He's cool. This white boy's sick. Plus he said he'd get me a beer."

"I'm Red. Just touched down from Seattle and I'm sick as hell. I'll hook you up if you can score for me," I said.

She looked me up and down and shook her head. "God damn. I just got back from over there and it's hot as fuck. I'm not walkin' back." Almost as an afterthought, she said: "How much money you got, white boy?"

"Twenty." I was a few dollars short, but I'd cross that bridge later. I knew she didn't really want to help me, so I had to upgrade my incentive plan.

"I'll buy you a beer too," I said, and suddenly she agreed to score for me.

"Ain't this some shit?" she said, bobbing her head from side to side. "Alright, let's get you well."

I started to run and yelled back at them, "I'm going to get the car; I'll be right back. Don't leave!"

Sara had gone to Portland's Pioneer Square to continue the search, so I grabbed my sister and Eric and said, "Get in the back." I didn't want to attract attention on a busy downtown street.

I sped west on Burnside, pulled to the curb, reached over and swung the door open. The two natives piled in the front. We were riding "dirty" for sure – no seat belts, junk strewn about the car and empty St.

Ides Malt Liquor bottles on the floor. It was around 2:30 in the afternoon and the sun was frying the city streets as well as the interior of my car. The humidity irritated us all. We crossed the Burnside Bridge and came to the corner of Burnside and MLK.

"Awright, Red, up two more blocks and take a right. My uncle should be right around there," Flea told me as she pointed to the right. Just off Burnside behind a Shuck's auto supply was the area known as Little Mexico.

"Bingo," I said as we approached. There were numerous strange-looking characters roaming around. I felt like I had just won a casino jackpot. This is what I loved. Chaos and disorder.

Empty beer bottles and trash littered the streets. Where most people saw discontent and desperation, I saw hope and tranquility. I knew that one of these footsoldiers possessed the black goo that would wash away my sickness.

We pulled into the parking lot behind Shuck's, and I took the spot closest to the sidewalk for an easy escape route. Lots can go wrong in a street deal, especially when you're sick and willing to do pretty much whatever it takes to get what you need.

We were immediately approached by some Mexicans. "What's up, homes? You lookin'?" a skinny Mexican asked me.

"Naw, motherfucker, he's with me." Flea cut him off before he could finish his sales pitch. "You seen Spider?"

"He's around, bitch. Damn, what's your problem?"

She ignored his remark, got out of the car and went looking for her cousin.

The Mexicans at the car started bombarding me with offers. Now what? If I copped from a Mexican, Flea wouldn't get a "kick down" so I'd have to break her off a piece of my already spoken-for kibble [heroin]. No option there. But I was hurting bad, and it was hard to resist the persistent dealers surrounding me.

Buying from any of them would cause a scene. But Flea was taking way too long, and I was too sick to wait any more.

I was about to give in and buy when Flea returned.

"Give me the twenty!" she said, seeing that I was right in the middle of making a transaction. I frantically sifted through my pockets. No money.

"Vato [homeboy] ain't even got no money, mija [little sister]," said one of the Mexicans -- a really big guy. These were the first words Juan spoke to me.

I felt like I'd just eaten a huge meal at a restaurant and discovered I'd lost my wallet when it was time to pay. My head shook uncontrollably. My sister got out of the car to try to help. Flea and the Mexican were getting into it. They were inches from each other's face, arms flailing. It was attracting all kinds of unwanted attention.

Chapter 4

The man was James T. Moran, who (when he used his name at all) called himself Juan Martinez. He would have a huge influence over me and lead to me into a place where death would have been a better option. He stood about 5' 7", had a stocky build, dressed in baggy pants and tank-top (a "wife-beater"), and had a sloppy demeanor. His head was down, his posture was slumped. It seemed the street had beaten him down. He introduced himself as Juan, and he showed me some court papers indicating his name was Martinez.

The way Juan's skin hung from his stocky frame indicated that he used to be a man of great size -- not that he still wasn't, but it was obvious he had fallen prey to some sort of misfortune that caused him to lose weight in a rapid manner. He was covered with stretch marks. It became clear from his posture and talk about "what he used to be" that he was self-conscious about his condition. He was homeless and penniless.

Juan weighed around 275 pounds. Novice tattoos covered his body in no particular pattern. His back was hunched over, his shoulders drooped and his head kind of bobbed in a tired, lazy fashion. I would have said the streets had drained his life force, but surprisingly, he had sprung into action like a gazelle.

Flea screamed, "Look, you good-for-nothing motherfucker, this is my sale, so back the fuck up, shitstack!"

"This is my motherfucking block, bitch, and I run this shit," said Juan as he circled around the parking lot, challenging anyone to disagree.

"You bitch-made mother . . ." was about all Flea got out.

Juan's fist shot out – directly into her eye. "Got me fucked up, I'll knock you out. Motherfuckin' dope fiend-ass junkie. Who the fuck's next?"

Flea took the punch pretty well. Her cousin tried to get out of the car but he too was met by a swift blow to the face before his feet could touch the ground.

"You want some from me too, Indian?" shouted the Mexican. "Get the fuck out of the car, homes." The native decided against it and shut the door.

Everyone on the block had circled around the scene now, and I still couldn't find my money.

"What a fuckin' nightmare. I can't believe this shit!" I yelled. "Molly, get back in the car! Goddamn, this ain't a game."

With everyone focused on the crazy Mexican, it gave me time to try finding my money. Molly, who had been up for at least two days, was visibly shaken from the fight and wasn't sure what to do.

Eric and the other native were still in the back seat, trying to avoid eye contact with anyone. I was grateful Sara wasn't there.

Half crazed, I started punching myself with both hands on the sides of my head. One thing for sure: you wouldn't be running into Mr. Rogers in this neighborhood. This was more like a scene from "American Me," a 1992 crime saga about street gangs and prison.

Flea was pouring out death threats, even though Juan outweighed her by at least 175 pounds. I gotta get that dope -- fast, I thought.

"Look, Flea," I said. "This is all my fault. Damn, girl, I'm sorry. That cat is trippin'."

She was holding her eye, but I think her pride hurt worse than the punch.

"That motherfucker's gonna get his, believe that!" she responded.

"Everything's gonna be cool," I said. "I'll give you a ride outta here. And you'll get your money."

As she went to check on her cousin in my car, I looked at the top-dog Mexican.

"She had that shit comin'," I said, "but you better get off the block before the police come."

"Nobody calls me a bitch, homes. Motherfuckers don't know who I am," Juan said, still hopped up on anger.

"Hey, man," I said. "I'll be back. And you'll be my first choice on the block."

That seemed to placate him, so I went to the car. I managed to come up with five dollars, and Molly had about $20 worth of weed she was willing to put up. I presented it all to Flea and she looked none too impressed. But she showed it to her uncle along with a pretty smile and persuasive vocabulary and he spit a tiny balloon out of his mouth and gave it to her.

Street dealers put their dope in a balloon, tie a few knots in them and keep them in their mouth. In the event of a police search, they can swallow the balloon with the dope inside. The rubber compound of the balloon protects the cargo all the way through the rigorous labyrinth of the digestive system. Or in most cases they usually make themselves throw up and retrieve it within minutes.

Amazingly, physical assaults, verbal assaults, a drug deal, and five people near a bright red BMW hadn't attracted the attention of the cops. So we all piled back into the car and sped away from Little Mexico, back to downtown Portland where I had first met the two natives.

We managed to scrounge up enough change for a beer for each of them, left the natives and promised to return with a third beer. Sara managed to scrounge up $10, but by the time we returned, they were no longer there. I felt bad for a minute, but that quickly passed, and I was on my way to make use of that money.

Two hours had passed since our initial visit to Little Mexico and we were nearly out of gas. Since I had to share my first kibble with Eric, I decided we could live without gas. After all, better to be well and out of gas than have gas and be sick.

"Mark, we're gonna run out of gas and you just scored," Molly told me. I ignored her. I was already circling Little Mexico, scoping out the scene, looking for a less conspicuous parking spot than before.

"Fuck the gas," I murmured to myself.

Now that I was well, rational thinking kicked in. My idea of rational thinking, anyway. So I parked about a block away from the blade this time.

"Should we stay with you? Or go?" asked Molly. At first I thought, what if they got hemmed up? But then another part of me thought, *Hey, these are two beautiful women, and I can get a better deal.*

Sara, Molly and I made our way across Burnside's busy four lanes of traffic and I zeroed in on my first choice. I could tell by the way he snapped out of his lazy jaunt that he noticed me as well. This was unmistakably the short, stocky Mexican who had caused a scene earlier. There was no avoiding him, even if we wanted to go through someone else.

"Órale, Rojo [Hey, Red], what's happening?" Rojo. That's what everyone called me on the street, since I had red hair. I gave him my best Spanish greeting and let him know what I needed.

“Damn, bro, I only have ten dollars. You gotta a ten piece [$10 worth of heroin]?” I asked.

“Ten bucks, homes. Fuck, no,” he replied. “Who are those hinas [girls] you with, homes?”

“Oh, they’re with me,” I told him.

“Alright, I’m gonna go try and get some more money.” My sister sprang into action as I walked off. Molly knew the game and was fairly street savvy -- more so than Sara, my girlfriend. Molly quickly slipped into character. While I pretended to try to get more money, I knew Molly and Sara would keep his attention and he would give in to a $10 sale.

All in a day in the life of Mark Tucker. Each morning was the same – consumed with fear, guilt, and desperation. Slavery. Every waking hour was dedicated to the search and consumption of drugs and alcohol. Every day, every hour was unpredictable and volatile. And I only knew one way to combat the feelings that constantly haunted me: more drugs.

A couple days had gone by since the Portland scores. Molly and Eric made their way back to Washington and I stayed behind with Sara.

Sara was already settled into a decent living situation with an aunt in southeast Portland, an area known as "felony flats." She had a modest job at a sandwich shop downtown and was an active participant at the local methadone clinic.

"Felony flats" is self-describing, and most cities have one. These areas are infested with minorities, white trash, low-income housing, welfare recipients and of course a high number of felons. So drugs and drug activity are commonplace. The crime rate is typically staggering.

There are always a select few residents who are hard-working citizens doing what they can to clean up their neighborhoods. Sara's aunt was one of those. She was a single mother with the chores of raising a healthy teenage boy as well as an impressive daughter who had just conquered her teens and was testing the waters of young adulthood. To judge from her unpredictable behavior, the daughter was toeing the line between experimental drug use and addiction.

Sara was now incorporated into the already-cramped household. Things were tense at times, with the normal "he said/she said" fights, but everyone was civil and operated with compassion.

Sara and I were most definitely in love. She stood around 5' 8," with soft auburn hair that twinkled with purple highlights and reached for her shoulders. Youth still had her pinned down in general life experiences but she was learning fast.

At age 32, in June 2005, I was homeless and in Portland, living in a the red BMW. It was parked in front of Sara's aunt's house. I was dressing from a backpack full of clothes.

My fortunes had changed drastically in recent days. I'd been on a real tear for the past 10 days, spending five days in Las Vegas and then five more days in Reno. I dropped thousands of dollars at the casinos and did $300-$400 a day in drugs. I used up all the $10,000 I had saved dealing heroin up on Whidbey Island and working with my Pops. I had been renting a house on Whidbey and a brand-new VW Jetta. Now all that had collapsed because of my drug addiction, augmented by a gambling addiction. One could probably say that my decision-making skills were a bit suspect.

I always told myself I could fall into the role of a functioning addict. "I can micromanage my heroin habit," I would tell myself. At the time my habit was well over $200 a day. This was some of my best thinking.

Sara had fibromyalgia and took a plethora of opiates to combat her pain already, but heroin proved to be a better painkiller than what her doctor was prescribing. Unbeknownst to me, she started taking heroin out of the packages I was selling. This lead to much strife, but she denied ever even trying heroin, let alone taking any.

I caught her one day stealing heroin and kicked her out of the house I'd been renting on Whidbey. She told her parents and they sent her away to Portland, to her aunt's house, where she got on a methadone program. We didn't talk for a month or so after that.

In the meantime, I squandered what was left of my savings and drowned myself in alcohol, heroin and methamphetamine. I was a mess. I lost my job, my Jetta was stolen from a casino parking lot and I was evicted -- all in a month's time. As unfortunate as this may sound, it was quite a familiar scenario for me.

In an act of desperation, I contacted a lifelong friend, John Smith (his real name), who was living in Portland, to see if he had any work. He said that he did and that he could use me as soon as I got there.

Thanks to the car my sister had given me, I had transportation. I packed up all my semi-valuable possessions, stored them in my dad's shop for the 100th time and took off to Portland.

Sara and I had been in contact in the latter part of my downfall, and she told me she would help me figure out a place to live. Out in front of her aunt's house was not really my ideal spot, but that's what ended up happening.

It was my own little RV park. Sara would come out and sleep in the house on wheels with me on occasion even though I would try to persuade her not to. I felt bad enough having to sleep in my car and though having her there was comforting, it was not the ideal living arrangement. The comfort level was definitely at an all-time low.

Daily life in Portland at that time consisted of waking up and wondering if I was late to work due to the fact that I traded my watch to the dope man, then running to Sara's window and waking her up to unlock the door. I would run into the bathroom, scrape some baggies (that contained some residue of heroin), "pound some cottons" (get residual heroin from the cottons through which I had previously drawn up heroin), rinse all my spoons, draw up the light brown liquid with a dull syringe and dig around for a vein. The bathroom ended up looking like a crime scene and I would usually just end up muscling the shot (shooting directly into the muscle, not a vein as is preferable) because my venous system was ruined.

After that morbid process, I would splash some water on my face, slick my hair back and clamp on a company hat backwards. I worked as a concrete pumper most of the time. I would place the call to my boss for the address of the job site or a convenient meeting spot. Then Sara and I would commute to a predetermined location and I would let her take the car so she could go to the methadone clinic to get her dose, which she needed as a direct result of the heroin "she wasn't taking" from me when we were living together on Whidbey, immediately before this time. I was usually either way early or nearly late to work.

When I was finished at work, I would call her to come pick me up. This was an everyday routine for weeks.

My job as a concrete-pump operator and business-getter for John Smith's pumping business brought me to different locations every day. A lot of times, John would drop me off downtown and I would go to Sara's work, get the keys and location of my car, then after work head straight to Burnside to score some heroin and escape the harsh reality that I had created for myself. Being 32 years old, living in a car in front of someone else's house, was actually not on my goal sheet.

I would usually make $300-$400 a week, and it all went to alcohol, video poker and of course heroin. Compared to my Vegas days, I had tapered my heroin habit way down due to lack of funds. This went on until I developed a nasty abscess in my upper thigh from muscling. It started out small, as they always do, and didn't interrupt my work. Neglecting it was easy at first, and self-medication was enough to keep the pain at bay. This was just another occupational hazard that I was all too familiar with.

Then I started having to walk with a bit of limp.

"Oh, my God, what's wrong with your leg, dude?" my boss would ask me. I would lie and tell him some tale about getting stuck with a rusty nail or some shit. He knew what it was from, but I still lied.

Work started to become an unmanageable task and the whole car thing was now out of the question -- it was too painful and difficult to live in it. The reality was that I had a late-stage abscess that rendered my leg useless. A trip to the hospital seemed inevitable.

I took my week's pay and had to rent a hotel room on 82nd Ave. in Portland, which is another notorious area for drugs and prostitution. Most of the hotels, like the Unicorn, were pretty cheap and came with the more horrible amenities: burn holes in the carpet, sheets that were suspect, cigarette burns in the countertops and the pleasant smell of an ashtray constantly tickling my nose. What more could you ask for?

Chapter 5

It was around July 13, 2005, and the sun was at its peak and on task, providing that soul-penetrating energy that makes your spirit glow.

While I should have been resting my abscessed leg, which was progressing into a life-threatening infection, I was out trying to score. In mid-search I realized I was late to pick up Sara, but I had just made contact with a Mexican.

He was actually the one who encouraged the contact. "Hey, homes, you lookin'?" he asked.

"Yeah, I'm hurtin'. You got shit on you?" I asked.

"Yep, I got you." Without hesitation, he hopped into my car.

"Hey bro, I'm in a hurry," I said. "Can you do two balloons for $30?" Each balloon is usually 0.25 grams.

"Yeah, I can do that." He spat out two balloons from his mouth. "You got the money?"

I already had the money in my hand and gave it to him. By this time we were almost in front of Sara's work on Portland's Fifth Avenue. So I swung into the nearest parking lot. The Mexican hopped out.

“Alright, homes. I'll catch you around," he said. "Hey," he added, sticking out his hand. "My name's Drew. If you ever see me on the block, hit me up."

I shook his hand goodbye and fixed right there in the car, trying to subdue the medieval suffering I was experiencing from my self-inflicted leg wound. I finished up and scurried to the entrance of the building where Sara worked. She was standing patiently.

We headed toward her aunt’s house, taking Burnside up toward S.E. Portland, when we spotted a man vigorously waving his hands trying to get our attention. It was Juan again. I pulled over, and he requested a ride.

“Hey, vato, drive me up to the Spot,” he commanded.

This referred to the entrance to a trail running along I-5 and eventually leading underneath a portion of the major interstate that had been inhabited by the homeless. Huge cardboard "condos" were scattered about, and the area was rank with the smell of human waste. Moldy, dried-up clothes and blankets littered the well-traveled path from the storage units.

I knew this place and had felt the pain of its inadequate living conditions many times. You could actually see the despair lingering above the camp. Long suffering was well represented here. Juan offered us some cocaine if we waited for him while he ventured to this forsaken wasteland of broken dreams and corrupted souls.

Reluctantly, we agreed to wait. It was dark by this time, and Juan disappeared as he quickly descended the winding trail. Roughly 10 minutes went by and he emerged with another Mexican. It was Drew. Apparently they were cousins. It seems like everyone is your cousin on the street.

They wanted a ride to Drew's hotel, and upon arrival he would give us the cocaine for our trouble. By this time I just wanted them out of the car.

Drew and Juan started arguing in Spanish. From what I could make out, Drew wanted to rob us and take my car. Obviously Drew didn’t know I understood any Spanish.

“Pull the fuck over, homes,” Juan shouted at me. As I was pulling over, Drew started swinging on Juan, punching him in the face.

“Oh, my God! What the fuck, you guys! Stop!” Sara screamed. She opened the passenger-side door and jumped out of the car.

Juan hopped out of the back seat first, and while Drew was trying to get out, Juan started a flurry of punches to Drew's head and face. Drew's attitude snapped like the hammer of a gun.

"Motherfucker, you gonna die now!" Drew shouted as he pulled out a decent-sized lock-blade knife. He snapped open the blade and started taking uncontrolled swipes toward Juan's sagging pot belly.

"Oh shit, Sara. Get the fuck in the car," I yelled.

As we looked on, Juan danced strategically around Drew's lethal advances and honed in on his face, delivering a swift blow right to his mouth and drawing blood. I was shocked that Juan stayed so calm and was able to land a solid punch that took Drew out of the game.

"Let's go! What the fuck are you waiting for?" Sara yelled at me.

"Hold on. I wanna see this," I responded.

Juan's punch knocked the wind out of Drew's sails but definitely turned up the heat for some revenge stew. Juan backed off and tried to talk Drew down out of his blind rage.

"Put that fuckin' knife away, esé ('dude'), before I take it from you" Juan told him.

Drew stumbled back over to my car, opened the back door and got in. "What the fuck, bro?" is all I could say. He still had the knife in his hand, so I didn't want to get too loud with the guy. Sara's eyes were wide with fear as she stared at the knife.

Unfortunately, my lingering to watch the fight had given Drew the opportunity to get back in my car like nothing had ever happened.

"Sorry, homes, I didn't know that shit was gonna happen," Drew said. "My cousin is always trippin'."

My mind was blown. *Drew was the one who initiated the fight*, I thought to myself.

"You're alright, vato. He likes you and your old lady," he told me as he patted my shoulder.

All this activity had drawn attention to us. Juan was already being approached by a fellow street dealer. Juan was coming around the car and heading toward my side when the street dealer called him out.

"Damn, homes, what was that about?" he asked Juan.

"Ah, it ain't shit, esé. Just my cousin trippin'."

They walked away from the car to have a sidebar and it looked like Juan was presented with a better deal than what he had going. He and the other fellow took off at a good speed.

"Thanks for the ride, rojo," Juan yelled as he disappeared up an alley. "Oh -- and this shit ain't over, Drew. I'll see you later."

"We gotta get home, Drew," I told him as we drove away.

"That fucker's dead," Drew declared from the back seat. "I'm givin' his ass a hot shot. They'll find him under the bridge dead as fuck, homes," he told us in a somber tone.

Sara and I kept our comments to a minimum. After seeing him trying to carve out Juan's whole stomach, we pretty much agreed with whatever he said. Luckily we were able to drop him off a few blocks up the street at a hotel.

Throughout the night, I suffered the wrath of my infected leg. My temperature was blinding hot and I was delirious.

Chapter 6

When morning finally came, Sara drove me to the emergency room at Providence Hospital.

"I've never seen you like this, baby. Oh, my God, you're so white," Sara told me as we drove up to the ER.

Because of the wound's severity, I was admitted immediately, and the tedious job that lay ahead of the phlebotomist was initiated: finding a vein in which to start an IV.

I myself could rarely find a vein when shooting up, but at least I knew where to look. I usually helped the techs find a good location. There is nothing more frustrating than having a rookie poke you with a needle the size of a turkey baster.

The first gal who tried starting an IV took a few stabs at it and had to call another nurse. She was nicknamed "The Best," but her failed attempts pushed me over the edge.

"Alright, we're done," I said. "We're gonna have to figure something else out." I looked like some sort of science project, with gauze pads taped on various parts of my body. Eventually a surgeon had to come in and start an IV in my neck. They immediately got me started on a morphine drip and a battery of antibiotics.

This infection had done quite the number on my thigh. There was a tennis ball-size wound deep in the muscle tissue, making it impossible to walk. The doctor came in with his prognosis

"Mr. Tucker, you let this infection go way too long, so you won't be going anywhere for a while," he said. "We'll do our best to stop the infection, but there is a small chance you could lose your leg."

"That's crazy talk," I protested.

"What's crazy is that you decided to just walk around with this thing eating away your flesh, with a temperature of 102 degrees," the doctor replied.

As the reality of my situation set in, pain began hitting me in tsunami-sized waves that made me grit my teeth and sent sweat down my face as if I had just eaten a ghost pepper. The doctor left shaking his head and told me the nurse would be in to check on me.

The morphine wasn't enough, so when Sara came by I begged her to go down to the block and score some dope. She was hesitant at first, but my words of desperation eventually broke her down.

This would be her first time to the Block [the area where the Blade -- the major site of gang and drug activity -- is located] without me, so I gave her a little pep talk and told her to try finding Juan or Drew. About an hour went by before she returned, and when she did she was not alone. She had brought a man with a farfetched proposition and a persuasive way of promoting it: Sara had brought Juan. He had some dope and a favor to ask.

Before I could listen to this proposition or do anything else, I retrieved a 20-piece (2/10 of a gram) of dope from Juan and hobbled into the bathroom. Anticipating this scenario, I had taken the special syringe from the nurse that screwed into my IV. I quickly cooked up the dope, pushed it into my IV and rinsed it with saline to get rid of the brown liquid that filled the tube into my neck. The pain and anxiety that had been boiling over were quickly subdued. Sweet, sweet "normalcy" was restored.

I sat in the bathroom for a moment and reveled in the magic of this insidious toxin that rushed through my battered body. I knew it wouldn't be long before the pain would come creeping back. Sara knocked. Reluctantly I arose and cleaned up any signs of foul play. I took a deep breath and opened the door back to reality.

I hopped back to the bed and let out a sigh as I eased myself down on the mattress. Sara joined me, laying her head on my chest, and we melted into a state of numb relaxation. Juan asked about the quality of his product and we both agreed that it did the trick.

He made small talk for a few minutes before dropping the bomb.

"So look, esé. I've been watching you and you seem like a solid vato," he said, pulling himself to the edge of his seat to reflect his seriousness. "My grandfather passed away and I would like to go see his grave and pay my respects." He didn't say when or how his grandfather had died. His demeanor stiffened and he looked me in the eye. "I need a ride to the Ozark Mountains and I'll shoot ya $1,500 and the rest of this dope." He used the terms "Ozarks" and "Missouri" interchangeably.

I looked at Sara and then back at Juan. I spent about five seconds pondering the question.

"Fifteen hundred dollars?" I asked.

"Yep," he replied. "We just gotta stop by the Tri-Cities to get the money."

"Fuck it. Let's go," I responded. I didn't even know where the Ozark Mountains were, but for that much money, I didn't much care.

Sara wasn't equally excited about the plan. "That's just silly. You're in no condition to go to the bathroom, let alone across the country."

But I think the money was just as enticing to her as it was to me. Obviously I was in no condition for such a trip, but offer a addict money and dope and all caution is thrown into the wind with little or no hesitation. I couldn't walk at all, and the constant pain was blinding, but not even Alexander's army could have kept me from the lure of dope and money.

There was one problem. I had to get my prescriptions for antibiotics and codeine from the doctor before I could leave. Upon admission, I was told that the severity of the infection could have easily progressed into a cardiac-arrest situation. So I had to get confirmation from the doctor that I wasn't going to die and have him sign for my meds.

Threats of death and incarceration are about the only things that can detour a heroin addict. Sometimes even the likelihood of death can't stop a determined addict. Believe me, I've seen it firsthand. People put off going to the hospital to the point of no return.

Chapter 7

It was the 18th or 19th of July, and Sara had to be at work in the next few hours, so I pushed the call button to inform the nurse I would be leaving shortly. Obviously shocked and taken aback, she stumbled over her words.

"Um, well, Mr. Tucker, that would be a bad decision. You're in no condition to leave."

"Thank you for your concern, nurse, but I'll decide. Can you please get me the doctor?"

"Mr. Tucker, you won't be going anywhere with that IV sticking out of your neck," she said as she exited the room.

She was right. As soon as the door shut, I proceeded to extract the IV. It felt like I was pulling a string out of my neck. I could feel the catheter sliding up and out of my vein. It made a sound like a zipper being zipped up as it exited.

Blood started to drain out from the hole at a high rate of speed and Sara lost it.

“Oh, my God, Mark. You're crazy! What are you doing?"

Even Juan was startled. "Damn, esé, you're loco," he said, shaking his head.

But for me, this was the norm. I had pulled out many an IV and left the hospital against medical advice to do more important things. I peeled the blood-soaked hospital gown off and had to take a little rest from the loss of blood.

After some time, a doctor blessed me with his presence. His face told the story of bewilderment as he saw that my IV had been taken out. I was trying to put on my clothes as he confronted me.

“Mr. Tucker, you can’t leave, but I can't force you to stay, and it looks like you’ve made up your mind,” he said. He cautioned me not to leave with an open wound that had not yet gone into remission. “This infection is still at large, so you’ll have to sign a waiver of refusal for care."

He agreed to prescribe the antibiotics and codeine that would be needed to keep the infection down and the pain manageable.

I summoned the nurse once again and told her I would be leaving against the doctor’s orders. Walking was not an option. I explained to the nurse that I would need a wheelchair or crutches. She brought a brand new pair of crutches and gave me a quick demonstration on their use.

With prescription in hand and pain shooting all the way down to my feet, I embarked on the agonizing route to the pharmacy, which was three floors down and a block away. I directed Sara to retrieve the car and meet Juan and me at the main entrance. The nurse tagged along to ensure my safety while still inside the hospital

Finally what seemed to be an eternity of labyrinths brought me to the proper exit. Sara hopped out and fell right into her natural nurturing role and assisted me to the car. She guided me to the passenger side, but after playing the tape through and considering Sara's awareness level behind the wheel, I decided to drive.

With Juan in the back among all the clothes, shoes, empty beer bottles and food wrappers and Sara sitting shotgun, we sped off to retrieve my prescriptions and take Sara to work.

Juan gave us more details about the trip we were about to embark on. It would take six days. Driving to Arkansas from the Tri-Cities, Washington, takes three days with no stops except to fill up for gas and the quick restroom break. So three days there, three days back. That sounded good to me. As it unfolded, the trip ate those six days, filling the rest of July and spilling into August.

Sara continued to express hesitation about the trip, but we had big plans for the money. We were going to get our own apartment and try building a life together.

We dropped Sara at her workplace. I was off to the Ozark Mountains. I didn't yet realize my passenger was a diagnosed paranoid schizophrenic. I learned of that diagnosis only during my trial. It came out in testimony that he had called a suicide hotline and said he heard voices telling him to kill. He was apparently told he couldn't be seen that day and would have to wait. He never called again. He made that call two days before he killed the Carrs.

Part 2
On The Road

Day 1
July 19, 2005
Portland, Oregon - Whidbey Island, Washington

We'd be heading southeast toward Arkansas, so it would have been faster to just leave from Portland. But we first had to go three hours north to Whidbey Island, in Washington's far northwest corner, so that I could pick up some valuables in case I needed money on the trip. I had stereos, big-screen TVs, VHF tapes, speakers, brand-new power tools, even a washer and dryer. All had been traded to me for the heroin I was dealing while living on Whidbey.

I found myself initiating most of the conversations as we traveled north on I-5 at a high rate of speed. I reminisced about my life on Whidbey.

My father had bought five acres there in the late 1970's and built the Flying "R" Ranch. The "R" represented the old Rainier beer logo, Rainier being a historic brew once produced in Seattle. An enormous "R" is carved into a plaque hanging over the drive leading to the ranch. The letter is part of the moniker "Tucker's Flying R Ranch."

This plaque is truly huge. Until recently, when they rotted, it was supported by two 30-foot totem poles that even the pickiest native would be proud of. All sorts of tribal-looking animals appear to be clawing their way out of the massive log they're trapped in. There's a somewhat more subtle nude carving of my Pops holding a can of Rainier Beer over his head. Directly below is a nude woman carrying him on her shoulders.

I'm actually surprised this isn't in the tourist handbooks, though the first sign you come to when approaching the ranch would probably deter anyone who didn't know us. This sign, also carved from wood, reads:

> Notice: IRS. Sheriff Subpoena. Bill Collectors. Process Servers, and Ex-Wives. Please Use Rear Entrance

Of course there is no rear entrance.

We finally arrived at the Mukilteo ferry landing, which is on the outskirts of Everett, Washington. Juan's interest was piqued by the sight of the massive ferry boat with the name *Cathlamet* on the side of the hull.

The moon was hanging low in the sky. It was around 12:45 a.m. We had made fairly good time considering we stopped by the Emerald Queen Casino in Tacoma to feed a few slot machines. Amazingly enough, we had won around $100 to help us with traveling expenses. I'm addicted to gambling as well as drugs, and the Northwest has been infected with the presence of casinos and "drift on in" card rooms. So for me, just traveling short distances in my home state of Washington is difficult.

While in Tacoma, we had stopped at the home of one of my dope dealers, and I had bought a half-gram ($20 worth) of heroin. That would have to last me until we reached Spokane, some three days later. It wasn't nearly enough.

We landed on Whidbey Island after the short ride across Puget Sound, and I drove straight to the home of my friend Orville Cordoba, because I knew he would be awake and be able to accommodate Juan's recently acquired hunger for meth. We hung out at Cordoba's until the sun made its presence known, pushing the darkness out of the room and creating the first shadow of the day. We said our goodbyes and headed for the ranch.

At the end of my prior stay on the island, which had ended in late May, I had left in a frenzy, leaving all sorts of my belonging in the house I was renting. I had managed to get most of my valuable items out of the house I'd been renting, but a lot of miscellaneous stuff was left behind, and my dad and his wife had brought it all to the ranch.

Juan and I pulled into the ranch around 11:00 a.m. It's located in Clinton, near where the ferry lands. The lawn is enclosed with cedar split-rail fences shaped into a circle. A giant finger carved out of wood in great detail with the words "That Way" engraved in the middle of the hand pointed to the left.

My Pops is a self-made man with workaholic tendencies. His property has three buildings, each roughly 20' x 30', for a store selling his hand-made, fine-grained custom furniture. Pops never took too kindly to having a boss or having anyone tell him what to do. So he has remained self-employed, using his love for wood and creating things with his hands as a means for survival for more than 50 years.

One section of one building had had to be cleared out to house my belongings, which placed a burden on my Pops and his wife.

This is another result of my selfish lifestyle that affects the people around me. My Pops and his wife have put up with endless letdowns and have been burdened with the chore of picking up my wreckage too many times to count.

I had called the ranch before arriving to let my folks know I would be showing up with company shortly. Juan was fairly impressed with the landscape.

The ranch houses not only people but also two Collies, Sunny Girl and Edward Francis. Also living there is Eleanor, a big brown cow that is hand fed and groomed on a daily basis and roams freely on the ranch's five acres.

Pops had recently acquired a beautiful horse named Cowboy. Apparently Cowboy had reaped the rewards of the winner's circle in his prime and was looking forward to his retirement. The ranch is a perfect facilitator for just that, and many pets have lived out their whole lives on this chunk of land.

I parked the car close to the building that contained what was left of my belongings. Juan and I were greeted by ecstatic barking and uncontrolled tail-wagging, followed by the custom Collie greeting of poking their long nose directly into your crotch.

My mission was to recover the items I felt could catch a few dollars at a pawn shop, visit with the family and be on our way. This all took a few hours. My leg was so bad Juan had to do all the work while my dad expressed much concern about my condition.

I could tell that Juan was feeling a little irritation and was not accustomed to helping someone to this extent. So I found myself apologizing for circumstances beyond my control countless times throughout the day.

We wrapped things up as the sun started making its descent. The BMW was packed to maximum capacity and we were ready for our next stop.

Juan was quite adamant about meeting some females, so our next checkpoint would be the house of a good friend. We'll call her Marina. Marina lived in the little town of Freeland, about five miles north of Clinton. It was a short trip, but turned out to be a long stay.

Marina is a slender-bodied girl with long, Shirley Temple curls and a vivacious attitude for life. She greeted me with a big hug. Marina displayed her assets very well, with pants that stretched across her hips, casually leaving a sliver of her underwear on display as she moved gracefully around the room. Juan was immediately intrigued by her presence.

35

"That's me, esé. I'm Grizz," Juan told me as he bobbed his head to the beat. I didn't know if this guy was telling the truth, but he sure was excited about the song.

Juan started telling me stories about transporting large quantities of drugs and weapons across the United States and living the high-roller lifestyle. This was hard to believe because of the way he presented himself now. He also explained how his people weren't aware of his recent experiments using methamphetamine, heroin and cocaine.

"If my homies knew I was fuckin' with dope, they'd have my head, esé" he told me. Using drugs is unacceptable in the eyes of his fellow gang members, and he would be excluded from the circle or killed if they knew that he had started dabbling in the product that he and his gang had been distributing nationwide for the greater part of his life. The gang demanded clear heads from those doing its business.

He also took pride in how "his homies" took care of him. Juan started telling me things that lead me to believe that this wasn't a trip to see his grandfather's grave. It seemed my passenger had pissed some people off enough for him to have to relocate.

Juan told me that he had relocated to Portland because the city didn't deport you if you were an illegal, and that his friends had put him up in an apartment and left him with enough meth to sustain himself temporarily.

It seemed, though, that his love for prostitutes and getting high became more than just having a little fun, it became a serious problem. I knew that from all his stories. Portland is littered with strip clubs and prostitutes, and most of them have a meth or heroin addiction.

Juan's display of anger the first time I met him confirmed his stories of violence when things or people didn't fall into line for him. According to him, the Portland apartment his comrades had rented him was taken over by one of prostitutes he'd consorted with. He had beaten her up for one reason or another and she called 9-1-1. She pressed charges, and he was now being sought after by the Portland police for domestic violence. So he couldn't go back to that apartment without repercussions. This woman was just another on his seemingly endless list of people to "take care of."

By this point in the trip, feelings of regret began to consume me. After hearing story after story about killings, violence and revenge, it was becoming very clear to me that I was in over my head with Juan. I simply wasn't used to violence, much less on the scale he presented.

I also felt I really wasn't free to go. Nor was he anything like willing to be dropped off. This is something I can't stress enough. I never felt safe leaving him. That's because he knew so much about me. He'd been to my father's house and my girlfriend's house. I didn't want to separate myself from him and have the threat lingering in the air that he could harm the people I loved the most. I couldn't tell my Pops or my girlfriend to keep a loaded gun around all the time just in case Juan showed up. Having him dead would be the only way out.

I also had no money, which would have made leaving him a difficult plan to implement.

By the time we reached eastern Washington's Tri-Cities -- Richland, Pasco and Kennewick -- we were both completely broke, and the car was running on empty. My leg was throbbing so badly I could hardly drive, and the pain pills were gone in the first two days. We found a park in Kennewick next to the Columbia River and rested.

Dehydrated and starving, we sought out some shade to rest. Eastern Washington's blistering heat was becoming a factor for both of us. The terrain resembles that of Camp Pendleton in southern California and becomes tiresome pretty quickly.

I wanted to get this trip started for real and conquer some highways, but we needed the help and funding for the trip that Juan insisted would be no problem -- once we contacted the right people at the correct time.

"I think I'm on Crime Stoppers, esé, so everyone is wanting to tell on me and collect the reward," he said. "We're gonna have to wait 'til it gets dark to hit up my homies."

"Fuck, bro, I need some dope," I responded. "I'm hurtin' bad. We need to get some money."

I completely disregarded his Crime Stopper story and was only concerned with surviving at this point. We hadn't slept or eaten since we left Portland four days before.

Night finally started to paint the sky with darkness, which provided Juan the safety net he needed to make contact with his homies. We crept down backroads and alleys, and he finally directed me to stop.

"Alright. Stay here. I'll be back in a few," Juan said.

"See if you can get some dope from your boy," I said in desperation. Juan concealed his identity again, with my hat pulled down over his eyes and his hood pulled tight around his face.

"Yeah, yeah, I'll see, homie," he said. "We need to get this money first."

I was so sick I would rather have had dope then money at this point.

Juan pulled the gun out and gave it a quick check, glanced at me and exited the car.

The thought of leaving crossed my mind, but I was out of heroin and had no money to get anywhere but the gas station. I convinced myself that all his talk about getting even with people, and the fact that he had a gun, were easily dismissed.

Being a heroin addict and being out of your normal environment is enough to cause stress and panic in and of itself. Having no money in an unfamiliar place is even more of a problem. So I had no choice but to sit tight and hope for the best.

Only about ten minutes went by before Juan reappeared and got back into the car.

"Damn, homes. Dreamer is trippin'. He didn't have all the money. I know he's holdin' out."

I just shook my head in disappointment. He returned with some weed, a little cash, a little meth (also known as speed) and some Ecstasy pills. No heroin! In my eyes this was almost a total loss. Juan said we would have to wait until the next day to obtain the necessary cash to accommodate our trip.

This definitely posed a problem. It had been two days since I took the last pain pill, so not only was I totally dope-sick, but the pain I was experiencing had me grinding my teeth and moving back and forth like a crazy person. In the past few days I had only got out of the car to use the bathroom.

We both did large shots of the crystal meth, which put my sickness in a state of remission.

A lot of heroin addicts, including myself, try to substitute meth for dope. It proves to be effective for maybe the first 36 to 56 hours with ridiculous amounts. Around the third day, though, you're at the emotional breaking point. All the symptoms of opiate withdrawal are starting to bleed through the intense high that the crystal is providing.

With a runny nose, watering eyes and cramped muscles, anxiety and stress infected my every thought. No matter how much you drink or how much speed you ingest, you cannot kill the symptoms of withdrawing from heroin.

I could tell that my opiate dependency, along with my handicapped leg, was wearing on Juan's patience, though he was constantly conveying his deep appreciation for the ride and company I was providing him. Having witnessed Juan's short temper and predisposition to violence, I tried to keep a calm demeanor while fighting off the inclination to go berserk from the pain in my leg and the anxiety that flowed through my blood from too much speed and not enough heroin.

More and more speed was the only logical cure. Juan was a speed machine, doing large hits every four or five hours. The track marks on his arm looked as though he had taken a paper clip and tried to extract his vein from his arm.

Though his techniques were definitely those of a rookie IV user, the amounts and the sadistic mannerisms he displayed were excessive and late stage. His self destructive attitude was very clear. This made me even more anxious and led me to wonder what he was really up to.

Juan loved to drink soda, and every time I would stop to get a St. Ides mixed-berry malt liquor, he would want a soda. So we pulled into a 7-Eleven in Pasco to purchase beverages with the little money "Dreamer" had given us. Juan stayed in the car with one of my hats pulled down tight as I hobbled into the store.

Dusk was upon us once again, but the air was still thick with heat left behind by the sun. The temperature was nothing less than perfect, as I tried to control my intake of beverages safely back to the car. Walking with crutches was a hindrance in everyday tasks. I was a walking train wreck and the crutches and this huge infection that had eaten a good chunk of my leg away were solid visual reminders of how addiction takes precedence over common sense. I wasn't even supposed to leave the hospital room, let alone take a trip across the country in a car packed to the dome light with clothes, video cassettes, DVD's, crutches, beer bottles, shoes, CD cases and a fat guy with a gun.

As I got back into the car, Juan had his eyes fixed on a man who had left the store just before me. He was a black man standing around 6' 3". He had shoulder-length Jheri-curled hair and was holding a 40-ounce bottle that poked out of a brown paper sack. It was apparent from his build that he had either been to the joint or had a membership to a fitness center. He strolled with a gangster-type gait, putting a little bounce to his step when he touched down with his right foot. The lights from 7-Eleven illuminated the parking lot and spilled over into the street enough for Juan to zero in on the man's direction of travel. Juan's interest in this man was intense. His senses were elevated and I could tell his mind was reeling.

"Pull out behind this motherfucker, esé," he told me. Adrenaline started to rush through my veins, but I didn't want to spook Juan by my nervousness. I tried to remain calm as Juan rolled down the window and made eye contact with the man in a provoking manner. I could tell that this guy was definitely not the type to just keep walking. As we coasted along the sidewalk at the same speed as this soon-to-be-victim, Juan started taunting him, saying, "Don't you know who I am, motherfucker?"

The man obviously didn't recognize him, but was definitely provoked. He replied, "I don't know you, motherfucker! What's up?" I could sense that Juan was holding back. It almost seemed like the man wasn't who he had thought.

I was hoping Juan would tell me to just keep driving away. I was thinking I wouldn't even be able to defend myself in my current situation if something went down.

I saw Juan pull the gun out of his pocket and cover it up with a shirt. Juan then directed me to pull ahead and turn the car around.

"Go up here and turn the car around. I want you to hit this fucker with your brights when we pull around."

I'm thinking, *Fuck! What am I supposed to do? This guy's got a gun, and if I say no, he could easily turn it on me.*

As we pulled ahead, Juan's target moved across the street. We were only about a block and a half away from the 7-Eleven -- not the ideal location for a gang-related homicide. Juan was seething with hatred.

"I'm going to buck this nigger in the head twice and he'll fall fast and we'll just take off like nothing ever happened."

Now I'm thinking, *This guy is out of his fucking mind.*

"What the fuck, bro? We're right in front of 7-Eleven," I said.

"What, are you scared, esé?" he sneered. "You gonna tell on me or something?" He stared at me with hateful eyes.

"No, I just don't think this is the best place to shoot someone," I responded, trying to stay calm.

As I started to turn around, the black man had almost reached the other side of the street. Juan directed me to turn my brights on and drive right for him.

"Hit your lights, homes. Blind this guy" he yelled. In a panic I fumbled for the lights and ended up turning them off.

"What the fuck? Turn 'em on!" Juan shouted.

Oh, my God, this is fucking crazy, I said to myself, closing my eyes for a moment and wishing it wasn't happening. I was not ready to assist in a drive-by shooting. So I proceeded with extreme caution, and tried to make my intended mistakes look unintentional, derailing his plan.

As we pulled to the curb, Juan positioned himself in the passenger seat so one foot was up on the seat, the other on the floor. He hung his head out the window and started yelling, "Come here, ya fucking nigger! Fuck you, nigger." I was looking around in all directions wondering who was gonna be the one to call the cops on us.

Juan's racial slurs did the trick. The black man was now enraged and coming for the car.

"Oh fuck, this is not good" I said under my breath.

"Get the fuck outta the car, fat ass," the black guy yelled.

He started falling into Juan's trap and moved closer to the car. I was a total wreck. I was looking all around and I had my foot on the gas ready to punch it as we coasted back toward the 7-Eleven and into the lights. The black guy had picked up his pace and was drawing the bottle back, getting ready to chuck it at Juan's face.

Juan's eyes were wide and crazy-looking. His bottom lip was tucked under his top teeth. Beads of sweat gathered on his forehead. Juan lifted the shirt that was concealing the .38. He cocked the hammer and moved the barrel in the direction of the man's head.

The noise from cocking the gun was loud enough to alert the man he was walking into a trap. I was unable to keep the car still, and Juan flashed on me for that.

"We're right in front of 7-Eleven. What are you thinking?" I yelled back.

In the heat of the moment, Juan was screaming at both me and the black man. My imagination was playing all kinds of scenarios through. I pictured the black man's head exploding in slow motion, his bottle dropping to the ground and the silence that follows a gun shot. Then I envisioned Juan turning the gun on me. All I saw was a bright white flash as I held my breath, waiting for oblivion.

Once the black guy saw Juan had a gun, he quickly turned around.

"Punk-ass motherfucker!" he shouted as he ran zig-zagging into the night.

Juan started cursing me.

"What the fuck is your problem, motherfucker? I sat in prison for a year plotting and planning on how I was going to kill that cocksucker. He fucked my wife. I can't believe I let him live. Why the fuck did you turn the lights off, dumb ass? I told you exactly what to do and you fucked it up!"

"Look, homie, we're right in front of 7-Eleven," I replied. "How do you expect to get to the Ozark Mountains if you start killing people before we even leave the state?" I said, trying to hold my ground. Juan was obviously upset and started banging the gun against his leg.

After he finally settled down, he turned and thanked me, with a startling change in attitude.

"You must be my guardian angel or something, homie. I ain't never not pulled the trigger." He shook his head and put the gun back in his pocket.

From the way Juan described his plans to kill the black man, it was obvious to me that in his many years of gang activity he had executed many an enemy in the same manner.

This incident was the first to show me I was in the company of a potential murderer. It was a chilling realization.

Now that the hostile situation was over, I tried to gain back a little composure. Without the aid of some heroin this was impossible. My mind was still trying to comprehend that the passenger of my car was a twitch of a finger away from committing a homicide in front of a 7-Eleven. God only knows why he didn't pull that trigger. Every muscle in my body was squeezing the marrow in my bones and trying to rip out of my skin. My toes were balled up into fists and almost breaking through the soles of my shoes. I will never forget or recover from that almost-fatal situation.

I figured at best Juan would shoot me in the arm or leg for disrupting his plan, or if the black man had a gun I would get hit by a stray bullet as we pulled away. All the outcomes that were playing through my mind were horrific. I am thankful for the outcome that prevailed. However if I'd known what lay ahead, I probably wouldn't have minded taking a stray bullet.

We drove away from the scene and across the Columbia River into Kennewick. It was dark enough now that we could try getting the package that would give us money to resume our mission. We stopped at a pay phone and he called a number that he had brought out with him from the first house we had stopped at. He returned to the car with some frustration.

"God damn, esé. These vatos are trippin'. They're lucky I don't just go rob them for their shit."

Whoever Juan talked to on the phone had told him he couldn't get his package until later that night, and it was already pushing 9:00 p.m. We drove aimlessly for awhile, then stopped off in a park and finished the last of the speed Juan had obtained the day before.

Now it was around 11:00 and we were sick of waiting, so Juan directed me to a little section of sidewalk that sat across from a car lot.

"This is my homie's car lot. Just park here," Juan told me. I was thinking, *There seems to be quite a bit of activity going on for a car lot at 11:00 at night.*

Juan suited up in his usual attire.

"Alright, homie. Let me go get this shit handled," he said. "Just sit tight. We'll get you well here in a bit." He was referring to scoring me the heroin I so desperately needed.

I hate waiting, especially when I've been up for almost five days. Things are not what they seem at that point. Living off handfuls of pain pills, a belly full of alcohol, bloodstream infected with meth and going through heroin withdrawal is not the ideal condition you want to be in when waiting for a deal to go down. I tried to sit still but couldn't. I tried to pretend to be asleep but couldn't do that either. All I could seem to do was sit there and look totally fucking suspicious. Ten minutes. Twenty minutes. Thirty minutes.

"Fuck! This is bullshit," I said out loud.

I looked over at the car lot, which was obviously a front for felonious activity. There were two taco trucks occupying the upper left-hand side of the lot, facing one another. Cars were randomly positioned around the lot. A small rambler-style structure sat in the middle of the lot, with wheelchair access on both sides leading to a sliding glass door in the middle.

I could tell Juan had told his friends I was with him. A couple of people gave a quick glance in my direction, which made me even more nervous. Ten to twelve people were gathered around the taco trucks smoking, talking and occasionally looking in my direction. I feel like a weirdo just sitting there, and I was positive I was being watched by Homeland Security and the Feds. I was thinking I should check under the hood or get something out of the trunk or just get out and walk away.

I started fidgeting around in my car, and in the midst of my flailing, I accidentally turned on my headlights.

"Oh, shit," I said, trying not to look over at the car lot. I fucked up again. It felt like I had just set off a car alarm and couldn't find the "off" button quickly enough. Almost everyone who'd been huddled around the taco trucks was leaving. I didn't know what to do.

Cars were filing out of the lot heading in every direction. Juan came running over to the car all freaked out and flung the passenger-side door open.

"What the fuck are you thinking? Are you trying to signal some-one or something? Now everything is fucked up. Everyone split, and they told me to call them later."

Oh, boy, here we go, I thought. This whole trip started out bad and only seemed to be getting worse.

Juan was shaking his head in disbelief at what just happened. I was scared to even drive away. I started in with my apologies.

"Sorry, homie. Fuck, I'm in critical condition here." This didn't bring any resolve to the situation. But I shouldn't even have been driv-ing, let alone be a part of a drug deal. I was upset with myself. Juan was upset that I screwed up the deal and raised everyone's suspicions enough to break camp.

We drove around for about an hour or so until Juan directed me to pull over at a pay phone and call his people to see if was cool yet. We scrounged on the floor for some change until we accumulated fifty cents. Juan put his hood up and hat down, walked over to the phone and placed the call.

"Alright, it's ready," he said.

He started giving directions to the outskirts of town. We came upon an auto body shop with a few cars out front, along with another taco truck. Juan directed me to pull into the adjacent parking lot. He hopped out of the car and walked toward the taco trucks. It appeared that he was ordering something from this restaurant on wheels. I could see Juan but I couldn't see inside the truck itself. Moments after his ap-proach, I saw an arm reach out with what looked to be a burrito wrapped in foil and a soft drink. Juan nodded as if saying thank you and started back toward the car. He set the drink down on the roof of the car and swung open the passenger side door, grabbed his drink and got in.

"You hungry, homes?" he asked.

"Does it look like I could eat some fuckin' food right now?" I responded sarcastically. Though I hadn't eaten in many hours, my sys-tem was in such turmoil that I had absolutely no appetite.

He gave a little chuckle and started unwrapping the burrito. As he peeled back the foil, I saw what looked to be several ounces of crystal meth.

"My homies cook dope in the taco trucks and blow the reaction out of the steam hoods. Pretty slick, huh, white boy?"

Now I'd seen it all. These were not just taco trucks. They were mobile meth labs. Apparently nothing is what it seems with this guy. You can either order a carne asada with cheese or a couple ounces of methamphetamine. This level of drug dealing is something I've only seen on TV. I tried to act like it was no big deal, but I was thoroughly impressed. Still, the reality of no heroin was closing in on my sanity.

"Sorry, homes. He couldn't give us any money, but we have close to three ounces of meth here we can sell."

This was catastrophic. I wanted to smash Juan's head through the windshield. But what could I do? He had a loaded gun and a pocket-ful of bullets. Plus I was so dope-sick, my leg hurt so much and I was so sleep-deprived that I wasn't myself. I just shook my head in disappoint-ment.

"When we get to the Ozarks I know people there, and this shit goes for $1,500 an ounce, homes," he told me.

"Well, that's real fuckin' neat," I finally said. "We're in the mid-dle of the desert, which is nowhere near the fuckin' Ozarks. We got three ounces of meth, no money, no heroin and we're almost out of gas."

I had never been to the Tri-Cities and certainly didn't know any-one there to sell meth to. Meth might have made us go faster, but it didn't make the car go any faster.

Day 4
July 22, 2005
Tri-Cities - Spokane

"Look, homes. I know you're sick and fucked up," Juan told me. "We can go wherever you want. I can't trust anyone around here, so I can't just go where I used to be able to go to score for you. Plus if any of my homies found out that I was doin' dope, it would be bad for both of us."

Now that I was in charge of our mission, it was off to Spokane, in Washington's northeast corner. By the time we got there it was 1 a.m. I knew where to get dope there at any hour. The city has a "ho stroll" -- a street where prostitutes work through the night -- and where there were prostitutes, there was heroin. I had been to Spokane a few times and never had any trouble scoring.

Juan's friends had given him enough money to fill the tank, though we had no cash to speak of. What we did have was a lot of crystal, along with a few blue dolphin ecstasy pills and some good weed.

Spokane is roughly 100 miles from the Tri-Cities. After we did a ridiculously large shot of speed, we were in Spokane in what seemed to be a jif. I was finally feeling a bit of relief just knowing I was in a familiar place.

While downtown we came across Dick's Hamburgers. Food was the farthest thing from my mind, but there were always quite a few people hanging out in front of Dick's. My first course of action was to get rid of the meth so I could buy heroin.

A lot of younger people were hanging out, trolling for action. Some were obviously intoxicated and looking to get laid or get into a fight. This kind of scene is truly a sublime environment for me. Some of the kids were hanging out in front of a van near my car. These cats looked pretty approachable, so I went up to them and struck up a conversation. These youngsters happened to be in one of those groups that traveled from state to state selling magazine subscriptions.

"You guys lookin' for anything?" I asked. "I got some some weed, a little ecstasy and some meth." I knew these guys weren't cops so I didn't hold back. All of them were enthusiastic about finding drugs, so I sold them a little bit of everything.

I sold everything we had except the speed, grossing only about $40. Juan and I drove around Spokane's hot spots looking for more customers or, better yet, someone with heroin so we could either buy some or make a trade.

The clock had almost come full circle again and it was pushing 4:00 a.m. After driving up and down the blade unsuccessfully for hours, we found a dusty back road that wound down underneath a bridge. We decided to rest our eyes for a bit and wait for the sun.

By this time most street folk had taken their nightly refuge somewhere in the midst of old battered buildings, under bridges or just laying their heads wherever they passed out.

Never really falling asleep, we both reclined our seats back as far as they would go. This wasn't very far because the back seat was packed with two big tall boxes filled with 240 VHS tapes I had brought from Whidbey if I needed some quick cash at a pawn shop.

I smoked a few cigarettes and drank the last remnants of a St. Ides. The sun drenched my windshield with its heat and danced on the back of my heavy eyelids. The first thoughts that infected my mind were these:

> This is pure insanity. My lifestyle has taken me a million miles away from normalcy. The demons that solicit addiction are cunning and crafty. Why am I subjecting myself to these extreme actions of self-destruction? I am failing to see the fun in dedicating every waking hour to a substance that has enslaved me.
>
> The only motivation that drives me to carry on is the thought of getting well. Constantly trying to kill away the pain, trying to suppress the feelings of shame and guilt and leading a life that is riddled with crime and corruption is strangely unrewarding. I've sacrificed everything for the dope and its game. I have suffered its wrath to epic proportions. I'm covered with track marks from my neck to my toes and I have drowned the ones I love in a river of deceit.
>
> All this sacrifice and not one ounce of return. Never once has the dope bailed me out of jail or offered to fix the problems it created, it took all my money and has left me for dead multiple times. These are not the qualities one would look for in a best friend.

Then I snapped out of my morbid reflection.

"Awesome! My life is awesome! And you're awesome," I said, my voice dripping with sarcasm. I looked at Juan and tried to hold onto my wavering sanity. I started the car and embarked on yet another mission to find dope, hoping it would bring calm to the storm I'd conjured in my mind.

Juan, like me, was unable to sleep. He woke up, lifting his seatback into the upright position. Also like me, he was ready to give up his time and energy to the same demons that tormented me. The sun felt good as it penetrated the toxicity enveloping my soul. It made me smile and gave me hope. With a new-found energy I pushed Play on the CD player and Jane's Addiction's "Nothing Shocking" album kicked off our morning.

As we drove into another day, I was patrolling the early-morning crowd looking for a someone to approach. Only about twenty minutes had gone by before I spotted a perfect portrait of poverty.

There she was, flailing about like she was being attacked by invisible ants as she crossed the street.

"Hey, girl!" I shouted. She was immediately distracted and came up to the car.

"Oh, hey there. You guys got a cigarette?" she asked, as she twirled a lock of her hair.

"Sure," I replied, handing her a Marlboro red.

"What's your name?" I asked.

She lit her smoke and leaned into the car.

"Mary, " she replied.

"My name is Mark, and this is Juan," I said. Juan nodded. "Hey, so we just got into town from Seattle and I'm dope sick. You know where to get any heroin?"

"Yeah, you don't look so good," Mary said. "You should come over. My house is just right there." She pointed to some run-down apartments on the corner.

Her energy was welcoming and her personality was bubbly. Mary was probably 24 years old, with light brown hair that waved down a little past her shoulders in disarray. Her makeup was put on way too thickly, and there was a definite line on her neck where the make-up stopped and her pale white skin began.

Hygiene was not one of her strong points, and her mental stability became more and more suspect as the conversation got deeper. Her body still sported the curves of a youthful woman but was camouflaged by a dingy wardrobe that hugged her body nicely but hadn't been washed for quite some time.

"Why don't you guys park right over there and come in?" She pointed to the curb in front of the apartments and started toward her unit. She was very excited to have us come over.

Juan and I parked and I gathered up all the paraphernalia to facilitate our mission. Juan checked his gun, as always, and we followed Mary to her ground-floor studio apartment.

"I live here with my boyfriend, Bob, and his uncle is the one who sells the heroin. But he doesn't live here so, we'll have to give him a call," Mary told us. She spoke like she was a bouncy 12-year-old.

It looked as though Bob had just woken up. He had bright red hair with big untamed curls that bobbed as he walked. He sported the typical redhead complexion: chalk-white skin peppered with freckles. He was exceptionally tall and had a slender build. It was clear both Bob and Mary had fallen prey to heroin by the track marks that tattooed their veins.

Bob and I started negotiating while Juan fixed up a hit of speed for us all. Bob agreed to call his uncle and have him deliver half a gram of heroin for me. As we waited for him to arrive, everyone fixed. Mary couldn't hit [inject] herself, so Bob did the deed without hesitation. It was my guess that Bob had got Mary strung out and was using her for her monthly check from Social Security.

My theory that Mary had a slight mental glitch was shortly confirmed. She started right in on stories of her childhood and the abuse that accompanied it. The story was similar to that of so many women who have lived a life of abuse from parental figures and siblings: sexually abused to the point of mental instability and then easily persuaded to a life of drugs and prostitution. The conversation got pretty uncomfortable as she told us about these dark events.

Luckily a knock on the door interrupted the story. My heart was skipping beats with anticipation. The feeling I had sacrificed fifteen years of my life for infiltrated my senses like a crashing wave. It was like a celestial wand gracefully waved from head to toe, washing away every ounce of pain, anxiety, sadness and self-doubt.

I felt like a nine-year-old at Christmas opening a present as I laid out the tools to quit the demons of affliction. The "uncle" came in with an air of confidence and moved with purpose. He was older, probably in his late forties, and his demeanor was that of someone who had seen his share of suffering -- both his own and that of others. He had the textbook biker look, with a leather coat, leather boots and a chain that hung from his wallet.

He got right to business. I already had the money out for a half-gram. We made the transaction and I got right to it. I drew up a nice shot to make up for the seemingly endless time I'd gone without. It had actually only been a matter of days since I bought some in Tacoma at my dealer's. This was only the second time I'd bought heroin during the trip.

Because I was so sick from withdrawal, I was shaking too badly to find a vein, so I muscled the first hit to gain my composure enough to find a one. I broke off a piece for Bob and Mary and disappeared into the bathroom to defile my battered body some more. At this point my physical body was merely a medium to facilitate a feeling of normalcy.

After about an hour I accomplished my goal: transitory tranquility. I rejoined the trio in the front room with a sense of serenity. The uncle had left and Bob was telling Mary that he was about to go pick berries all day so they could stay well, with enough money for heroin.

"Honey, where are my baskets?" Bob asked, a bit panicked. Juan and I looked at each other in disbelief.

"Berries," I said out loud. I wasn't aware that there was a market for people foraging through the woods picking berries, let alone people who actually held themselves in high regard for having such a job. "Bob the Berry Picker," which was his new handle, told us that it was cool to hang out and that he could probably sell some of our speed for us when he got back.

Now that I was well, I had energy and a bit of clarity.

"Alright, I'm going to the pawn shop to get some cash for these tapes," I said with confidence. Now that I knew where to get dope, I had to get some money, score enough dope to last the trip and get on the road.

Juan and I told Mary that we would be back and that she would have to call her uncle as soon as we had money. She told me where the nearest pawn shop was and we were on our way.

Juan and I were both anxious to get on the road. He even got out of the car to help me with the transaction. The two huge boxes were too much for me to contend with, especially when it literally took me three or four minutes to get out of the car. Even with my body saturated with heroin and alcohol, the pain in my leg was undeniable.

As soon as the boxes were in the store, Juan disappeared. The owner was a little reluctant to take all the tapes, but I was persistent. Nearly all were of popular movies. We agreed on a little more than a dollar apiece for 240 VHS tapes, and I left with almost $300 and a big smile. This was the first time I had held this much money in a while. The only thing as exciting as getting heroin is getting the money to get more heroin.

Night had snuck up quickly and surrounded us as we pulled up to the rickety old apartment complex. The door was partially open, so we took the liberty of entering. Mary was alone and anxious for conversation. Her energy was like that of a puppy that had been home alone all day and whose master had finally come home. I hardly had time to respond in between her questions. She asked whether she should call her uncle, and I told her to go ahead.

She got on the phone and made the order. “OK, he’ll be here in a few,” she told us as she hung up the phone. About twenty minutes went by before the knock came. Mary had been keeping us entertained with her adolescent-type antics and her failed attempts at seduction for more speed. The uncle came in as before, but with a little more hurried this time.

”Hey, I got some more money this time, but you wanna do any trading?” I asked.

“What do ya got there, Red?” he replied as he broke out his scale and a chunk of heroin.

I pulled out some of the crystal and showed him. “Got some of this shit,” I said, flicking the bag with my finger.

“Oh, you mean this stuff,” he replied, pulling out a bag twice the size of mine and giving me a quick smile. "Nope, probably not there, partner. I’m all set."

Feeling a bit deflated, I put my little bag away.

“Alrighty, then. Let me get a couple grams of black,” I said.

Dope was way more expensive in Spokane than Seattle or Portland. I could only afford a "teener," which is 1-3/4 grams, and at that time cost $150. That would barely last me the trip to the Ozarks, let alone back. I would have to curb my heroin habit. Now that’s a funny concept.

I concluded my business and felt a huge sense of security and relief. Finally having a nice piece of dope in my pocket gave me the confidence of a king. Even though I couldn’t walk unassisted and hadn’t slept in almost a week, I was now ready to dive head-first into the trip.

Day 5
July 23, 2005
Spokane - Idaho Falls, Idaho

It was early evening and still light out as we traveled east on I-90 toward Idaho. We were finally on our way to the Ozarks (which run through Arkansas and Missouri), I thought. Thoughts of the open road, especially with a chunk of dope in my pocket, boosted my spirits. But memories of Whidbey Island and our visits to Marina's and Mary's seemed to occupy Juan.

”That girl was loco, eh, esé?”Juan said, referring to Mary, laughing and shaking his head.

"Yeah, she won't be forgotten any time soon," I responded.

Unfortunately for me, the memory I was playing through was the one where Juan almost shot some dude in front of 7-Eleven. I saw the rage in his eyes and the insanity on his face when that fella started toward the car. There'd been no doubt in my mind he was going to pull the trigger. I knew I was in the company of a killer by the energy he had given off. There was no denying the deep-seated evil that came over him when he had that dude in his sights.

Juan and I still hadn't had a good night's sleep since we left Portland five days ago. Chalk that up to large quantities of meth, plus the sleeplessness that accompanies withdrawal from heroin. We hadn't touched a shower either, so both of us were looking rough. Since I lived in my car already, I was set for traveling. I had most of my nice clothes in the trunk, so I would hit the rest stops and convenience-store bathrooms to clean up.

Juan, on the other hand, didn't really do well in this type of environment, and his weight was a factor. The smell that started seeping from his pores infected the air with a chemical fog that started punching me in the face. Eventually I had to let him change into some of my clothes in hopes of containing the odor. I didn't want to confront him about his body odor, but he smelled like a rotting corpse. After a while I had to hold my head out the window to avoid throwing up.

I could see that Juan was starting to crack like a dam, from the inside out. This lifestyle was eating away at his mind. The smell he was exuding, the tattered clothes that hung off his dying body and the lethal amounts of meth he was ingesting were all taking their toll.

He broke out a picture that he got from our Tri-City visit and started telling me about how he used to live. "That's me right there, esé," he said, pointing to a guy who was at least 100 pounds heavier then he was now. But I could tell it was him. Two other gang members stood next to him, along with three beautiful women. They were all dressed in suits and sparkled with expensive jewelry. It seemed that talking about his past eased his frustration a bit.

"This shit ain't me, homes," he said. "Fuckin' punk-ass wife-beater and these old-ass jeans. I used to run these highways, Rojo."

His voice had conviction as he pointed to the road ahead.

"I can't even see my kids, esé. I'm about ready to just buck myself in the head and get this shit over with," he said.

All signs were pointing towards disaster for me. The more this guy told me about himself, the more reason he had to take me out in a fit of rage. So I refrained from inquiring about anything he was saying. I just wanted this trip to be over.

Now that we were truly on our way, we seemed to be making some pretty good time. But because of lack of sleep, I was drifting in and out of consciousness and swerving on and off the road.

"Goddam, esé, you're gonna kill us. You better let me drive," Juan yelled at me, trying to snap me out of my sleeplessness-induced psychosis.

The next couple of hours, Juan drove and I drifted. We passed through the Montana panhandle and then back into Idaho. The scenery was beautiful. Huge shafts of granite shot through the dense forest of evergreens, hemlock and cedar trees.

Exhaustion was feeding on us both, so we decided to pull into a rest stop. At this point the conversation took a turn for the worse. Juan was writing down license plate numbers. His reasoning panicked my already paranoid mind.

"You see that SUV over there, esé?" he asked, pointing to a white Explorer a few spots down from us. "Homeland Security and the Feds are deep on these roads. That's why I write the plate numbers down -- so I can tell if they're following us."

Yep, this cat is losing it, I thought to myself. "Ah, I see" is all I said.

"Me and my carnal [brother] used to run big dope on these roads, esé. You gotta know who's around you at all times. They see a gringo with a Mexican and they're already gonna be suspicious." Apparently the roads we were traveling were well-known drug-trafficking routes.

The car trip was turning into an ambiguous situation. The car was becoming my classroom, and I was Juan's pupil. He went into detail about things I'd never even thought of before: what kind of vehicles to look for and whether they had government plates on them. SUVs seemed to be the most popular choice for government vehicles, and on occasion the Ford Taurus.

All this stuff made sense to me, but the facts that I met this guy on the streets and that all he had to his name was a backpack seemed to indicate he wouldn't be under such a high level of surveillance. Then again, not too many people can make a call and have a covert meth lab disguised as a taco truck deliver large quantities of dope to a car dealership on a hot summer night. So I didn't know what to believe.

My lack of sleep and large consumption of drugs and alcohol fueled Juan's paranoia in me. Now I was looking at every vehicle with extreme suspicion. I found myself trying to down play all this talk of U.S. Marshals, Homeland Security and federal agents. The sincerity in his voice and the diligence of his counter-surveillance were hard to overlook.

Juan looked around the car and said we needed to get rid of all the crap that had accumulated.

"You gotta clean this car up, homes. This shit will have you buried in prison. We're in a zero-tolerance state," Juan exclaimed, pointing to the floorboard of the car, which was littered with drug detritus. The longer I was strung out, the less time and effort I put into being discreet and trying to hide the fact that I was a total train wreck.

As I sifted through the layer of felonies that littered my car, I was reminded of how far from hope I had fallen. A small army of orange caps that never found their way back to the needle they once housed were randomly scattered throughout the car. Old cookers that were used to mix dope in were casually strewn under both the seats, along with a small collection of needles. It was basically a mobile sharps container. I found an old convenience-store bag and cautiously placed the contraband into it and put it in the nearest trash can. I saved two needles and put those in my pocket.

What's strange about all this is that I used to freak out if there was even a pine needle on the floor of my car. Those days were long gone. By this time the innocence of my youth had been eaten away by cancerous cells. Moral prudence and a hopeful future were mere memories now.

My reflections were rudely interrupted by an older man who was watching us with intensity. His stare had us convinced that he was a federal agent and that we had better be on our way.

So with all of the junk out of the car besides Juan, myself and the dope, we set back out on the road to misery. The sun was blistering, and it was around noon when we took off. The heat was not helping the smell lofting from Juan's pores. So I kept my head partially tilted out the window to obtain fresh air.

Juan started giving me a game plan if we were confronted by law enforcement.

"If we get pulled over, esé, you better get as far away from me as possible, cuz I'm not goin to jail," he said. "You get what I'm sayin', vato? I'm gonna empty this gun and they'll have to kill me, and if they don't kill me I'll kill my own self."

Now, I've heard people say things like this before, but this was much different. This was real and solidified by his tone and demeanor. His having a gun and a pocketful of shells really sealed the deal for me. If I hadn't been so out of my mind on meth, pain, sleeplessness and dope-sickness, I'm sure fear would have affected me more.

We drove for several hours, consuming nearly the whole length of Idaho. The terrain went from beautiful forest and mountainous rocks to sage brush and rolling hills that seemed endless and hypnotic with repetition.

Juan's grim mood was creating a tense feeling. My paranoia was becoming too much to handle. I needed to try and calm down. Guns, ounces of meth, federal agents and the smell of rotting flesh were driving my anxiety into the stratosphere.

"Look, bro, I gotta do a hit. It feels like there's a rat eating the flesh from my leg," I told Juan.

The pain in my leg was never-ending. It felt like pins and needles were flowing through my veins.

"Alright, esé," he replied. "We'll pull off in the next town. You don't look so good," Juan told me with wide eyes.

I was thinking that if *he* thought I looked bad, we must look like we just escaped from a morgue.

We pulled into the next little town and I purchased a can of Pepsi and some water. We had thrown out all the spoons and cookers, so I had to improvise. That's where the Pepsi can came in. The can is easily converted into a cooker by cutting the can down by the bottom all the way through so you have two pieces, then discarding the upper portion. The bottom portion can be turned over and used as a disposable cooker. After purchasing the necessary items, Juan jotted down a few license plate numbers and we resumed our travel south.

Juan had me so freaked out I hopped in the back seat to cook up my hit. Trucks that passed us could see in the car but if I was in the back seat I could conceal my activity a bit better. Then I thought it would be an awesome idea to cook up all the dope I had and put it into one needle. This way if we did get pulled over, I only had to deal with one thing. I could use the other needle to dispense the reserves as needed. Unfortunately this stayed in the idea stage .

"God damn, homes, aren't you done yet? You're gonna get us busted!" Juan pushed me into a frenzy. The lack of sleep and ongoing use of meth had me twisting and flailing around like a wind sock. I was having a hard time keeping anything steady.

I had all the product boiled down into liquid and was about to extract it from the disposable cooker. The anticipation of relief was ripe as I started the final process of drawing the liquid up. Just when I thought my anxiety would soon be silenced, a sweat-soaked tank top came flying over the seat and landed directly in the cooker. For a split second I was in disbelief that something this terrifying could happen, then reality set in.

"What the fuck?!" I screamed. "Oh, my God." Panic hit me fast. I pulled the wife-beater off the cooker, but it had already soaked up every last drop of heroin that was seconds away from being safely quarantined in a rig.

This catapulted me into a blind rage. I was consumed with despair and sat with tears blurring my vision as my tragic reality set in. I held my head in my hands. "No, no, no," I chanted. This was the worst-case scenario.

To try putting this in perspective for a person who's never been strung out, it's similar to the feeling you'd get when you turn your back on your child at the county fair and when you look again, he or she is gone. Or losing your wallet or purse after you just got paid. It's an immediate feeling of panic, triggered by the fact that you have no power or control over what has just happened. Like watching your house go up in flames or falling prey to some sort of natural disaster. You can't change it.

After wallowing in despair for a few minutes, I tried to salvage what little product was left in the can. This resulted in another letdown, because there just wasn't anything other than a rinse. I attempted to wring out the precious liquid that was encapsulated in the nasty tank top, but again this turned up nothing.

All my extraction techniques were in vain. This tank top didn't have any intentions of returning the product that held my fragile world together. I couldn't let this shirt get away with all my goods. So I took a small pocket knife and cut out the 2" x 3" piece that had my medicine hostage. I then cut that piece into three little sections. I rolled one of the three pieces up and put it in between my cheek and gum like a Skoal bandit tobacco pouch.

While this traumatic event was evolving, Juan was showing a little bit of sympathy while he tried to calm me down.

"Damn, homie, I'm sorry. That's fucked up. I didn't mean to do that shit," he said. I just gave him a blank stare. I know it was an accident, but this didn't stop me from wanting to smash his head into the window. The fact that he had a loaded gun tucked under his leg stopped me from verbally assaulting him with too much vigor.

A physical assault was out of the question with the amount of pain that constantly surged through my body. I found myself in acute isolation staring out the window, as I silently prayed for death to find its way into my shattered life. Guess I should have been more careful what I wished for.

"You alright, esé?" Juan asked with genuine concern. He could see the psychic change that had happened.

"Does it look like I'm OK?" I snapped back. "I'm pretty sure we're in the most desolate place on earth. I haven't seen a tree in like eight hours, we're out of money and almost out of gas. Let's not forget that I'm probably gonna lose my leg, my dope is all gone and there's not a city or even a person in sight. I don't even think we're on planet fucking Earth anymore!" I finished up with as much sarcasm as I could muster.

We had traveled nearly the whole length of Idaho by this time -- nothing but desert, hills and tumbleweeds. At this point I felt my passenger was transforming into my captor. I entertained the thought of jumping from the car at a high rate of speed. That felt like a better option than continuing this trip with a rage freak on colossal amounts of meth.

"Fuck this, homes, we gotta do a hit," Juan said as he scanned our surroundings looking for a place to pull off.

"Yeah, that's just what we need -- another hit of speed. That'll make things much better," I replied, shaking my head. All this chaos definitely warranted another pit stop, but I wasn't going to do any more speed, that's for sure.

Juan pulled off onto a old dirt road that wound down to a small creek. Tall brush grew along its banks but was interrupted as it twisted its way under the highway and disappeared into a sunburnt terrain.

"God damn, homes, I'm fuckin up," Juan said, cursing himself for pulling off the beaten path. This was a violation of one of his cardinal rules. During the trip he kept saying that by pulling over we were highly susceptible to an interrogation and possible search.

We parked amongst the brush, which offered no real protection from the gaze of passing motorists. Juan pulled out the needle he had saved and put a good amount of speed into the same half-can I had used.

No sleep, lots of speed, and Juan's constant threats of violence were taking their toll on me. Persistent paranoia about federal agents closing in on us scrambled any rational trains of thought or sound decisions that might have entered my mind.

Juan had drawn up his hit and was driving a dull needle through the layers of scar tissue he had created from his abuse when I hopped out of the car.

"This is crazy!" I said. I couldn't take it anymore. I felt like a little teapot filled with liquid anxiety, about to blow my top.

I hobbled around the car, using it as a crutch and positioned myself in a way that would block someone's initial glance. Sometimes Juan would practice sound decision-making, but most of the time he seemed to invite danger. I was not ready to spend my life behind bars, and at the same time I didn't want to be shot dead.

While he was recklessly probing for a vein, a car emerged from further down the dirt road. It was coming right for us. I was in a state of pure panic. A rooster tail of dust followed the suspicious car and next thing I know, they drive around us and parked right along the creek about fifty yards from us.

It was a white, dust-covered Ford Bronco. The two men occupying it looked pretty official to me. They both had hats and wide metal-framed sunglasses. I was thinking it was all over for us and this was just the first truck on the scene. The rest of the squad was close behind, and I figured the ground troops who were embedded amongst the brush were just waiting for me to make a wrong move. Juan had the gun out in plain sight and was looking pretty nervous.

He apparently fixed his hit and was observing the truck with intensity. After a minute or so of standing there looking like I had just planted a bomb nearby and waiting for it to explode, I made my way back to the passenger seat. I got in and Juan started the car. We turned the vehicle around and began the 100-yard drive back to the highway.

To my disbelief, no one trapped us. We weren't attacked. The heroin Skoal Bandit I had been chewing on this whole time, along with the small amount I recovered from the cooker and muscled, was finally kicking in. This brought a wave of calm to my body, and the raw terror I had conjured up vanished. I tried not to think about the harsh reality of not having any more heroin as we forged on, but I knew the inevitable sickness would return soon.

I can't remember where we slept that night, or whether we slept at all. It may have been at a park. Sometimes we didn't sleep -- we just closed our eyes for a few minutes after pulling off the road.

Day 6
July 24, 2005
Idaho Falls, Idaho

We pulled into a park in the town of Idaho Falls, Idaho, at mid-day. Sweat was pouring off us both, and we looked defeated.

"My leg is throbbing so bad I can taste blood," I told Juan. "And we gotta get rid of some of this dope or we're gonna be settin' up camp in this little-ass Mormon town." Being so close to Utah, the Mormon population was large here.

I was so exhausted I just wanted to lean the seat back and let the sun melt me into a pool of toxic matter. However, I knew I had to seize this short reprieve from heroin withdraw to make something happen. In a couple hours I would be too sick and anxious to accomplish anything.

Desperation is always a powerful motivator, and when you're broke, out of gas and badly wounded, ingenuity springs up fast. I looked at Juan with a veil of disgust.

"Well, bro, looks like we -- or should I say I -- gotta go try and find some gas money," I said. My only options were to sell some dope to a stranger or to panhandle. Neither one sounded like a good idea, but something had to be done.

We were still in a zero-tolerance state, and the consequences of a delivery charge start at about 110 months in the penitentiary. Unfortunately, I had to chalk this risk up to another "occupational hazard." It was either that or just sit there and wait for someone to call the cops on us for looking crazy. The last thing we needed was to be approached by some type of law-enforcement agency. Juan had already made it clear that he wasn't going to prison.

I let out an exaggerated sigh and grabbed my crutches. "Fuck, this sucks," I said in frustration at the task that lay ahead. Juan came around to help me out of the car and gave me some words of encouragement.

"Sorry I can't help, homes, but someone might recognize me. You'll do OK. You look like a nice white kid." He paused and smiled.

"You never know. One of these Mormon girls might just take you home and put you to work." He gave me a pat on the back.

"Fuckin' right," I replied. "Look at me. I look like a toothpick with hair on top and I walk like a rusty robot that's lost his way."

I had to slip into character fast if I was to approach anyone with success. I drearily scanned the area, looking for a potential customer. It was hard not to be distracted by the beauty that encompassed me. The Snake River carved its way down a narrow ravine, jumped off the cliffs and danced on the rocks below. People were swimming, laughing, and celebrating life. Humans in harmony with nature -- such a sight of beauty. In contrast, I was stuck in survival mode, skewed by addiction, slavery and bondage of self. I had more pressing issues to deal with.

I had peeled my shirt off and tucked it into the back of my shorts. It was time to go to work. I moved slowly and winced each time the crutches touched the ground. As I moved through the freshly paved paths in the park, I thought of the words I would say to someone who looked like a drug addict. *Hey, sure is hot out. Wanna buy some meth?*

This whole thing was getting beyond ridiculous. I had to make the effort, though. This wasn't like the inner city where half the people on the street were either selling dope or looking for it. We were in a little tourist town where most of the natives were Mormon or country folk just working to make a living. Drugs, prostitutes and gang members were not mainstream down here, that's for sure.

After a half-hour of searching the park and riverbanks for a shady-looking person, I finally saw a young couple sporting punk-rock attire and approached them.

"Hey, you guys got, like . . . a bad part of town around here?" I asked them.

"There is no bad part of town. This is Pleasantville USA," the guy responded with a laugh.

The guy had spiked hair dyed blue, a Misfits shirt on and a chain dangling from his wallet to his front belt loop. His girlfriend had green hair, a nose ring and heavy black eyeliner staining her eyelids. She wore a studded leather choker around her neck, tight black pants and a Vandals shirt.

Having grown up listening to Bad Religion, NOFX, Penny Wise, Rancid, Operation Ivy and the Dead Kennedys, I definitely knew my punk rock. These two fell into the poser category.

"Damn, do you guys know where to get any pain pills or heroin around here?" I asked, already knowing they probably didn't.

"Um, no. We might know where to get some weed," the wanna-be punk responded.

Fuckin' weed. I'm so far past weed it's pathetic, I thought to myself.

The punk rockers I kicked it with, traveling from city to city, put hygiene and morals last. Drugs always came first. Panhandling and selling drugs were their main sources of income. These two looked as though they had to be in by 9:00 p.m., and their outfits looked more like costumes, without the punk-rock attitude. The clothes just didn't fit them.

Still, I continued to probe them for information and direction.

"Well, you two looking for any speed? I'm trying to get some money to get to Salt Lake."

"What do you mean? What kind of speed?" the guy asked.

Rookies, I thought to myself.

"Meth, crystal. You know -- shards."

"Oh, no, we don't need any of that," he said, taken aback.

"Alright, do you know anybody that might?

The girl chimed in, "No, we just smoke pot. No hard stuff for us."

I sighed with a disappointed nod and laughed at their attempt at being punk.

"Well, you guys have a good day," I told them. They scurried off, giving me one last look over their shoulders as they pushed on.

"Hmm, that didn't go very well," I said under my breath.

I was surrounded by tourists, travelers and farmers. Feeling tired and defeated, I took refuge on a contoured rock underneath a bridge. The scenery was in every way sublime as I sat and pondered my existence. *What the hell am I doing in Idaho Falls with no money, no home, no sense and now no heroin to suppress the misery I have so masterfully created for myself?* I wondered. Sobriety was nowhere near an option, so I had to spring into action with much diligence or suffer the wrath of heroin withdrawal in a small car with a mentally unstable passenger.

My leg was hurting so bad I just wanted to curl up into the fetal possession and slip away. But I moved on. I did one more lap around the park and saw no opportunities.

Juan was sitting in the passenger seat with his eyes closed as I approached. I opened the driver's side door and threw my crutches in the back in frustration.

"Dude, this is bullshit. There's not one shady-looking cat in sight. We gotta find a better spot. I was just told that this is Pleasantville USA".

My anxiety was creeping back up. It seemed like everyone in the park was staring at us.

"Yeah, homes, you're looking rough. We better find a new spot," Juan told me.

At this juncture, panhandling seemed to be my next logical move. I knew Juan wouldn't be joining me in that festive adventure either.

I needed to rest my leg -- it throbbed with every heartbeat -- but the sun was disappearing fast and I had to make something happen. I went to put the car in reverse and back out. My energy level was so low that it took all I had to just put the car into gear. Reverse on a manual BMW is up and over to the left and as a result of my exhaustion I hadn't quite pushed hard enough over and to the left, therefore putting the car in first gear. I was looking behind me and popped the clutch suddenly I felt the car slam into the curb. I slammed on the brakes but it was too late.

A loud crunch, followed by the sound of metal scraping on concrete, filled the air. This did not sound healthy. I slowly backed off the curb. The same noises emerged from under the car, but a bit slower and more drawn. This captured the attention of every person in the park.

Humiliation took me by storm. I punched the steering wheel in frustration. "Fuck, what an idiot!" I yelled.

After backing completely off the curb with my teeth clenched, I saw the oil stain on the brand new curb. I got out of the car in time to witness five quarts of the blackest oil I had ever seen pour from the wounded oil pan.

The oil spread like molten lava from a volcano, slow but unstoppable. I watched helplessly as it made its way to a storm drain that was framed with stenciled pictures of small fish. The words "Don't Pollute Our Rivers" were written on the drain.

I stood in shock for a moment and then started to scan the area for dirt, sand or anything that would impede the oil slick. This black creature was almost 8 feet in diameter. As I looked around, I noticed three children around 10 years old standing with a Native American, each one with a pole cast over the railing.

Watching the oil slowly disappear through the slats of the storm drain, I began digging in vain through the trunk of my car looking for something to block its path. Then I noticed some beauty bark scattered around a small tree on the backside of the parking lot, about 30 yards away. I limped over to the tree and scooped up as much bark as I could with both my hands, dropping most of it by the time I made it back to the scene of the crime.

Juan followed my lead and took over the relay race. I was making the first trip when I heard one of the children yell, “Eew! What’s that slimy stuff?”

Next thing I knew, up came an Indian with cowboy boots, cowboy hat, long black stringy hair and a classic Native American choker necklace with long black and white horizontal beads. The native came close enough to see that the oil from my car was what was polluting the river.

“What the fuck is wrong with you white people?" he demanded. "I should start kicking your ass right now. How can my grandchildren catch fish when they're dead, asshole?”

I felt like an asshole, that was for sure, but at the same time the situation was so outlandish that a part of me wanted to laugh. I was at a loss for words. By this time Juan had thrown enough bark in this black abyss to stop it from causing any further damage. With oil dripping from my hands, I started my apology with all the sincerity I could muster up.

“Look, friend, I am trying everything I can to stop this from going in the drain. We are stranded here with no money, no gas and now, no oil. So it is not the best of days for me."

The Indian seemed to appreciate my apology and realized that it was not an intentional act.

“Well, good luck to you son, I hope your day gets better.” After the Native spoke his piece, he turned and made his way back to his pupils and the outdoor classroom we had interrupted.

It took us roughly a full day -- 24 hours -- to get the car repaired and functional again. I cadged $10 for gas from a guy I met in the men's room. Then I let the pump run to $14 and blamed it on Juan's inattention. The cashier let me slide.

“Hey, have you ever heard of a town called Pocatello before?” I asked Juan as I got back in the car.

"Yeah. Why?"

"I had this dream and I don’t remember what it was about but when I woke up the word 'Pocatello' came out of my mouth."

“That’s like a couple towns down the highway. That’s about as far as were gonna make it with the amount of gas we got,” Juan told me.

"Well, looks like that's our next stop," I said as we pulled back onto the highway.

I took the opportunity to review my situation.

Since I met Juan, I'd witnessed three assaults -- one on Flea and her cousin in Portland, Oregon; the second on Drew, with the near-knifing; and the third with the black man in Pasco, Washington. Either of those could have easily escalated to murder. I hadn't slept for at least a week. I was on the brink of losing my leg to self-inflicted and negligent activity.

I'd agreed to give a total stranger a ride across the United States with a promise of a cash bonus that had yet to be seen. I put more than 1,000 miles on my car before we even officially started the trip. I hadn't eaten anything for at least two days. I had no money left and was robbed of all my heroin by a toxic tank top. I was hauling around a guy who was obviously suffering from some sort of paranoid psychosis, thinking Homeland Security, FBI and DEA agents are on our tail, which in turn has me believing him. Let's not forget the fact that he smelled like a rotting zebra carcass and looked like he was dying.

We had scored large quantities of methamphetamine wrapped in a burrito from a taco truck in the middle of the desert, met a professional huckleberry picker and been verbally assaulted by an Indian. I was constantly withdrawing from heroin in the middle of nowhere. I was too tired to even drive a stick shift, which caused a minor oil spill.

Day 7
July 25, 2005
Pocatello, Idaho

Running on fumes, we took the Pocatello exit off the interstate and drifted into the city center. We were again in the familiar predicament of no money, no gas and no heroin. This was so redundant I thought I was trapped in a scene from *Groundhog Day*.

We found a big grocery store parking lot, parked and started scanning for potential clients to buy our meth. I had to do some more speed to summon the energy to go use the pay phone. It was time to use the "call for help" card.

I knew what the answer would be but had to exhaust every option. I hopped over to the pay phone and called my boss, John Smith. His tone told me he thought I shouldn't have gone on the trip in the first place. I was on my own.

Back in the car Juan was still using the "I'm a Mexican and no one wants to help me" thing. The days of traveling had taken a toll on the interior of the car. The floorboards of the back seat were cluttered with empty cigarette packs, Big Gulp cups, napkins, a tank top that looked like it ran into the business end of a wood chipper and other miscellaneous trash that had built up. I figured it was time to clean up a little. While flailing threw the rubbish I discovered a $10 winning Washington lottery ticket. At this point, $10 seemed like a $100.

I hobbled as fast as I could over to the store to collect my winnings. My excitement was quickly shattered when the clerk told me that they couldn't honor the ticket because it was from Washington. I figured we just needed to find a vehicle with Washington plates and sell them the ticket. I drove the car to a better position, close to the entrance of the parking lot so I could get a good surveillance system set up.

We sat and examined license plates. About twenty minutes went by before we scored a winner. We approached the driver, but he wasn't interested. "I don't believe in gambling, but good luck," he said.

This was another blow. I thought about lying under his tire and hoping he would run me over, then back up to see what he had hit.

We coasted down the hill and pulled into a 7-Eleven with gas pumps out front. Juan and I started profiling every passerby in hopes to find a buyer for our meth. My patience had dwindled. I felt like making a sign or banner that read "We got meth!"

Thirty minutes passed with only two customers, but the third customer had major potential. He drove an old Chevy pickup with junk crawling over the sides of the bed. The man driving had a shaved head, a wiry build and a long pointy nose. I saw him take a pull off a can of Budweiser before exiting his rig. This was a perfect catch.

I let him take care of his business in the store before I came at him. I walked up to the pay phone and pretended to use it while he chatted with the clerk. His body movements were quick and sporadic. These were tell-tale signs that he used speed. The confirmation came when he exited the store with a six-pack of Budweiser and started digging aimlessly in the back of his truck.

Most meth users are always in the midst of a mission that never gets completed. Another mission or project distracts them from the first, so nothing ever gets accomplished. It's called "criddling": doing meaningless tasks at a high rate of speed. Washingtonians call it "diggaling." This guy was criddling big-time.

"Hey, brother, my friend and I are from Seattle and got some killer speed and we're out of gas and trying to get to Salt Lake," I said to the guy, who said his name was Cisco. "You wanna check some of this shit out?"

While I was breaking the ice with this guy, he was trying to tie down a washer and dryer with some jumper cables, so I knew he was probably pretty high already.

I offered him $20 worth to shoot up with his girlfriend, the store's cashier. When they disappeared into the back room, I took the opportunity to do a little shopping. Juan stayed behind. I filled my pockets with energy drinks: Red Bull, Rock Star, Venom and Sobe. I had tucked my pants into my socks this way I could load each leg up with candy bars and protein bars. My pockets were thoroughly stuffed, as were my pants and both hands.

Just as I was leaving, the couple emerged from the manager's office with bright eyes.

"Just grabbed a few sodas for the road here," I said. I scrambled for the door. It sounded like I was walking through a pool of tin foil. It was pretty obvious I had a little more than a few sodas, but they didn't say anything.

Ever since I became a slave to heroin, I had boosted (shoplifted) to support my habit. This was now another addiction of mine. It was rare for me to actually buy something when I go into a store.

Cisco came to the car to say he was disappointed in the quality of our product. He agreed to give us $20 but said, "We didn't really feel that stuff." They also gave us $10 worth of gas. This marked our first sale for actual cash. It was a glorious moment.

We had been using so much for so long that we couldn't tell anymore ourselves whether the quality was good. We had gotten two kinds of meth from the taco truck. The big batch we had gotten was lithium meth, and it was pulled prematurely due to Juan's persistent bickering. This meth was made with lithium strips from batteries. Its shelf life can be shortened by exposure to the sun. The other kind of meth we had was much better, but we saved that for ourselves.

We were at least 1,000 miles from our destination, with a quarter-tank of gas. I put $10 of the $20 into the tank. We left Cisco in the rearview mirror flailing aimlessly in his truck's sea of junk.

Pretty much everything we were doing was related to the getting or using of drugs or money. In Pocatello we met Craig, who said he wanted to buy some of our meth. He agreed to take us to his house but was so high that he couldn't give us correct directions.

Juan sat in silence and sat cocked to the side so he could keep Craig in his sights as I navigated through the hood.

"OK, now where?" I asked.

"Umm…" Craig said, looking very unsure of himself. "Damn, I thought this was the street. Turn around. I think it's back there."

"What the fuck, homes. You don't know where you live?" Juan asked him.

"I just moved there today so I've only been there once," Craig said.

We drove down a couple more streets and the tension started to boil over.

"Check this out, esé," Juan said. "If we gotta turn around one more time I'm gonna shoot you right in the face!" Juan made sure he made eye contact with Craig and exposed the gun briefly to let him know he was dead serious.

Craig sat back a little, shook his head and blinked his eyes as if to make sure he was really in this situation.

"Yeah, OK, umm, it's right up here. Yes, this is definitely it," Craig shouted with excitement. "Sorry about that, guys. I'm pretty spun out and haven't had a lot of sleep."

Juan just shook his head.

We sold $30 worth of meth to Marvin, a guy we met at Craig's house. He paid entirely in $2 bills.

Juan and I discussed our next move and agreed to embark on an opiate mission ASAP. We figured it would be beneficial to both of us if I was well rather than going through late-stage heroin withdrawal for the remainder of our trip.

Marvin directed us to a house where he said a woman lived who could supply me with some methadone. As we approached, adrenaline raced through my body. The excitement of someone possibly having some sort of opiate was enthralling. Plus the nervous tension generated from going into a unfamiliar place with unfamiliar people was making it hard for me to even swallow. The company I was surrounded by was heavy with discontent that was subject to spill over at anytime. Basically, nothing on this trip was easy or comfortable, and this would be no exception.

As always, Juan had his gun stuffed in his pocket. I leaned on my crutches as Marvin knocked on the door.

A young, attractive female stood in the door way with a defensive stance and a confused look. Marvin had to refresh her memory of who he was. She stood there and searched her memory for a moment and let us in with a reluctant "I guess you can come in but I'm leaving here in a few." This was Carrie Blackford, who would accompany me on the rest of my tortuous journey with Juan.

She whipped her hair around with attitude and disappeared into the back room. It was a small one-bedroom apartment. The living room was cluttered with clothes, and a single wide bed sat in the middle. The living room led to a small kitchenette that was more like a hallway leading to a back door. Juan and I took a seat on the bed, and Marvin found a chair in the corner.

Carrie came back into the front room with a compact in one hand and a tube of lip stick in the other. She was meticulous in the application as Marvin and I explained my dilemma.

She was a Caucasian women who was raised with a great deal of Hispanic influence. This was apparent by the way she presented herself. Her lips were defined with a dark brown pencil and her eyes were accented with heavy black liner and brushed lightly with a touch of blue.

Her hair was still wet from the shower and was streaked with blond highlights. It cascaded well past her shoulders. She sported a sexy figure and advertised her features well. A tight shirt stretched across her full breasts, and her pants hugged her hips just right.

Marvin wasn't too much of a talker and was beating around the bush way too much for me so I stole the conversation with my words of desperation. As soon as she admitted to possessing some methadone, I really laid on the syrupy words.

"Listen, girl. I've been driving for days, my leg is rotting off and I am in late-stage withdrawal. I need something before I lose my mind. We've got some meth and a little bit of money I can give you."

I could tell she was the type that didn't give in easily to anything.

"I already have some meth, and these are my prescription methadone pills. I don't ever sell those," she said.

"Damn, girl. Help a guy out," Juan chimed in. "This dude has been going through it for days. Just give him a couple of pills."

She put her hands on her hips and gave out a sigh.

"Alright, I guess I can sell you a few."

She left the room and came back with a pill bottle in hand. She shook out four 10-milligram pills and handed them to me. That was barely sufficient to quell my sickness but was greatly appreciated.

I gave her $20 and a line of meth for her pills. Finally my sickness was extinguished and a feeling of tranquility rested squarely upon my shoulders. This would be the first time in what seemed an eternity that I wasn't at the brink of a total nervous meltdown. I embraced the feeling for all it was worth and disappeared into a bubble of relief.

As my thoughts drifted far from my present situation, Juan's were locked in on Carrie's every move. Juan told her his name was Johnny. His face gleamed with infatuation. The two of them seemed to be very content with each other.

Carrie bragged that she knew everyone in the area and could easily help us sell off the rest of our meth. I didn't believe a word she was saying.

The night dragged on and the sack got smaller. The pills I had taken, plus a constant flow of alcohol, had put me under sedation. By this time I felt that we were in a safe environment and had retrieved all the dope that was hidden in the car. Juan for a change was displaying normalcy: laughing, smiling, talking with a positive and energetic flow of conversation. Carrie was captivated by his stories of his gang activity and responded with stories of her own.

I broke out the big sack of meth to see how much was left and in the process, I nodded off and dropped the sack on the floor. Carrie zeroed in on my careless action and made a comment that set Juan off.

"You know, I could have my brothers come over here and rob you guys so easily."

Juan lost it.

"Bitch, you have no idea who I am or the shit I've seen," he said. "I wish you would call someone to come rob me or Red."

I hadn't seen the determination or hate that filled Juan's eyes since the incident with the black gentleman in Pasco. This comment would send the conversation into a dark argument about power for the next thirty minutes.

Carrie started back-pedaling.

"I'm just sayin' that your friend is pretty loaded and he needs to be careful."

"He don't need to do shit," Juan snapped. "He just needs a little sleep is all."

All this ruckus snapped me out of my nod and and I snatched up the bag like I hadn't missed a beat.

Juan and I went outside onto the porch to discuss our next move. I was concerned she really couldn't or wouldn't help us unload the meth but was only hanging out so she could help use it up.

"This broad is trying to just stay in the sack, bro," I told Juan. "She ain't tryin' to help us get rid of shit."

But he was too blinded by lust. "No, she's diggin' me, homes. I can tell."

I just stared at him for a second, thinking there would be a smile, but he was serious. I was thinking, *You are 300-plus pounds of stink. The only thing she's probably digging is a grave for your ass.*

I couldn't reason with him. It was becoming clear that Juan didn't even care about going to the Ozarks anymore. And in fact, we never got farther east than Idaho.

I could tell Juan's infatuation couldn't be deterred and agreed to help her fix her car in turn for her trying to sell the remainder of our meth. But I knew that after we finished our end of the agreement she wouldn't be able to keep her promise. Juan disagreed and was thoroughly convinced she would deliver. I was in no position to argue with him -- or his gun -- so we agreed to disagree and made a little bet. There was no real wager. Just the fact that either I could say "I told you so" or vice-versa.

Day 8
July 26, 2005
Pocatello, Idaho

Morning crept upon us quickly. Juan and Carrie were snuggled up on the bed and looked to be in a state of hibernation. I had found refuge on the floor.

As we made our way to the car the sun greeted us in all its glory. Summer was definitely in full swing. It made me smile as we navigated through Pocatello.

Now that it was light out, it was much easier and less stressful to drive. Carrie and Juan occupied the back seat. Carrie narrated directions to me while I took in the sights and street names. Whenever I drive somewhere I always take careful notice to my surroundings in case I need to return to that same location or just for common knowledge.

I helped Carrie start her broken-down car, which was at her father's house. That took hours. The intense heat conjured heavy beads of sweat that were dripping down my face and into my eyes. I was in desperate need of a shower. Juan could get a flow of sweat just by standing and was also in need of a good cleansing. I'm not sure how Carrie could stand the pungent smell that surrounded Juan but she was always within arm's reach of him. After a quick stop at the store for malt liquor, we arrived back at Carrie's abode.

I grabbed some clean clothes out of the trunk and some CDs. The rest made their way inside. I stayed behind and enjoyed the fact that I had completed my end of the bargain with success. Now it was Carrie's turn to deliver on her promise.

By this time the methadone had lost its kick, and I was once again at the mercy of my self-appointed affliction of opiate withdrawal. A decent shower and another bit of speed were the only remedies I had available. Carrie wasn't willing to sell any more pills.

I found my Sade "Lovers Rock" CD and slapped it in the CD player. Sade always brings serenity to a stressful situation. At this point I was missing my girlfriend and was depressed and angry that I agreed to embark on this disastrous journey.

I stepped into the hot spray of water and let the heat absorb into my flesh. The water slowly began its comforting assault on my tense, aching muscles. Songs number one and number seven took me far away from Pocatello and guided me through precious memories of my first love and all the adventures we experienced.

Being young, innocent and full of life -- and then the reality of "Look at me now" -- set in as I inspected my legs, which looked like I had been wearing socks made out of barbed wire, and my thigh, which looked like I'd been shot with a musket.

I would definitely be hesitant in narrating the events of my life at my 20-year class reunion. I was imagining what I would say to a long-lost classmate.

"So Mark, what have you been doing with your life since graduation?"

> Well, it's been nonstop excitement. I've accumulated five felony convictions, which include three possessions of heroin, one possession of crack cocaine and one possession of stolen property. My misdemeanor record is also quite impressive, with 14 counts of shoplifting and 20 moving violations for a total of 39 convictions and a total of approximately five years of incarceration behind those convictions.
>
> I've also experienced multiple years of being homeless and witnessed countless stabbings, overdoses and deaths. I even

had the privilege of finding my best friend after he had been dead for three days in his van due to an overdose.

My step-sister jumped off the Narrows Bridge and committed suicide after a night of drinking and drugging. My step-mom died in her sleep due to a mixture of heroin and pills. I watched the love of my life overdose multiple times, one of which put her on life support for three days. I shot dope with Kurt Cobain and Lane Staley, who are both now dead because of drugs.

I myself have been hospitalized multiple times due to my drug addiction either for a life-threatening infection or a drug-induced psychosis. I have also managed to thoroughly destroy my vascular system and constantly lose feeling in all my extremities at various times throughout the day.

I've systematically destroyed every aspect of my life due to my heroin abuse and furthermore have been diligently strung out for more than a decade.

But other than that life's been good, Bob!

I can only imagine the response I would get. I doubt it would be anything like, "Oh, that sounds great. I wish I had decided to pursue a life of drugs and crime. Damn, you sure are lucky."

Just after I got out of the shower, Carrie's so-called brother, Diego Mogonia, appeared at the house. He's the one she had said earlier would be happy to rob us. Both Juan and Diego immediately became agitated at the other's presence. I could see Juan holding the gun in his hand through his pants pocket.

I thought for sure there was going to be a shooting. I was once again stuck in the middle of a potentially violent situation.

Traveling with Juan for a week, I had come to the conclusion that his best thinking was subject to get him put in either a mental hospital, prison or a shallow grave. The things he said and the extreme actions he displayed were bizarre. I've been around a lot of bizarre people and seen some pretty extreme and tragic events. But the way Juan lost control so easily and quickly was scary.

Even though I was riddled with fear, I had to remain calm in his presence. I felt that if I were to break down and show weakness or act as though I was against him, it would have been detrimental to not only myself but to everyone in close proximity.

The mental instability and lack of human morality Juan displayed were in every way discomforting. I had never been in a situation where I was actually at the complete mercy of another human to this degree.

I had to think about everything I said and everything I did. If I wasn't careful of my actions I could have evoked my own demise at any given time. Not only did Juan know where my girlfriend and close companions live, but he knew where my family lived. All these factors were running through my head when Juan's anger was unleashed.

But the men's meeting ended peaceably, with them discussing California and certain gangs in different areas. It never did become clear exactly what the was relationship between Carrie and Diego.

Carrie was getting ready to leave the house. I was basking in the relief that Diego hadn't provoked a fight and there hadn't been a shooting. I was also careful never to let on to this constant feeling of tension Juan gave me. I felt that he was on some sort of last hurrah. His health was definitely failing. His breathing was labored and he smelled sick. Then there was his extreme paranoia of law enforcement. The guy was a loose cannon. Needless to say I agreed with Juan on most things and was careful not to provoke him in any way.

Carrie finished up in the bathroom and returned to the front room. She was in a perky mood as she bent over slightly and shook out her hair into a towel. I'm definitely a hair fanatic when it comes to females, and she did have some gorgeous hair.

She had decided to wear an extremely tight shirt that showed off her breasts in an encouraging manner. Nicely advertised breasts always seem to have a positive effect on the male species and blind us from rational thinking.

Carrie, Juan and I drove around town looking for buyers for our meth. We all consumed some more of the speed. Still, pain was chomping its way into my muscles. It was impossible to find comfort in even the simplest of tasks. I couldn't wait till this was all over.

Carrie directed me to the highway, and we were making our way to the Blackfoot Indian reservation. Apparently Carrie had some friends out on the rez who she was sure would buy enough of our product to get us to the next city, Salt Lake City.

The reservation was only 40 minutes from Pocatello, though it seemed to take a lifetime to get there with the hot sun draining my energy and the misery of withdrawal. The scenery was desolate. As I suspected, there was no one home at this house or any other house we stopped at in Blackfoot. So we had to drive back to Pocatello empty-handed.

This confirmed my thoughts on Carrie's promises to come through on her end of the deal. She insisted it was just an off day and any other day she would have no problem getting rid of our product. It was just a matter of time. Almost completely out of gas, we made it back to Carrie's.

I was already at the breaking point and wanted nothing more than this trip to be over. I was missing Sara and tired of being puppeteered by a hostile and unstable madman. Again my options at this point were limited by multiple factors, the biggest one being that Juan knew where my whole family lived and was crazy enough to follow through with any threats he might make if I were to piss him off. So I held my tongue as much as possible.

At one point, Diego and I had a chat about how poorly Carrie was executing her promise to sell our meth. When Juan found out about the chat later, he seemed jealous.

"I hope you're not plotting against me," he said to me. "I know a lot about you, and it wouldn't be a very good idea for you to turn me in."

I told Juan I'd only been trying to find out whether Diego was plotting against us. Juan calmed down a bit but let it be known to everyone that he would shoot Diego down in an instant if he were to push Juan in the wrong direction.

Carrie got a phone call, then announced she had a sure sale lined up at the other end of Pocatello. For a moment I forgot about the troublesome position I had put myself in and observed the fact that I was in a town I had never been in before. Even though it resembled so many towns that litter our country, it was the adventure of it all that I reveled in.

The buyer wanted 1-3/4 grams of speed, known as a "teener." But he said he wanted to drop it off at a friend's house, get the money, and come back to pay us. He offered to leave a camcorder as collateral. I agreed to the deal.

When he left, Juan and Carrie grabbed a blanket and cuddled up on the couch in the buyer's apartment, while I sat in a recliner as we all watched TV. I started getting anxious just sitting there watching Juan and Carrie doze off. Plus the snuggling was reminding me of my girlfriend and how we would fall asleep in the comfort of each other's warmth. So I grabbed Juan's cell phone and went out to my car and gave Sara a call.

The buyer's apartment's parking lot was virtually empty, and darkness enveloped my car. The long day of constant sunshine had left behind a gift of warmth that filled the night air.

Sara picked up the phone. It was comforting to hear her groggy voice. My need for female attention runs deep, and I am forever searching for the nurturing comfort of even a female voice. Counselors have told me I seek this attention due to being abandoned by my mother at such a young age.

My mom went blind when I was young and had to leave me and my dad due my father's drinking and philandering. So I've always sought the attention of older women in particular to fill that hole. Growing up I clung to the mothers of my friends like they were my own, and they returned the action with genuine love and concern. As I reveled in the soothing words of concern that Sara was conveying, I climbed in the back seat of the BMW. I grabbed a blanket and snuggled up with the phone and began to enlighten Sara on the events that had transpired thus far.

She had just crawled into bed when I called and was in her sleeping attire. Picturing her in this position quickly turned the subject to sex. Sara is very beautiful and has a gorgeous body. Her skin is dove white and soft like velvet. I wished I had never embarked on this foolish trip.

Her voice was the only thing in my life that made sense at that point and brought peace to the insanity I was currently consumed by. Sara and I indulged in some phone sex for quite some time until I was interrupted by Carrie knocking on the window.

Apparently Juan was concerned about my whereabouts and sent Carrie to investigate. She said that Juan needed to talk to me. This was a very rude and upsetting interruption but I complied. I told Sara I would see her soon and hung up.

Carrie and I made our way back to the apartment. By this time we were getting suspicious about the return of the youngsters. Juan was suspicious of me, asking me where and what I was doing. I could tell he was tired and wanted to take Carrie into the spare bedroom. So we all decided to take a little nap. They disappeared into the back room and I was left to my own devices.

My first thought was to see if they had anything cool to take if they decided not to come back. After creeping around the house peaking in drawers, cupboards, and boxes, I found nothing worth taking and went out to reorganize and clean my car. What better thing to do at 3:00 a.m.?

Empty fast-food wrappers, cigarette boxes and beer bottles made up the majority of the junk that littered the floor. The trunk held clothes, my computer and all the accessories, miscellaneous bolts, screws, washers, pieces of a jack, and weird little trinkets my sister Molly left behind.

Day 9
July 27, 2005
Pocatello, Idaho

By the time I had restored order to the trunk and categorized my clothes by color, the sun was sneaking up over the hills.

Damn, I thought. *Another day has passed and we we're still nowhere near our destination.* Plus these youngsters hadn't come back with our money.

By this time I was acting as if the apartment was mine, going through cupboards, making breakfast, taking a shower and using the computer. I quietly opened the door to the spare bedroom to find Juan and Carrie still sound asleep. I was frustrated but knew Juan needed the sleep.

It was 6:00 a.m. as I pondered my next move. I figured I would kill some time by going to the store to check out the sights. So I wrote Juan a note in case he woke up while I was away.

"Hey Juan I went to the store. I left the sack in your zapatos but I will be right back." Zapatos is Spanish for shoes. I then snuck back into the spare bedroom and left the note on the floor right by the bed.

I crept back out and made a swift departure. It was so nice to have the car to myself. Sleep deprivation was playing tricks with me as I drove into unfamiliar territory. The sun was still rising and darkness lingered. After you've been up for a while, you start to see shadows out of the corner of your eye. You know they're not really there but you have to look anyway.

Then there are tree people, which are also shadows but they are up in the trees and look as though real people are up there spying on you. Here again, they looked so real that it distracted me.

OK. Got to get a hold of myself before I re-enter a semi-social activity such as driving and going to the store. With very little gas and only change for money, I stopped at the first mini-mart I saw that was accommodating morning commuters. Even though I probably looked like a chemotherapy patient, I still thrived on partaking in the daily rat race of life: people late for work, getting gas, snacks, cigarettes and energy drinks for the long day of endeavors that lay ahead.

Then there were those early-rising families, tourists and travelers excited to make unforgettable memories and conquer new ground. All this social integration is the fabric of our existence. Everything we do is based on a relationship in one way or another. I was consumed with a sense of clarity at this epiphany and was happy being part of it all.

I went in the mini-mart and got myself a breakfast brew to take the edge off. I also got a 32-oz. fountain cup and straw to conceal my beverage. Back in the car I poured the 22-oz. bottle of St. Ides mixed berry malt liquor into the cup.

I decided to stop by Wal-Mart and check out some car stereos. My stereo was currently not working very well so I figured I would at least see what they had. I finished off my beer, parked and entered the store.

One of my favorite parts of the Wal-Mart experience is the greeters that stand vigilantly to acknowledge your entrance. My grandparents used to be Wal-Mart greeters so I am always reminded of them when I enter. Sometimes a smile and cheerful hello from a stranger is enough to brighten your day.

After efficiently inspecting all the systems, speakers and stereo accessories, nearly two hours had passed. I forgot that I had Juan's phone still and was startled by the loud ring that echoed from my pocket. I actually jumped as if I had been shot with a taser. After being up for this many hours and the profuse amount of drug intake, my motor skills were nowhere near normal. I'm sure to the casual observer I looked like a little kid trying to hold out on taking a piss.

I answered the phone expecting to hear the tired voice of Juan telling me that he was awake and the youngsters along with the money had returned. Not the case.

It was Juan, but he was enraged and going on about how could I abandon him like that and that he was on his way to the Greyhound station because he thought I had intercepted the money from the youngsters, taken the rest of the dope and left him.

"Didn't you get my note?" I calmly replied.

"Fuck, no! What note?"

I told him to look on the floor in the spare bedroom.

"That would be pretty hard since I'm not at the fucking apartment anymore."

Now I was stricken with disbelief.

"You mean you didn't see the note? How could you not see the note?"

Juan, still very angry, replied, "I'm back at Carrie's. We thought you left us. Why didn't you wake me up? What the fuck is your problem?"

I tried to explain the note and that I had left the dope in what I thought was his shoe but apparently wasn't and I lost track of time.

"Did you find the dope in your shoe?" I said. My face was tensed up and my eyes were squinted as I awaited his response.

"Fuck, no, I didn't get the dope. *You mean you left an ounce of dope in some stranger's shoe?"*

Feeling like a complete ass, I told Juan I would be right over to pick him up. I didn't want this guy to make it his life's goal to seek revenge on me. Of course I got lost trying to find my way back to Carrie's and it took me nearly an hour to get there. Juan was pacing out front.

From his demeanor, I figured we were going to fight as soon as I stepped out of the car. We came chest to chest and he cocked his head to one side and began a sustained verbal assault on me.

"Don't you ever leave me again, motherfucker! See what happens when we split up? I thought I was going to have to hunt you down. Now you forgot the only valuable we had left at some tweaker's house that already ripped us off for the teener you fronted them."

All I could say was, "My fault and I'm sorry, bro."

We sped across town praying the dope was still there. Not many words were spoken on this trip. We both knew we would be screwed without any dope to sell. I didn't even have any change left at this point.

The gas gauge was dangerously close to empty as we sped past vaguely familiar establishments. My mind was converting into pure anger the mixture of feelings that had overwhelmed me since the delivery of the bad news. Pure anger that I justified by the lack of payment from those little fucking rave kids.

The apartments radiated with a ghostly absence of people. *Is this a set-up?* I wondered while hobbling up the stairs to the apartment.

Juan followed close behind. Disregarding the pain, I dropped my shoulder and rammed the door. The place was empty. I rushed to find the shoe.

"Please be there. Please, please, please be there."

I swooped down to pick up the shoe and gave it an aggressive shake. The sound of a sandwich bag crinkled and boom! the wondrous bag of dope parachuted into my hand.

"Oh, shit. Got 'em, coach!" I shouted and did a little dance back into the living room. Juan wasn't as joyous as I was, but he was happy.

We decided to take some collateral. After all, they owed us $150 for the package I had given them the night before. Plus, they had told us to make ourselves at home. We took the stereo and some CDs, but there was nothing else in the house that was worth taking.

Back at Carrie's apartment we met Diego again. He agreed to sell some of the meth for us. He made a few calls and in no time said he had a $400 deal. I'm sure he had told the buyers the price was $500, but if he made a profit, that was OK with us. The deal went down smoothly, and we found ourselves with $400 in cash.

Carrie inquired on our whereabouts and if we had any shit left. I replied, "We have a little left, and I'll hook you up with a bit if you'll let me get some sleep". She agreed. So I went into the bathroom and made her up a small package.

Even though she hadn't sold a single bit and had pretty much reneged on her end of the bargain, I was in no mood to explain ethics to her. I returned from the bathroom and gave her the package.

Lighting my final smoke of the day I found a blanket and a pillow and curled up in a quiet corner. Juan and Carrie retreated to the porch.

Day 10
July 28, 2005
Pocatello, Idaho

It only seemed like minutes but it was well into the afternoon before the racket from the front door woke me up. When I got my bearings together I noticed a not-so-friendly Diego standing above me.

"Get up, boy!" he shouted at me. "I need my money back. That shit was weak."

I shuffled to my feet with a dazed look and responded, "What are talking about, dude? There's no refunds, plus you said it was all good last night."

Diego explained that the people he sold it to were not pleased and sent him to collect their money. Meanwhile I was wondering where

Juan and Carrie were. After a quick look around it was very clear they were gone.

While I was checking the house for life forms, Diego reached under his shirt and pulled out a gun from his waistband. I knew what he was doing, but I turned away and stepped out onto the porch before he could confront me.

There I was met by five gang members leaning up against Diego's car. Two of them were holding guns. This was a situation I was not well equipped to handle. I assured everyone that I didn't have the money and pulled out my pockets to show them.

Diego had stepped around me and was in the front yard pacing back and forth. He kept repeating, "Man, give up the money. I don't want to have to shoot you."

I kept telling them that I didn't have the money, that Juan had the money and had gone to the store. I figured Juan's absence was actually a good thing, because he would have started shooting. It was a good thing they didn't strip-search me, because I had the money deep in the confines of my chonies [underpants].

Still I was overwhelmed with fear that I was about to be shot. These fellas were all tatted up, with blue bandanas stretched across their foreheads. They were putting on quite a show. I figured one of them was going to shoot at any second. I kept talking and trying to defuse the situation. I was telling them that Juan would be back in a little while. After a few threats of being shot if Juan didn't have the money, Diego swore he would be back shortly to collect.

Then one of his friends said, "Let me just smoke him, esé."

"No no, we need the money. We'll be back."

They piled in his car and took off.

I've been jumped before, hit with baseball bats, even had knives pulled on me. But this was the first time I actually had guns pointed at me, threatening my life. So I was a little shaken up.

Juan and Carrie returned shortly after. I gave a shaky description of the events that had just transpired. Of course Juan's desire to retaliate was immediate.

"Where the fuck did they go? I'll buck that fucker in his head," Juan shouted. This was his favorite pastime: to gang bang. And since Diego was also in a gang, it would now be a gang war.

Juan was completely fired up and ready to unleash some built up aggression. The only thing I was concerned about was getting a few more methadone pills from Carrie. Juan, seeing the desperation and physical bankruptcy in my eyes, apparently sympathized with me. He turned to Carrie and convinced her to come clean with a couple of methadone. She was a little reluctant but did give a couple up.

They had also been thoughtful enough to purchase me a St. Ides mixed berry malt liquor beverage. I cracked open my beer, popped my two pills and greedily tried to drink my troubles away.

Meanwhile, Juan was mentally preparing for battle as he paced back and forth in the little trampled-down yard in front of Carrie's. He walked with much purpose. One hand clearly clenched the .38 revolver that never left his pocket.

I began to think of the odds while sitting on the steps of the front porch. It seemed to me that there were at least six of them, and three of them were actually holding guns. We only had one gun, which was a revolver at that. No match for the small arsenal they displayed. At best, Juan would get a couple shots off, maybe even wound one of them while I sat unarmed and hoped I was only wounded by a spray of small-caliber projectiles.

So without sounding like I doubted Juan's capabilities, I suggested we take this opportunity to disappear. I explained to a very serious Juan that it was getting dark. We were way past schedule. My leg was getting worse, not better. And having a shootout with odds of six to one was not good. I also explained to him that since doing dope and hanging out with gang members and prostitutes wasn't curbing our lust for action that, the only logical thing to do was to find a casino. Still frustrated and clearly angry, Juan agreed. Carrie chimed in, "There's a casino on the Blackfoot Indian reservation just right up the road."

Earlier in this book, I merely touched on the depths of my gambling habit. See, when I was in Reno attending my sister's wedding, I had just recently gotten back from Las Vegas. While I was in Vegas I dropped a good $5,000. When I went to Reno, my money situation was pretty grim but what the hell, it's my sister's wedding and maybe I'll win something this time.

I brought all the money I had in the world ,which was about $3,000. By the second day I was down to $2.00. Seriously, $2.00. On my way back to my room to pout, I figured I might as well spend it all.

So I found a slot machine and wouldn't you know it? On my last pull I hit the big one. This machine did everything but shoot out fireworks. Bells, whistles and the click click of the machine counting out credits. Security came running over along with a very beautiful girl all in glitters with a fanny pouch full of money. After a good five minutes of this machine spouting off, the credits totaled $1,500.

I phoned my sister and gave her directions to my slot machine. She showed up while the long legged cashier was still handing me hundred-dollar bills. I gave her a nice chunk for a wedding present and disappeared into the sea of slot machines, forever plagued with "The Fever."

Ever since then, even if I only have a quarter in my pocket, there's the little voice in the back of my head telling me that I could win it big. That little voice was cheering me on as soon as Carrie said there was a casino nearby.

We all agreed it would be best that we made a swift and stealthy get away. Unfortunately Juan's lust for Carrie was so great that he insisted on her coming with us.

I took him aside and observed we'd encountered nothing but trouble since we met her and it would be best to move on without her. Juan again insisted that we bring her along and that we would drop her off on our way out to town. Juan wasn't really making a suggestion. He was saying how it was going to be.

Carrie agreed to go to the casino, but she insisted on driving her own car. I learned later that he had stolen her keys in the casino so that she would have to ride with us after that point. That's how she came to be a hostage to Juan.

Once again, Juan had to suppress his anger that was obviously becoming an issue with his ranting about wanting to kill Diego. Plus the fact that I kept spoiling his abnormal thirst for homicide. He was persistent in the way he talked about getting revenge on people. It seemed like I kept having to remind him that there were actually punishments for such things.

About 20 minutes into the drive, Juan seemed to have calmed down a little, so we fixed up a hit. Juan and Carrie did theirs and I saved mine for when we stopped. I didn't want to kill the little feeling of serenity I was experiencing from the methadone and alcohol. Plus the damage I've caused to my vascular system is so extensive that I had to search, sometimes for hours, for a vein.

It was evening by the time I found a parking spot at the Blackfoot Casino. For me, it was like pulling into Las Vegas. Big bright lights in the middle of the desert. I gave Juan the money because my money-handling skills in a casino are not good. Although I did keep $50.

Juan and Carrie made for the entrance and left me to poke and prod myself. Finally I achieved my goal and hurried into the casino. The sounds of slot machines hit me in the face as soon as I opened the doors. I got an "I just won a shopping spree at Costco feeling" as I made my way through the forest of lights.

The penny slots and nickel slots were about the only thing I could afford so I stuck with these mostly. After an hour or so of playing the not-so-lucky slot machines, I had squandered my $50 and started looking for Juan.

It didn't take me long to discover Juan and Carrie huddled around a nickel slot machine. By the look on their faces it was clear that luck had passed them by as well.

We wandered around the casino for a bit. Our eyes were like big black headlights from the speed. The people surrounding us were mostly country folk. Cowboy hats, cowboy boots and obviously cowboy roots were the theme.

So our presence was like that little black unidentified object floating in your drink. You had to look real close to see what it was. What seemed to be the treatment we were receiving? I think all three of us had come to the same conclusions as we made our way to the exit signs.

Juan's constant feelings of being followed had corrupted my thinking deeply. Ever since the stop at Moses Lake, Juan had shared his thoughts of being followed by any number of agencies: FBI, Homeland Security, State Patrol, FTA, DEA, you name it. I figured that the huge amounts of methamphetamine he was consuming had obscured his mental capabilities to tell truth from fiction. Still, everywhere I went, I felt that I was being watched and that "they," whoever *they* were, were just waiting for the right moment to swoop in on me.

Then there were the gang members. Every time I saw a Mexican I figured that we were about to be sprayed by gunfire.

The initial excitement of traveling across the country had been dissolved into a series of mind-bending events. I lacked the motivation to go any further. I had pitched my crutches out of the car in a frustrated fit of anxiety earlier that day. So it took every ounce of strength I could muster up to limp ten feet. After ten feet I had to pause, grit my teeth with pain and try and gain some composure before moving on.

To an onlooker I probably resembled someone who had just been shot in the leg. The pain I was experiencing was insufferable, but I had to keep moving. I had to fill this craving void to overcome, to adapt, to explore this infectious self destructive path to the end.

Why can't I stop? Why don't I stop? I remember wishing that somebody, anybody would save me from my worst enemy. Myself!

As I looked to the sky and begged the stars for mercy, two official-looking cats came out of the casino and were coming towards us. I felt it necessary to spring into action and vacate the premises. Cringing with pain, I hopped in the driver's seat. Carrie sat in the back, while Juan sat shotgun.

Day 11
July 29, 2005
Pocatello, Idaho

It was well into the small hours of the morning when we drove over same ground back toward Pocatello. Shortly after making it to the highway, a familiar-looking car came creeping up on my bumper.

"Oh, shit! It's the cops. Fuck!"

Carrie turned around to look. Juan had his eyes fixed on the cop's reflection in the side mirror. We all tried to remain calm, which worked until a second highway patrol car came into view.

We were approaching an exit, so I decided to take it. I wanted to see if they were really following us. When I exited the highway, to my dismay, so did they. OK. Now I started to panic a little. There was still enough dope left to put me away for a decade and probably another decade for the paraphernalia.

As soon as Juan saw they had followed us off the highway, he pulled the gun from his pocket and spun the cylinder.

"If we get pulled over, I'm gonna wait until this pig comes up to the window and buck him in the head." Juan said. He was definitely not joking.

Carrie stuck her head between Juan and me to see the gun.

"What the fuck, bitch? Sit back and put your seat belt on," I said.

I had no clue where I was or where I was going. Now all of us were frantic. Carrie and Juan started to argue about what we should do. I asked Carrie if she knew where we were. She said she did.

"Which way? Which way?" I shouted.

Carrie told me to take a left and Juan told me to go right. I figured I would follow Carrie's direction since she knew where she was. Big mistake. Juan's temper boiled over, and before I knew it he had stuck the gun into my ribs.

"Motherfucker, if you ever do what she says again, I'll shoot the shit out of you."

I was waiting for the bullet to rip through my gut. I was thinking, "OK, I'm either going to get shot by Juan, get shot by the police or go to prison forever." I felt like just letting go of the wheel and crashing into a ball of fire.

With the police still trailing behind us, I pulled into the first house. Before the engine even stopped I opened my door and was acting as though I lived there. The police crept by and stared my car down but kept going. I figured they were going to surround us. Juan was going to start shooting and we would all be dead in a matter of seconds.

A wave of relief rushed over me when the police disappeared into the darkness of the desert. But that relief was only temporary. Juan himself was a cause for greater concern. I felt he had become a fearsomely evil character. I could feel the evil seeping from his pores. Negative energy flowed out of his eyes and penetrated my very soul. I tried not to even make eye contact with him as he directed me to drive.

Carrie was oblivious to Juan's threat to me. She was a no-nonsense, strong-minded female. A queen bee if you will. I would even go as far as calling her a smart ass. She wasn't about to be bossed around by some stranger, even one with a gun.

Carrie and I were never alone long enough for me to convey to her Juan's mental instability. I cringed when she made smart-ass remarks. I knew there would come a time when Juan's anger would outweigh his lust for Carrie.

Unfortunately, that time was upon us. Juan and Carrie started to argue a bit as we drove. She wanted to go home. It was apparent that she thought Juan was just trying to tell her what to do.

Juan started to spin the revolver's cylinder. I was trying not to look in his direction but I caught a glimpse. To my dismay, Juan was swaying back and forth and mumbling unintelligible words.

Then he opened his eyes with a look of insanity and said with a sadistic smile, "Sorry, man. I gotta get rid of you guys. These voices in my head won't shut up until I do what they say."

It's hard to overstate the terror that erupted in my heart. I never thought I would live to tell this story.

Juan directed me down a desolate dirt road that wound its way deep into the rolling hills of southern Pocatello. The barrel of the gun swayed back and forth.

He began to apologize for what he was about to do.

"Sorry, man. These voices are telling me to kill her, and I can't leave any witnesses." I was trying to hold it together but my emotions were starting to spill over.

Carrie kept inquiring about Juan's plans. He replied with a sinister laugh, "Heh, heh, heh. You'll see. Oh, you'll see."

Fear infected even my motor skills. I found it almost impossible to shift, steer or push the clutch in. I didn't even feel comfortable breathing. Darkness and desperation enveloped any words I tried to speak.

He ordered me to keep driving deeper into nothingness. All I could think about was the last time I saw the people I love. My Dad, my sisters and brothers. What would be their last memory of me? What would they say at my funeral? Images of the Flying 'R' Ranch flashed in my mind, and memories of all the growing up I had done there.

Day 12
July 30, 2005
Pocatello, Idaho - Northern Idaho

The farther we drove, the more reality set in. I was sitting across from an angel of death. A hollow feeling set in when Juan directed me to stop and kill the lights. We had driven for so long the sun was starting to eat through the darkness and shed the first rays of light on the dirt road.

"I'm going to kill her first. Depending on how you react, I'll see if I'll let you live."

By this time I was fighting back the tears trying not to just curl up in a fetal position and give up. Juan got out of the car, lifted the seat forward and ordered Carrie out of the car.

I kept repeating, "Oh God please no please no oh my God."

Carrie's attitude was now drastically different. She could see the craziness that filled his eyes.

I had to do something, but what? My leg was virtually useless and Juan seemed possessed. Truly possessed. When actually faced with a life or death situation, your mind is clouded with emotions that are so overwhelming, you feel frozen. Unable to respond or react to such a catastrophic event, let alone engineer a plan to subdue a murderer.

Do I stay in the car? Do I get out of the car? Should I try starting the car and running him over? Or should I try reasoning with this now-psychotic tyrant?

Juan dragged Carrie about five feet from the car and threw her down onto her knees. He raised the pistol to the back of her head and pushed her head all the way down into the sand. She whimpered desperately. Juan's mouth was tensed. I couldn't bear to look but couldn't look away. This was the most frightened I had been since the trip began. I was about to witness a cold-blooded murder, and I was sure I'd be next.

Then, out of nowhere, a small red pick-up truck appeared on a distant dirt road with a load of hay on the back. I announced this to Juan and he quickly put the gun away and ordered Carrie back into the car.

Now Carrie and I were forced into a dictatorship. Indecisive, irrational and hostile would be words to describe Juan's attitudes and behavior as he directed me to turn around and head out of the hills. An eerie silence plagued us as we drove into a red dawn. The car seemed different. The hills seemed unreal. Everything was quiet and distant. The world took on a distorted and sinister existence.

A pungent chemical odor flowed from Juan's pores from the massive amounts of meth that swirled through his blood. My senses seemed heightened. I felt like a celestial being or something not of this world.

Did that really happen? Is this situation I'm a part of even real?

These thoughts traversed through my mind as we made our way back to civilization. The highway finally came into sight and was a sign that the world was still functioning. I'm not exactly sure what the first words were that broke the ominous silence, but I'm pretty sure Juan told me to "take a right" or "take a left."

We drove back the same way we had just come. I pretended nothing was amiss and ignored the fact that Carrie and I had been seconds away from being executed.

I drove on wondering how to approach Juan. It seemed like he was normal and relaxed, but who knew what twisted thoughts raced through his mind? I figured I would let him strike up the conversation.

It had become apparent I was dealing with a couple of different personalities in Juan. Now that I had witnessed the devilish metamorphosis Juan was capable of displaying, it was a question of how long Carrie and I would live.

Carrie calmly asked to go home. She had not packed any provisions. Not even a purse.

"Please take me home. I just want to go home."

Juan's reply was, "I thought you wanted to come with me." As if nothing was wrong. I wondered if Juan even remembered that he had a gun to her head not that long before.

Carrie persisted in her request, and Juan started to rock back and forth as he had before. I shook my head and let out a soft, drawn-out sigh, because I had a feeling Juan was going to snap again. As we drove down the sun-baked highway, Juan told me to take the next exit.

Here we go again I thought to myself.

Sure enough, a desolate dirt road came into view and Juan directed me to turn onto it. Old barbed wire fences leaned down toward the overgrown grass that lined the road. There were no structures as far as the eye could see.

Juan directed me to stop the car and removed the keys. He got out, lifted the passenger seat forward and told Carrie to come with him. I was directed to stay put while he had a little chat with Carrie.

The sun was beaming down so hot it felt like it was trying to kill us. When you breathed in a deep breath, it was as though no air was consumed. The simple task of breathing was odious.

Juan held Carrie close to him and walked slowly up the hot and dusty road. He leaned into her ear and spoke with a serious look upon his face. They walked about 50 yards up the road and then back again. This was repeated a couple times, consuming about a half hour.

I never heard a word of their conversation but Carrie's expression was sullen and she had a melancholy demeanor when they finally returned to the car.

"So what's up?" I said.

Juan told me we were heading back to the Tri-Cities.

All this time dedicated to absolutely nothing but total fuckery! I thought as I pulled back out onto the highway.

I felt like the world's biggest fuck-up. But we were still alive and heading back to my home state.

My opiate withdrawal was again in full swing. My eyes watered as though I was crying and my body ached with every heartbeat. The muscle spasms and severe leg cramps came non-stop.

We again started back toward Washington. Conversation was minimal. The only words spoken were little threats by Juan. For example, when we stopped for gas he would have the gun in his lap and tell me not to take too long as he looked at me and then at the gun.

Juan told Carrie that if she tried anything, she and her children would be killed. "I know you have two kids who live at 333 Swan Lane in Pocatello, and I won't hesitate to snatch them up and make them disappear." Carrie was in shock at those words. It was obvious that was in fact the address where her children lived from the way she reacted. I was also taken aback that he knew her children's address.

Then Juan turned to me.

"Can I trust you, esé?" he asked. "Cuz I would hate to have to kill you or your girlfriend. And you know I know where your family lives. You see, I have these voices in my head that get so loud sometimes that I have to kill. That's my job. To kill. Or they will just get louder and louder."

By the look in his eyes you could tell he was not kidding. I believe this was some sort of death march he was acting out, the last chapter in his life of lunacy. Maybe that's why his words and actions seemed so profound.

After Carrie and I were thoroughly threatened, we finished fueling up and returned to the highway. I flashed back to happier times as I drove. Thoughts of high school, when everything was new and adventurous. The burden of moving from middle school, where you were top of the social food chain, to high-school freshman. My school had a "freshman pond" where you were subject to take an unexpected swim.

Then the stress of changing schools trying to find a social circle to ease into. That first day of school is the meaning of pressure and the definition of anxiety. Sports, my first love, prom night, and dreams of all the goals I had. All those things have been displaced by deep-seated addiction. Drugs have affected every aspect of my life, wreaked havoc in every relationship I've ever had: family, friends, teachers, bosses and most of all, myself.

Now here I sit. With a deadly infection running through my blood, a half-inch of flesh eaten away in my right leg from careless IV drug use, haven't slept for more than a week from excessive amounts of meth, put myself into a situation where I'm a hostage and my captor is obviously suffering from schizophrenia and maybe from demonic possession and now, there's been a female incorporated into all this who is agitating the highly volatile combination of personalities. All of this suffering because I wanted to get high.

I wished with all my heart I had never agreed to this so-called trip. I wished I wasn't high when I was high and wished I was high when I wasn't. I wished I was in my girlfriend's warm embrace and most of all I wished I was free from this poison. This destructive disease of addiction. I begged God for another chance.

There was no room for smiles. No need to laugh. No reason to be happy, and the future was not bright. What used to be an experimental and moderately social intake of drugs was now an out-of-control storm of misery.

Although things were grim, Juan remained placid. "Do you want me to take over driving? You've been driving for a long time," Juan offered.

Driving was the only thing left that I controlled -- when I wasn't at gunpoint, anyway. So if I wanted to ram into a telephone pole or wall at a high rate of speed, I still had that option. Unfortunately Juan always made sure he had his seat belt on, so that idea really wouldn't accomplish a great deal.

"I think we could all use a little rest, and I saw a rest-stop sign a minute ago," I said. He agreed, so I pulled off the highway and descended into the rest area. We were clearly back in the northern Idaho now. Big pine, hemlock and fir trees graced the area.

Carrie had been cramped in the back seat with blankets, clothes, CDs and an assortment of shoes, so she wasn't in the most comfortable of positions. Nor was she in the best of moods. We all got out and took a much-needed stretch and a deep breath of Pacific Northwest air.

We were disoriented and wandering around the car. The darkness gave way to an eerie medieval ambience and my imagination was in full swing. I peered into the ghostly forest that seemed to hold us captive while we rested. The woods only amplified the feeling of pending doom that I had been experiencing for quite some time now.

We decided it would be an unnecessary risk to return to the highway at this hour, so we agreed to wait until daybreak to resume our trip. Juan migrated to the back seat to seek out some elusive comfort while I embarked on a reconnaissance mission and a detailed perimeter check.

I'm not sure what I was looking for, but the more time I spent away from Sir Psycho the better I could think. My fragile state of mind was under a barrage of ominous thoughts as I crept through the rest area. I could feel the amphetamines waging war on my neurotransmitters. Opiate withdrawal infiltrated my bone marrow and sent shivers through my body as I walked. Definitely not a good time to be out in public.

I checked out the restrooms and lingered on the small paved path that wound back to the parking lot. A huge hemlock tree found its home a few feet from the path and littered the area with an onslaught of pine cones. The dense forest extended about 50 feet in three directions.

As I paused to analyze my surrounding I could hear the whispers of conspirators from the army of darkness that was surely mounting an attack. Or maybe I just needed some sleep. Regardless, I saw it best to return to the car.

Upon my return I found Juan had been watching me and said that I needed to sleep because my actions had become suspect. Everyone was far too paranoid to sleep. Carrie didn't even want to come out from underneath the blanket and I knew she was too terrified to sleep. So we all just rested our ravaged bodies and stewed in a vessel of misery.

Day 13
July 31, 2005
Northern Idaho - Tri-Cities

The clock read 5:30 a.m. Early go-getter types were making preparations for a fun-filled day of traveling. What lay ahead for us would fall far from the fun tree.

At this point, Juan felt it was safe to return to the highway. It had been dark when we exited into the rest stop, so I wasn't exactly sure where we were other than near the general area of northern Idaho.

Juan had to point out the way back to the Tri-Cities, which obviously irritated him. It seemed he had a hard enough time contending with the voices in his head. Any added voices such as mine were not welcome.

By this time, the bag of not-so-good meth had been reduced to crumbs, and Carrie was desperately conserving the few methadone pills she had left for herself. Juan consumed the bulk of what remained and left Carrie and me with very little.

"What the hell! Are you guys plotting against me? Did you guys do something to the dope?"

I could tell that this was going to be another long day. Juan drew the ominous liquid from the spoon and told Carrie to give him her arm. She was not cooperative at first and tried to take the needle from him.

"I'll do it myself," she said.

Juan did not take kindly to her response and directed me to pull over. Carrie then changed her tune.

"OK, OK. Here," she said, holding out her arm.

The gun rested between Juan's legs virtually the whole time. Occasionally he'd grab it and cock it to remind us -- or maybe the voices that screamed in his head -- that he was in charge.

"I run this fucking show," he blurted out.

Carrie teared up as Juan emptied the contents into her arm. Juan told me to give him my needle and drew up what remained in the spoon.

"Here. You can do this when we stop," he told me.

When we reached Kennewick, we were as empty-handed as a newborn baby. The money we'd obtained from the only profitable drug deal out of the few ounces of meth was now gone, along with the product itself.

Juan's mood was once again volatile. He was sweating profusely while he swayed back and forth in his seat. We drove down alleys, through neighborhoods, orchards, businesses and parking lots.

"It's not safe to contact my people during the day, but I need some fucking help. I'm about ready to kill my homie and rob him if he doesn't answer his phone," Juan said.

He directed me to drive in front of his friend's house. As we drove past, a few gang-affiliated friends of his were standing out front. Not more than a minute passed before Juan's phone rang.

"What's up, esé? Oh, she's just a friend. Oh, no, no. I didn't kidnap her. She's here on her own free will. She wanted a ride to Oregon."

Then the conversation changed into Spanish. High-speed, agitated Spanish. It ended with, "Alright, alright. I'll be there."

Juan hung up and told me to pull over so he could drive.

"What's up? What's the word?" I asked.

"My people think I kidnapped the girl and told me to quit fucking jeopardizing everyone and get rid of my baggage."

"What's that supposed to mean?" I said.

"Sorry, bro. I have to bring you both to the pig farm. A few of my partners are going to meet me there. Everyone wants their turn with the girl. Then they'll shoot you both and make sure the pigs dispose of the evidence."

"What the fuck are you talking about, bro?" I responded. A pig farm? I immediately thought of the movie *Snatch* with Brad Pitt. One of the characters gives the gruesome details of how fast a pig can consume human flesh and bone.

"I'm sorry, dude. I tried to talk them into letting you go, but they're afraid you know too much and you'll tell on me. Maybe while they're having their way with the girl, you can escape."

By this time, we were heading out of the Tri-Cities and toward Walla Walla, Washington. I tried to figure out whether he was being serious. Either way, we were traveling into a secluded area. We drove higher and deeper into what seemed to be uninhabited forest.

Juan's phone rang again.

"What's up? I can't remember where the driveway is. Alright, alright. I'm almost there. No, no, everything's cool. I know what I'm doing. Alright, don't trip. I'll be there. OK, later."

Juan was visibly anxious and threw the phone down.

"Fuck, esé, I'm sorry I got to do this to you. I liked you, homes. You were gonna give me a ride all the way to the Ozarks to see my grandfather, but the people I work with don't want any loose ends. I asked if I could just drop her off, but the risk of you telling someone about what you would see is too great and they're not willing to do that."

"Come on, man, you can't just drop me off? How do you know they're not going to kill you too?"

The people who had called Juan were definitely upset and I could hear them yelling through the phone. I was desperately trying to say something, anything to plant a seed of doubt about his friends' motives.

"That's my family, esé. They're not going to kill me."

I started in a new direction.

"Hey, I know you want to see your kids before you go back to Mexico or wherever you're going. So why don't you let me go into Kennewick and find them and bring them to you? That way no one will see you, and no one knows me, so you wouldn't be in jeopardy."

This piqued his interest. But he responded, "I can't just not show up. They're all waiting for me, and if I don't show up they're going to think I'm a bitch, and I ain't no bitch."

Carrie was sitting up, taking in this whole conversation with an abstract look of concern but not sure how much validity this whole pig farm thing held. Just like me, though, she was again starting to panic.

"What's going on? Please don't take us there. We're not going to tell on you."

"Don't you see? It's too late. They already think I kidnapped you." Juan was highly agitated, swaying back and forth and fondling the revolver.

Trees were whizzing by as he looked from side to side for the entrance of the farm. His pupils were dilated so severely that only black remained.

Juan started mumbling to himself and firmly gripped the revolver's wooden handle. "Fuck you. Shut up!" He tapped the end of the barrel against the side of his head as if he were trying to beat the voices into submission.

"These voices are getting louder again. I have to get rid of you guys."

Being within arm's length of Juan I could see the mental instability and anger that overcame him. I felt the only thing plausible was to keep talking to him and try and keep him focused on something positive instead of the voices in his head.

"Look, homie. I'm your only chance. If you want to see your kids, let me go find them. You and Carrie can sit in the car and I'll go into Kennewick and bring them back to you and you can see them before you leave."

Juan slowed down to a crawl, and a driveway came into sight. "There it is. That's it right there!" Juan said.

The pig farm

I'm thinking, *If we go down this driveway it's all over. Especially when his cohorts see us. We're going to be trapped. Carrie's going to be raped and then we'll both be shot, killed, chopped up into pieces and fed to the pigs.*

Carrie's feistiness came back as she leaned forward a bit and said, "This is bullshit. I never asked for this, man. What the hell did I do to deserve this? I don't understand why you are doing this. I just want to go home."

Juan's phone rang again. This pissed Juan off. He picked it up off the floor where he had thrown it minutes before, looked at the caller ID and hit the silence button.

"Fuck! They're getting pissed. I gotta do something."

We had passed the driveway and turned around about 50 yards ahead of the entrance and were heading back.

The phone rang again.

This time he picked up. "Yeah. I'm coming down the driveway right now. I'll be there in a sec."

Now that Juan's friends knew our location, we were definitely in harm's way. Juan was so visibly nervous and indecisive in every action or decision he made that it gave me the impression he was in trouble with the people he was taking us to.

The driveway was overgrown with tall grass and barbed-wire fencing lined each side of the road. Broken-down cars were scattered randomly throughout the fields. Driven by fear and will to live, I made one last, desperate plea. It was a pig farm. I could tell that because a few pigs grazed within an electrified fence.

"C'mon, bro. We can't go up here. They're going to kill us all and you'll never be able to see your kids. Let's turn around."

Juan raised the gun up and was flailing it around, complaining about the caliber and the fact that it was a revolver. "Just shut up and let me think. All I have is the weak-ass revolver. I need a better gun. I don't know what the fuck to do."

"Let's just turn around and get out of here before they see us and trap us," I repeated.

The driveway widened a little as we pushed ahead. An old, broken-down Buick consumed by blackberry bushes sat on one side. The other side of the driveway had a little turn-out spot.

"Right there! We can turn around right there and go find your kids!" I shouted. Juan was looking in all directions with confusion. "C'mon, you don't want to kill us. Let's get out of here" I kept on trying to capitalize on his muddled state by talking like I had a plan. It seemed to be working. Juan was so shaky and would change his mind faster than he changed gears.

The phone rang again. "Don't answer it. Let's just go" I said.

"If I don't answer it, they're gonna find us and we'll all be screwed," Juan replied.

"We're screwed anyway. Let's just go."

Juan hit the silence button and turned the car towards the fence. "This is stupid. What's wrong with me?" Juan mumbled. We couldn't make the turn the first time so Juan had to back up and make a fresh start at it. The whole time I was just waiting to see some gang of Mexican hillbillies swarm the car with machetes, pitchforks and automatic weapons.

Fortunately, we made it out of there and back to the main road unharmed. Juan was swearing at himself, "I can't believe I just did that. Now I'm really out. They're not going to help me now. Fuck!" He slammed the gun against the steering wheel. "I guess I'm a big 300-pound bitch!"

This was a desperate man in a desperate situation. I have never witnessed such drastic transformations in another human being. His moods would switch from psychotic to bizarre to normal in a 20-minute period. I never knew what to expect or when to expect it. The one thing I was sure of is that our chances of living through this were not good.

My nerves by this time were shattered. Carrie had been reduced to a traumatized school girl and hid under the blanket as Juan drove erratically and hastily out of Strangeville.

Anger, misery and a sense of uncertainty loomed in the air, but the fact that we were leaving the mountain prison that nearly became my final stop brought a small sigh of relief. Juan's inability to make decisions was, in a way, helpful at this point. I believe his conscience was starting to play a role in his actions.

I feel that Juan was losing his mind. Trying to contend with someone like that is extremely difficult, especially when your life is randomly and erratically flashing in and out of his gunsights.

Not knowing whether he would actually pull the trigger was such a great source of anxiety. Bobbing back and forth, trying to keep out of the line of fire, was the norm at this point. The gun could have very easily been fired by accident countless times, not to mention the times it was pointed with malicious intent.

As twisted as Juan's mind was, though, I had tapped into a layer of remorse. My only hope to survive this siege was to bring those feelings into the light.

I think Carrie was so disoriented that she wasn't sure what to say or what role to play. This volatile situation forced both Carrie and me into survival mode. We had to counteract each of Juan's personalities with a different role. The problem with role playing with a killer is that if you assume the wrong role, your character could be terminated.

Another problem was that Carrie had said some things that reverberated in Juan's head and were a catalyst to a lot of his anger --for example, when Carrie told us that her brother Diego could be quickly summoned and would rob us. That statement embedded a seed of betrayal in Juan's mind. Juan kept asking me if I trusted Carrie, if I thought she was going to tell on him. He was obsessed with the whole trust issue.

He would repeat her statement mockingly when he had her at his mercy. "Where's your brother now?" or "Why don't you call your friends and see if they want to come rob me?"

Juan's teeth were gnashing as he tried to shift into the proper gear. His nerves were so strained that simple tasks had become cumbersome. His phone kept ringing, adding to the tension. Juan was once again swaying back and forth trying to decide whether to answer. "If I don't pick up they're going to kill us for sure," he said.

Juan's driving was terrible, but we were putting distance between us and the pig farm. That was pretty much the only good action of this scene.

Juan picked up the phone and had another conversation with his "family." Apparently he was conversing with his brother. I determined he was getting directions to another secluded spot along the Columbia River. My first thought was, *Oh, how joyous that will be. Another secluded spot where Carrie and I can be disposed of.* We were yet again close to being out of gas.

Juan fell silent after his conversation, seemingly lost in contemplation. I could no longer stand the silence.

"Hey, bro. Are we going to go find your kids?"

"No, esé. My brother wants me to meet him. He's going to give me a ride back to Mexico and he's totally pissed, homes. I shouldn't have turned around. I'm trippin'."

I could tell Juan was feeling like a total failure. I believed he was experiencing a nervous breakdown and was on the brink of lashing out. I wondered if I should take a chance and try to snatch the gun from him. Even with the flesh that dangled off Juan's body, he was still twice my size. I might be able to get away, but Carrie in the back seat wouldn't have a chance. I knew in my heart of hearts that the only way Carrie or I could escape would be if Juan were killed. And I was not ready to take a human life -- even his.

He constantly talked about suicide and having a shootout with the cops if we were approached by any. It seemed that the only thing that deterred Juan's destructive tendencies were his kids. Or at least the mention of them.

Now, I'm no hostage negotiator. I knew it was only a matter of time before the whole kid tactic would fail. Aside from his kids, Juan apparently didn't have any reason to keep trudging through his chaotic life.

Soon we were driving alongside the mighty Columbia River. The sun warmed us. We had traveled for a good 40 minutes before Juan's phone rang again.

"Hey, what's up? Alright. Alright, cool, I'll see you in a bit."

With a look of calm, Juan hung up the phone.

"Didn't we just pass a trailer park a second ago?" Juan asked.

"Yeah, it was a small one on the right," I replied.

"OK. There's supposed to be a dirt road coming up on the left." Juan leaned his head close to the windshield, peering through the dust.

"So what's going on? What are you planning on doing?" I said in my most compassionate voice. He didn't respond.

The road we were traveling was once again desolate. On the right was nothing but scorched farmland, with little evidence of human life. To the left were steep rugged hills that blocked the view of the river. The hills were a mixture of sharp rocks concealed by short sunburnt grass and sandy dirt. It looked as though the road was carved right down the center of these hills, so on either side of the road was an uphill shoulder.

The shooting range

About two miles past the run-down trailer park, a dusty driveway came into view. It was barely visible. It was questionable whether we could even travel up it. A four-wheel-drive vehicle would have had a little trouble conquering the hill it led up, but our slightly lowered BMW was hardly the vehicle for this job.

Juan, however, didn't hesitate and turned off the paved road onto this questionable trail. The road became so steep that all we could see was blue sky in front of us.

After sixty seconds of climbing we came to the top of the small mountain. Plumes of dust kept rising into the clear sky as we scanned the area. The view was of postcard caliber. The river was huge and wound its way through grassy plains and disappeared into the sun. There were no signs of life. No houses. No businesses or roads in either direction.

Juan inched the car down a steep incline until the road vanished into nothing but sharp rocks.

"What are you doing? Where the hell are we?" Carrie said in a tired and agitated voice.

"This is your stop," Juan replied.

He opened up the driver's-side door, grabbed the keys and hopped out. He demanded that Carrie exit the car. Juan caught my eyes and held a sinister stare followed by a laugh as he led Carrie away from the car.

Again I questioned my grasp on reality. Was this really happening? Was I about to witness a homicide and then be shot myself?

I heard Carrie pleading for mercy. I opened the door and went to step out. When I looked down, the sand was littered with hundreds of brass shell casings. Now it was clear that this was real and that this spot had a specific purpose.

Juan was about thirty feet from the car, and Carrie was crying and pleading for sympathy. Juan made her get on her knees and face the river.

He drew the gun up to the back of her head. He shouted, "Turn your head, esé. You don't want to see this."

I was immobilized with panic. But I had to do something. I opened my mouth but no words came out. I started looking around in all directions hoping something or someone would help.

When I looked across the river to the other side, I saw a light brown truck sitting in the middle of nowhere. When I looked closer I saw a man standing outside the truck with what looked like binoculars.

"Hey, Juan, stop! Stop! There's someone watching. Look way over there on the other side of the river. He's looking right at us!" I shouted.

Juan paused and lowered the gun from the back of Carrie's head.

I pointed to the truck. "See it?"

"Yeah, that's my brother. He told me someone would be watching to make sure I got rid of you guys. After I shoot you, he's going to come get me."

Carrie, still on the ground, was sobbing and pleading for Juan to stop. "Please, I'll do anything. Don't kill us!"

Carrie leaned forward until her face was almost touching the sandy ground. Her face was red and puffy from the flow of tears.

Juan had the gun pressed to the back of Carrie's head and was leaned down close to her ear, whispering. Then he looked up at me and said, "Do you trust her, esé? Should I shoot her?"

I had to think about my answer, because the way Juan processed information was not normal. I had to take into account that he was paranoid, so that if I said, "Yes I trust her," he might think Carrie and I were plotting something. If I said no, he probably would have killed her.

It was clearly easier to hold the gun up to Carrie's head and question her loyalty to him then mine. I felt responsible for her life because Juan seemed to listen to what I had to say. By this time I had a silent bond with Carrie. A bond that was, to me, one that would normally take a lifetime to develop. I thought to myself, *If we make it through this, only we would understand how close to death we were.* It was the kind of feeling that might arise in the midst of a natural disaster.

The best response I could muster up was, "Ah . . . I don't know, but I think I hear somebody coming." I really hadn't heard anything. That was all I could think of to say.

There was nowhere to turn around, and the road was barely wide enough for a single car. Nor was there anywhere to run. If Juan shot us, whoever came over that hill would easily be able to see what had happened. The truck that sat on the opposite side of the river still remained in the same place, with its occupant standing outside the driver's-side door.

Juan had a panicked look in his eyes and raised a finger up to his lips and said, "Shhh."

"Please, Juan, let's get out of here," Carrie begged. "You don't want to kill us. Let's go find your kids. Please, we're not going to tell on you. C'mon, let's just go."

I saw hesitation in Juan's eyes as I too started in on him.

"Yeah, homie. Let's go find your kids. If you go through with this, your brother won't let you say goodbye to your kids. Bro, we're going to be totally trapped if we don't get out of here." I was trying to play on the "I think I hear someone coming" statement.

When I said that, I think he really did hear something or maybe he just needed an excuse not to kill us. Either way, I could feel the tension dissipate a bit.

"Alright, fuck, get up. I don't know what I'm going to do. I guess I'm just a bitch," Juan said. Once again I could sense Juan's disgust with himself.

Carrie's hands were shaking as she wiped tears from her face. Juan had her arm and was leading her back to the car.

"Here, let me drive, bro," I said. Juan threw me the keys and I hobbled over to the driver's side. I glanced across the river and noticed that the truck had sped off. This added a sense of urgency to the situation.

Was that truck really watching us? Is he after us? I asked myself as I frantically put the key into the ignition.

There was no place to turn around, so I had to back the car out all the way. The incline we were at was pretty steep. Now the rear window was filled with blue sky, so I had to guide the car out by looking from side to side. Juan acknowledged the hasty departure of the truck and told me I had better get somewhere fast.

As soon as I made it up over the peak of the small mountain, it was a little easier to guide the car towards the paved road. Dust engulfed the BMW, making a ghostly trail that hovered in the dry summer heat like fog.

Carrie was trying to regain some composure. I backed the car out onto the much appreciated paved road and floored it. Shifting with clarity; first, second, third. Nothing like the immaculate sound of a BMW engine. The RPMs racing. I shifted into fourth. The speedometer read 95 mph. Finally, I eased it into fifth gear: 110 mph. The fast-moving air chiseled the layer of dust from the car as we made our geta-way.

I checked the rearview mirror for the mysterious truck. Juan's demeanor was jumpy and frantic. Desperation filled his eyes. He was once again swaying back and forth. Self loathing and self pity seemed to cry out from within his disturbed world.

"I'm such a bitch. I don't know what's wrong with me. My brother is going to kill us for sure now. I'm going to be totally cut off and all I have is this little-ass revolver. I should just kill myself right now."

Juan looked at me as if waiting for a response. I could feel him analyzing me. With the gun in his hand, he tapped it against his leg. The tension was thick. What's a good answer to a question from a clinically insane, strung-out paranoid schizophrenic? I'm not sure but, silence is definitely not the way to go.

"Let's just go back to Portland, bro," I finally said. "I'll call my girlfriend. She gets paid tomorrow, and I'll ask her for some gas money to get home. Maybe we can go find your kids and you can say goodbye to them before you go back to Mexico."

I'd slowed down a bit while conversing with Juan. We were still parallel with the Columbia River and it would come into view occasion-ally. About five minutes had passed when I noticed a truck in my rear-view mirror. I was still traveling 90 mph. The truck in my mirror was getting closer.

"Uh . . . is that the same truck that was across the river?"

Now the truck had closed the gap to about 100 yards. Juan turned around in his seat to check it out.

"Shit! That's my brother, esé. I told you this wasn't no joke. We're fucked!"

I pushed the gas pedal to the floor, but the truck was keeping up. There was no doubt that the truck was pursuing us, especially when we were reaching speeds up to 130 MPH and the vehicle behind us was keeping up.

"Go faster, esé, they're gonna shoot us."

Then the phone started ringing.

"Answer it, bro. See what they want," I said.

Carrie sat up and said, "Let me talk to them. Maybe I can talk them out of killing us. I'll tell them you didn't kidnap me and I'm not going to say anything."

"Bitch, are you crazy?" Juan responded. "All they want to do to you is fuck you and then kill you. I'm trying to keep my own self alive and if there's a shoot-out we're fucked! All I have is this weak-ass revolver. These guys are killers. I don't think you understand what's going on here. On any normal day, you both would have been dead a long time ago. I just can't bring myself to pull this fucking trigger."

The phone was persistently ringing, intensifying the situation. I was so disoriented I was having trouble keeping an eye on the road. I was more worried about bullets shattering the back window. I was slouched down in my seat. My head was level with the dashboard and I was looking through the steering wheel.

Juan was doing the same. Juan checked the revolver by spinning the cylinder. Each of the chambers were full. Then Juan opened the glove box, where he had put a whole box of .38 shells. He shook out all the bullets into his hand. Several fell onto the floor. The phone kept ringing.

Juan stuffed the bullets into his pocket. I had slowed down considerably because I was driving from such an odd position. At speeds of a 100-plus mph, the chances of surviving a crash were slim.

Finally Juan answered the phone. "What's up? What's going on?"

I can only guess what was being said, but it was obvious the truck was trying to get our attention. Finally it pulled alongside us. There were two occupants. The passenger brandished a gun and grinned as the truck kept trailing alongside us. Juan was still on the phone and was talking to the driver. Both had dark-brown complexions, were in their late 30's and were fairly well dressed, with their eyes covered in dark sunglasses.

Carrie was underneath the blankets in the back seat, inflaming the situation by repeatedly asking, "What's going on now?"

I replied, "Just stay down."

The sturgeon hole

With guns on both sides of us, I figured this would end with my being shot and the car spinning out of control. I could picture the car rolling over and over -- glass shattering, bones crushing and the metallic smell of blood filling the air. I was actually ready to accept any kind of closure to this mayhem. If this was going to be the end then, so be it.

I managed to glance over at the newer-style Ford truck. The passenger was waving the gun to the right. Juan was still on the phone but was speaking mostly in Spanish. As he was hanging up, he told me to slow down.

A red Topaz was blocking my side of the road. The truck was signaling me to turn right, which was my only option. With the Ford truck on my left and the Topaz turned sideways blocking the lane, I had to turn right.

"That's Gocho in the Topaz," Juan said. "They're Mafioso. I really fucked up, homes. I should have gotten rid of you guys back there. I knew they would be watching."

"What's going on, bro? Where are we going?" I asked.

"We're going down to the Columbia. There's two big rocks that mark a sturgeon hole along the river bank," Juan replied. A sturgeon hole is the deepest part of any river.

"This is crazy, dude. They're going to get rid of all of us!" I said in a panicked voice.

Then Carrie again suggested she be allowed to talk to the men.

"I don't think you fucking get it," Juan replied. "These guys are killers. They don't even speak English, and they're not interested in what you have to say. Gocho has Down syndrome and does the killing. The Mafioso has these people do their killing because they are easily manipulated and submissive."

The passenger in the Topaz did fit the description of someone with Down syndrome. His face was abnormally long and his eyes were exceptionally close together. He too held a pistol up into my line of sight.

"I've had beef with that vato before. I hope he doesn't think he's going to try and buck up on me" Juan said.

After I turned, the river came into sight The road we turned on was covered with a thick layer of sand from the desert terrain surrounding the whole area. No houses, no businesses, no sign of life in any direction. An all-too-familiar setting.

The truck sped up and passed us as soon as we turned and the Topaz fell into place behind us. I thought briefly about what Carrie had suggested and I joined Juan in rebuking her.

"You don't even fucking know Spanish good enough to try and talk your way out of this shit, and what the fuck would you say anyway?"

I asked her. I pictured Carrie trying to reason with a Down-syndrome Hispanic carrying a gun. Juan had already clearly stated what they wanted to do with her.

As I drove, my composure was crumbling. Somehow I'd been able to flood Juan's mind with distracting thoughts in the previous episodes of near-execution. Not this time. Not only was Juan under supervision, his supervisors were now directly involved.

I believe Juan was having trouble killing us because he had gotten to know us. Especially me. And there's the fact that he hadn't succeeded in obtaining all he desired from Carrie, so he didn't want to kill her. Now the situation was out of his hands.

The speedometer had descended down to around 40 mph, and I was still boxed in. We traveled toward the river in motorcade formation. The truck led the way and the Topaz followed close behind me. The temperature inside the car was well above 100 degrees. None of us had slept more than a few paranoid hours in the last nine or ten days. We hadn't eaten any real food in days, and no water had touched our dry lips in the past 48 hours.

Juan told us he wasn't supposed to have left Mexico. He said he had done some dirt in the Tri-Cities and Chicago, so his affiliates had paid for him to obtain a new identity and a safe passage deep into Mexico. That's where he was supposed to be now -- in seclusion down in Sinaloa.

His colleagues also gave him a job while in hiding. His job, as he put it, was to get rid of people's unwanted baggage. Juan went on to tell us that the ID he'd been given was no longer any good. He'd grown tired of Mexico and had traveled to Portland, where he was selling dope on the streets and was arrested for possession of cocaine under his alias. The justice center in Portland booked and then negligently released him. Juan was both jubilant and baffled that they had let him go.

"Someone fucked up real bad, homes. I should have taken advantage of that and went back to Mexico. Now I have to explain to the patron [boss] why I came back and why I haven't gotten rid of you guys yet. Fuck, vato, I should just get this over with and buck myself in the head."

The river was now in plain sight. The Columbia is powerful and extraordinarily deep, a perfect example of nature's raw power. The paved road turned sharply to the left once again running parallel with the river.

The truck slowed as it rounded the corner and came to a stop. The Topaz was inches behind us. A dirt road veered off to the right and proceeded down farther toward the river.

Juan directed me to turn onto the dirt road. Waist-high foliage burnt from the sun lined each side of the trail. The truck took off and the Topaz closed in behind us. I looked in the rear view mirror hoping that they hadn't followed us, but there they were. The dust that lofted up from behind my car obscured the predators' faces, which made the scene that much more ominous.

The road wound down into thicker foliage. The paved road quickly disappeared. Any chance of a passer-by's seeing us was now lost. Within a minute the trail came to a small clearing. Trash was scattered everywhere. Empty beer cans, Big Gulp cups, plastic bags and a ripped-up blanket. It looked like someone had been squatting there.

To find the right words to describe the fear and adrenaline that resonated in my veins would be difficult. If you've ever been on the edge of a cliff, roof or steep drop off where death would most definitely be the result of a fall, then you've tasted this level of fear. Or the feeling you get when you witness a child walking out into the road and oncoming traffic is approaching. Your heart races out of control. Your throat constricts, making breathing impossible and your basic motor skills are delayed and fumbled. This is the level of fear that I was experiencing.

The clearing we had just come upon gave way to the river. A shroud of trees blocked out the sun. The water rippled on rounded rocks only 10 feet from the car. About a 15-foot arch of tangled branches revealed a small panoramic view of the Columbia's murky waters.

I had to say something. Juan was constantly looking behind us. Carrie was still hiding under the blankets in the back.

"Fuck, esé. My brother took off. I think this vato might try and buck me, too," Juan said.

"Yeah, bro, this isn't cool," I responded. "Now we're trapped. You can't just let these guys kill us. Plus you know what they're going to do to her."

"They ain't doin' shit to me," Carrie chimed in from the back seat. "Let me talk to 'em."

"Turn the car off, homes," Juan said flatly. "This is the end of the road."

The dust had cleared and the Topaz and its sinister passenger emerged.

"Fuck it, esé," Juan said. "I'm gonna do us all and you're first, bitch." Juan pointed the gun at Carrie's head. She quickly covered up once again and let out a cry for help.

I turned my head and covered my face with my hand to try deflecting shrapnel from the blast. With one hand on my face and the other on the door handle, I popped open the door.

"Where do you think you're going, homes?" Juan asked.

I had noticed that the Gocho had exited the car with a gun in hand.

"Look, bro," I said. "Gocho is creeping up on you." The back window was so caked with dust he couldn't see what was behind us. I had the advantage of my side mirror. The passenger-side mirror was missing.

Juan hopped out. He raised his revolver and put Gocho in his sights.

"Qué onda, esé? Qué vas a hecer hoy? [What's up, homeboy? What are you doing today?]"

Gocho's gun was still pointed toward the ground. Juan was speaking Spanish, but by his tone and actions I could tell this was a power struggle. Gocho had a permanent grin on his face displaying rotten, jagged teeth. The driver of the Topaz remained in the car. At a closer glance he looked to be in his late forties. He wore a thick mustache and slicked-back hair. His expression was stiff and seemingly unaffected by the situation at hand.

Juan's voice was growing louder and more intense. Carrie was now out from underneath the blankets and panic stricken. I was out of the car and nauseous from tension.

Juan closed the gap between himself and Gocho. He was standing about five feet away from the back of the car. By this time I had made a decision to make a break for it, because it seemed obvious we were about to be killed.

I leaned back and told Carrie, "I'll lift the seat for you, but I'm running for it. This is our only chance." I reached in, depressed the seat lever and flipped the front seat up.

Carrie jumped out in a disheveled state. The only place to run was into the water, which was so close to the car that we were splashing through the water in seconds. The river was shallow at first but dropped off immediately.

As we swam I could hear Juan's argument with Gocho continue. I heard gunshots. I had my back to the clearing and with every frantic stroke, I anticipated a bullet striking me in the back. A few seconds went by and Carrie and I were a good 20 feet out into the river. The water was murky and the current was getting stronger as we reached deeper water. A combination of fear and curiosity provoked me to finally turn around. Dirty river water stung my eyes as I tried to focus on the clearing. I floated on my back briefly. Carrie was bobbing up and down, only exposing her head for air and quickly disappearing back under the water.

The Topaz was slowly backing up, with Gocho walking backwards behind the passenger door. Juan was yelling, "Back the fuck up, esé." He fired his gun at the front of the Topaz, pulling off four shots.

He still had his gun pointed at Gocho and was stepping toward him. I saw Juan glance toward Carrie and me, but only briefly. His attentions were directed more towards the Topaz and its passengers.

With one hand on the passenger door and the other still gripping his gun, Gocho slowly got back into the car. He was still sporting the same grin and, like his driver, appeared unaffected by the confrontation. Juan still had his gun pointed at the Topaz as it pulled away in a cloud of dust.

After the Topaz disappeared, Juan turned his attention to us. By this time Carrie had also turned toward my car and was wiping water from her eyes. Her hair was pulled back and her eyes filled with despair.

I wanted to embrace her and tell her everything was going to be alright. Unfortunately, everything wasn't alright. The fact that we couldn't swim any farther out without being swept away by the current was another pressing issue.

While we tried to catch our breath, Juan started wading out towards us.

"Everything's alright, but we have to get out of here. Those guys are going to be coming back with more people," he shouted toward us.

Carrie looked at me.

"What should we do? I can't handle this anymore."

I just wanted to let the river sweep me away from all this misery. All I could say was, "Me neither, girl. Me neither."

Carrie's eyes sparkled in the sun and her lashes clung together. A flash of blue eye makeup showed when she blinked.

I was still in full-blown opiate withdrawal and battling ferocious bacteria that had consumed a fist-size hole in my leg. Juan and I had consumed roughly 1.5 ounces of meth in a week. That's approximately 42 grams. That's a lot.

Carrie's consumption was minimal. Her sleep deprivation was a combination of terror, methadone and meth. I believe any opiate addict would agree that sleep is impossible coming off dope. Even without adding the intensity of crystal meth, you can be sure you will find no comfort, no sleep and no remission in opiate withdrawal.

Skin constantly clammy, leg cramps so severe that it feels as though you just ran a 10K. Your eyes water, your nose drips, you feel the sporadic beat of your heart pumping anxiety into your veins. The only thing that gives you enough energy to move is the thought of getting more dope. Your life force is directly connected to the opiates that are driving you mad.

Up till now, my life had never been threatened with violence. Being a heroin addict I have seen my share of death and come close to it myself. Death is a very real aspect of not only heroin, but the whole drug community. If you are an active participant in a drug circle I'm sure your chances of being killed are only slightly increased from that of a normal citizen. That is if you are just an average user and maybe sell a little product on the side to support your own habit.

Unfortunately, I had run into Juan, a street dealer who was involved in a higher level of trafficking. Violent assaults, stabbings, drive-bys and vandalism are commonplace for street-level drug activity.

Murder is more intimate, more personal. It takes a certain breed to commit such an act. Kidnapping is also an up-close-and-personal act. These crimes usually occur in a higher level of drug activity. So witnessing events like those I've described was foreign to me.

Out of all the dealers on the street, I had to pick up the one who enjoyed acts of brutality and displayed the most recklessness in the taking of human life.

I was dope sick and drained of life. I wanted to die. Drowning felt like a feasible escape from this bizarre situation. But I didn't have the courage to take that first breath of water. The only option I had was to swim back to shore. Swim back to an armed, delusional dictator. A person who didn't value his life or any other life. A person who had been exiled from his family and now his friends.

The only reason we weren't dead is because Juan thought Carrie or I could help him arrange a meeting with his kids. That option now seemed our only hope. I believe that neither Carrie, I, nor our families would be safe as long as Juan drew breath.

Carrie and I treaded water and prolonged our immersion as long as we could. This was one of the only times we were together without

Juan being within five feet of us. That brief moment felt like freedom. Unfortunately it was short lived.

With gun in hand, Juan, only a quarter submerged, shouted for us to come back to shore.

"Come on, let's get away from this sturgeon hole. People disappear way too easy here." This, too, was a familiar place to Juan, and he had obviously participated in one or more disposals there by the way he spoke of it. Carrie and I accepted our fate and swam back to the shore.

I looked at Juan and shook my head. "I just can't take it anymore. Maybe you should just get this over with, since we're already here."

"No, esé," he replied. "You're gonna find my kids for me. They're all I have left. My homies are done with me. My life is over, homes. I want to see my kids before I die."

I felt a glimmer of hope as I stood there, dripping wet. Carrie emerged from the water slicking her hair back. I wasn't in too much pain to notice that her shirt stuck to her large breasts, displaying the details and contours with precision. This encouraged a brief distraction from our conversation. She chimed in, "I'll help you find them, too. I love kids."

It seemed Juan was having a change of heart. At this point I was happy to still be alive and equally happy I didn't have to watch Carrie being killed.

We all started making our way out of the water and back to the car. The sun dried us quickly. The wound on my leg was itching and stung with each beat of my heart. Now that the adrenaline had left my body, pain had replaced it. I limped back to the car and copped a lean immediately. As I caught my breath, Juan and Carrie started rummaging through the car trying to find a towel to dry off with. I wished I had a hit of heroin to ease the pain.

Juan directed me to drive back to the Tri-Cities. What a relief it was to see people and houses and the normal functioning of life -- something I thought I would never see again.

But the pain and anxiety of withdrawal were seeping into every part of my body. The cramps in my legs were so painful it was almost impossible to work the pedals. Shifting gears was annoying to no end. Even turning the steering wheel was frustrating.

Juan obviously didn't know where his kids were. He didn't have a clue. We drove through Kennewick, Pasco and Richland.

"Take a left. Take a right. Stop here. Turn there" is what I heard for four hours straight. We had put a few dollars in the gas tank but were burning through that quickly. There was no meth left and Juan probably had only about $30 of the money we had from Idaho. Carrie was once again in the back dozing.

Juan was losing his hope. The sun was almost gone. We drove to parks and through neighborhoods looking for his kids. He had no idea where the kids were living or where they might be hanging out. So he shortly gave up on the idea of finding them, and that was the last we heard of the idea. He didn't know what to do next.

Juan couldn't make up his mind about anything. "Just take me to the police station, esé. Fuck it. I'm gonna just turn myself in," he told me. This of course was the best idea I had heard him come up with. But when we would drive past the police department he would say, "Yeah, you probably would turn me in, huh, esé?"

Every time he would direct me to do something, he would get pissed off when I did it. "Alright, homes. Let's go over to the Columbia Park," he said. Then when we got there, he said, "What the fuck are we doin here, homes? Are you trying to set me up?"

"You told me to come here! What are you talking about?" I replied. This went on and on.

As we were driving through downtown Kennewick, we pulled alongside a car occupied by two males and a female driver. Juan threw up a gang sign and yelled out the window, "18th Street kills the most!"

The two male occupants immediately responded by throwing up their sign, that of the Black Gangster Disciples, another popular gang in the Tri-Cities, which is mostly black. 18th Street is Chicano and Hispanic.

Juan turned to me and said, " Alright, homes, I'm gonna buck this bitch in the head and take the car. You meet me at the I-395 on-ramp."

Juan raised the gun up and out the window, pointing it toward the car. The female ducked, as did the two brothers. They sped off through the red light. There was traffic everywhere. I couldn't understand: if this guy was so wanted, why isn't anyone calling the police? We had driven by the Kennewick Police Department several times. It was like he was trying to provoke a fight. I could tell he wanted to go out with a bang. Carrie and I would be caught in the middle. There would be no time to explain to the police or to one of Juan's rival gangs that we were not part of the chaos he was stirring up.

I felt like pulling out into the middle of the intersection and just sitting there, waiting for the police to come.

Juan had told us many times what would happen if we were approached by authorities. He explained very earnestly that he would "buck" the first cop that approached in the head, then turn the gun on us and then take his own life. So here again the options available to me were few: either do what he said or be killed. Run away -- or in my case, limp away -- and put my family on his list of people to kill. Or keep playing this psychotic charade until an opportunity arose.

The day dragged on into night, and I was falling asleep at the wheel. Juan would quickly wake me up. "What the fuck, homes? You trying to draw some attention or what? You want me to just buck you in the head and get it over with?"

I thought, *That that would almost be better than driving for one more second.*

"Damn, bro," I said. "We've been up for almost two weeks. I need to crash. We should just get a hotel for the night and get some sleep. I'll call my girlfriend in the morning and have her Western Union me some money."

By this time my driving was radical. I was swerving and hallucinating pretty bad. The road was blurry, and it was difficult to keep the car between the lane lines.

Carrie was still sleeping in the back seat. I noticed Juan was nodding off too. The gun rested between his legs, with his hand loosely holding the wooden grips.

The thought crossed my mind to grab it, but I would have had to shoot and kill him. This is something I was not prepared to do. To think that Juan would cooperate with my demands is ludicrous. The only way Carrie or myself could successfully escape this ominous situation is if Juan were dead. Even if Juan was captured by the police, we would have the constant fear of retribution agasint our families. Juan knew where I lived, and he even had the street address of Carrie's children. We never did figure out how he'd learned that.

Finally Juan came to the conclusion that we all needed rest. At this point, nothing seemed real except the pain and misery we were all experiencing. My brain was incapable of normal thought. I felt like I was moving by remote control.

I just wanted to lie down in a real bed. I missed my girlfriend and my family and wished I could see them one more time.

Just one month before this crazy trip began I was living in my own house on Whidbey Island and going to work with my dad every day. Now I was a captive in my own car, which we were essentially living in. I felt I had lost everything I had worked for and numbed it all out with excessive heroin abuse.

My self-esteem had fallen. I was caught in a situation that was forcing me to take my own inventory. I never thought we would make it out of the mountains of Idaho, let alone the pig farm, the shooting range or the sturgeon hole. All these places and traumatic events had dredged up buried memories and feelings that had been diluted into a spoon.

An addict never wants to take his own inventory. That's why we do more dope. To forget. To forget all the bad, all the hurt. But in the long run, you're still left with yourself. A portrait of misery. There was no more dope to suppress the reality that surrounded me. I had no energy to move on and nothing to look forward to. Juan had virtually drained the life from me.

I think he could tell I just didn't care anymore and was jeopardizing his rendezvous with his kids. So he directed me to a little motel in Pasco, Washington. "OK, homes. We'll get some sleep here. I'll stay in the car and you go rent the room. If I think you're trying anything, the bitch is dead."

Carrie had popped up out of her slumber. "Oh, thank God," she sighed. "We're finally gonna get to take a shower and sleep. I never thought I'd be taking another shower or see another bed again."

Carrie had been unwilling and unprepared to go on a tri-state adventure and had no clothes and no makeup. Her clothes and body were in desperate need of washing. For that matter, we were all in need of an aggressive scrubbing. Sweat, sand, dirt, river water and chemicals had made their way deep into our skin and clothing.

After I parked, I sat back into my worn, sweaty seat. I had to find the strength and the right frame of mind to interact in the social setting of renting a room. At this point, that seemed like a three-dimensional NASA project.

Juan dug out a crumpled up ball of wet money and handed it to me. "Here, esé. This is the rest of the money. Get us a room in the back."

I walked into the seedy office, where the manager was on the phone. I considered urgently explaining to him what was going on and asking for his help. But I was sure the manager wouldn't understand the urgency of the situation, and in any case, because of Juan's intention to kill us, cops and himself, asking the manager for help probably would have been suicidal.

I succeeded in renting a room for me and my "girlfriend," advising the manager that her "brother" was traveling with us but wouldn't be staying the night. The room cost $29. We got room 23.

“Do you think that vato called the police, homes?"Juan asked me when I returned to the car. "I’m gonna wait right here for a minute and make sure. These fucking pigs aren’t gonna catch me slippin', homes.”

“No, bro. It’s all good. Don’t trip. Everything’s cool. He didn’t act weird or anything. Let’s just get some sleep,” I replied.

I went to the trunk and started grabbing some clothes. I overheard Juan asking Carrie if she thought I told and if she thought the cops were coming. She had to play her role with conviction.

“No, he’s your friend just like I’m your friend. We’re not going to tell anybody anything. I have kids and I want to see them again,” Carrie told him.

James Moran, aka Juan Martinez

Carrie Blackford

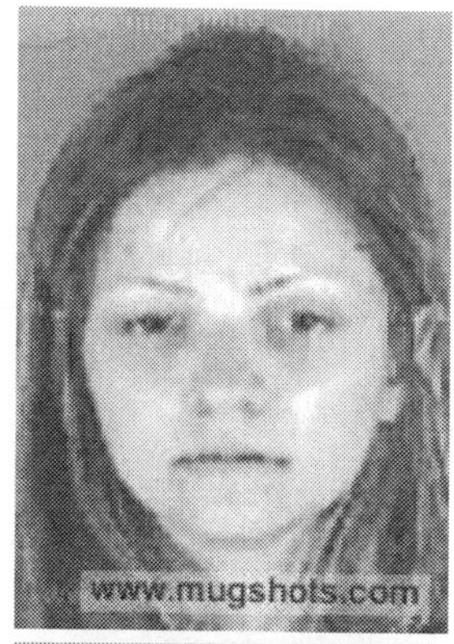

Carrie Blackford (2005)

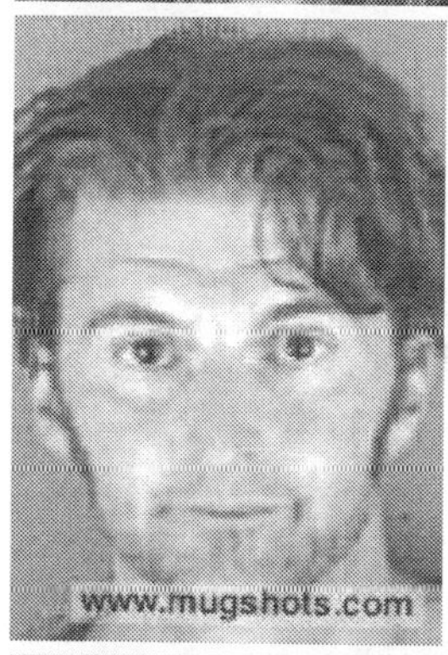

Mark Tucker (2005)

Mark Tucker (2005)

Juan told me to go open the door to the room and leave it open. "Leave the door open a crack and back the car up to the room. I don't want anyone to see me going into the room."

Room 23 was small, with worn-down shag carpet. Everything was a dingy brown, and the musty smell of cigarettes lingered in the air. A single bed with an autumn-colored bedspread stood in the middle of the room, talking up most of the space. In other words, it was your run-of-the-mill dive.

It took every bit of energy I had to move the car as Juan ordered. I felt like I had been walking through the desert all day with a 100-pound pack on.

I took the liberty of showering first. Juan was so paranoid he told me to leave the bathroom door open. I was too tired to argue.

The hole in my upper thigh was healing but still looked infected. I was careful when I scrubbed around the wound. A build up of bandage glue had surrounded the hole and had collected a lot of dirt. It was far too painful to get all the dirt off the wound and I just didn't care.

After a five-minute shower I got out and sat on the toilet. The steam swirled around me and I felt a sense of relaxation. The shower has a transitory healing power for a dope-sick individual. For a few minutes, the aches and pains of opiate withdrawal subside. Unfortunately that feeling quickly dissipates.

I managed to put on some semi-clean shorts that were falling off me because I had lost so much weight on the trip. I fell like a freshly cut tree onto the worn mattress. Nothing short of a nuclear bomb would have woken me up.

It had been nearly a week since I had actually ingested a shot of heroin, and the methadone I had taken had only prolonged my withdrawal. For me, the third and fourth day of this epic detox were the worst. The frustration of not being able to sleep is the worst. Meth speeds up the withdrawal process a bit, but the level of anxiety it adds makes it worse later.

Day 14
August 1, 2005
Pasco, Washington - Portland, Oregon

I got up in the exact same position I had fallen in. I looked on the floor, and Juan and Carrie were uncomfortably sprawled out there at the foot of the bed. As soon as I made a move off the bed, Juan woke up.

I felt refreshed but frantic to get going. Portland was only three and half hours away. I was thinking more clearly now and was ready to leave the Tri-Cities.

"Alright, bro," I told Juan. "I'm gonna call Sara and ask for help. We can be back in Portland by 3:00 p.m."

I had a calling-card number with some minutes left on it, so I picked up the phone and dialed Sara's aunt's house. I was silently praying that she was home.

When she answered, Juan was standing right beside me, trying to listen to her words by holding his ear close to mine. This of course made it hard to communicate my true feelings to her. I had to respond as if nothing was wrong.

"Hey, baby. I'm alright but I need your help. I mean I really need your help. Can you please send me some money? Like right now? I'm stuck in the Tri-Cities and I can't really explain everything right now."

I could tell she got the hint that something wasn't right. "Um, sure" she responded. "Are you coming home? I miss you."

"Yeah, baby, as soon as I can get some gas money I'm coming straight to you."

I loved Sara with all my heart and felt she would make an excellent mother. She was young and vivacious and still possessed an innocent quality. Even though she had gotten a glimpse of the street life, she hadn't been tainted by it.

Sara was still young enough in life and her addiction to have the unconditional love and support of her parents. Although her curiosity was leading her deeper into one of the worst addictions known to man, she hadn't crossed the threshold yet. Sara was also very much in touch with her emotions, and her feelings were easily hurt.

The last thing I wanted was for Juan to think Sara knew anything that had transpired in the past couple of days. Even if I could have told Sara a little bit about the insanity I had just been a part of, her reaction would have added fuel to a fire that already felt out of control.

Juan told me to have her send the money Western Union to Atomic Foods, a small grocery store in Pasco. I told her I loved and appreciate her, and hung up. I was relieved she hadn't asked too many questions. She did ask why I didn't have all the money that was promised to me and why we didn't make it to the Ozark Mountains. As she was inquiring, Juan's stare became sinister.

But overall, Juan seemed happy that I talked to her and let her know I was still alive. I hadn't called since we left Pocatello, and Juan was worried she might have called the police and filed a missing-persons report.

Carrie's attitude had changed drastically. She was far from the spunky, argumentative and gregarious spirit she was when I first met her. It was a sad sight. Just like a dog that's been beat once too often, she sulked. Her spirit had been shattered and she had lost hope. As I was gathering my bags I saw a silent tear slowly streak down her face. My heart went out to her, but Juan would have misinterpreted as a conspiracy any sign of compassion. He kept such a vigilant watch over us that we were unable to communicate, anyway.

We got ready to pull out of the room. None of us had eaten anything substantial, and we were all dehydrated. Even with six hours of sleep, my energy was zero. My muscles still ached with blinding intensity and I could feel the anxiety rapidly building. I tried to replace these feelings with happy thoughts -- thoughts of seeing and holding Sara, feeling her arms around me and her perfect breasts pressing against my chest. I pictured kissing her and nibbling on her full lips. I could hear her soothing words of comfort float into my ear. I truly missed her, but at the same time my addiction screamed for attention. Even the powerful nurturing powers women possess can't curb the suffering of opiate withdrawal. So just hearing Sara saying she was on her way to the Western Union brought much relief.

With some sleep, even Juan seemed to be a bit calmer -- even rational there for awhile. Juan pulled his hat down to his eyebrows and scrutinized the parking lot. He threw me the keys and we loaded our meager belongings into the back. We piled in our mobile jail cell and set off for the grocery store.

It was close to noon when we arrived at Atomic Foods. Juan still had the gun on display, and his pockets bulged with bullets. Sara had to get a ride to the Western Union in Portland, so we had to give it a little time. I found some shade in the parking lot.

All the talk of being followed and stalked started reverberating. Every car that pulled into the parking lot drew my attention. *Oh, shit. Are these people after us?* I kept wondering.

Pasco has a lot of Hispanic folks, so the majority of people around us were suspect to me. There were two taco trucks directly behind us with a beehive of activity surrounding them. I was starting to lose it. Any one of these people could be looking for us. I kept my eyes peeled for a red Topaz or a big Ford truck. I stayed low in my seat, praying we didn't have a shootout in the parking lot.

Carrie was lying down in the back, silent. Juan sat with the rearview mirror tilted to help him see what was behind us.

About 30 minutes passed with little conversation. It felt like an hour. I couldn't take it any longer and told Juan that the money was probably there.

"Andale [come on], homes. Don't take too long or you'll be hearing some shots. Know what I mean?" Juan said with a smirk as he waved the gun around.

I think I was the only white person in the store, which attracted some attention. Being around all these people made me feel alive for a moment. I began to tell myself that I just might make it to Portland. My mood started to improve as I progressed in the line.

The clerk handed me a $50 check to endorse. I signed the back and she cashed me out two twenties and two five-dollar bills. My very own money -- what a feeling.

Juan was sitting low in the seat with his hat pulled down tight. Sweat was gathering on his face. I'm sure it was close to 100 degrees. I was sweating pretty good myself. Carrie's hair was sticking to her face and she looked pale.

"Alright, guys, I got the money, so let's get something to eat, fill up the tank and get the hell out of this desert."

Juan suggested we eat at the taco truck behind us. Of course I had to go and get the tacos. After the first trip through the Tri-Cities and its meth lab/taco trucks, I would never look at a taco truck the same.

Unfortunately there was no $.99 menu. My main concern was to save enough money for a shot of heroin when we got to Portland. So I ordered three basic tacos and three ice waters. Now I was $5 poorer and still starving. But the important thing was that we were heading back to civilization.

As we pulled in to gas up, Juan was once again slouched in the seat. "There's cameras here, homes. Hurry up!"

Here we go again, I thought. He was already starting to get weird again. I had to get on the freeway fast, before he decided to take us to another death camp or just snap and do us on the spot.

I filled up the tank. Before I went into the store to pay, Juan flashed the gun and told me to hurry up. I just shook my head. Carrie had laid back down and covered up her face with a blanket to block the sun.

Finally we were off. Juan had to direct me everywhere. Sometimes he would forget that I didn't know where the hell anything was and we would miss a turn. This pissed him off.

"What the fuck, esé? You were supposed to turn back there!" he would scream. Then the gun would start flailing around in all directions.

We made it to highway 395, which leads to I-82. Now I-82 was familiar territory for me. That road goes directly to downtown Portland.

As we turned onto 395, Juan started complaining about his friends not helping him and his lack of money.

"This is bullshit, homes. I feel like just buckin' myself in the head. I don't even have any money. What the fuck am I going to do in Portland? I should have went back to Mexico, homes. I'm trippin', esé."

He was tapping the gun against his head again. The only thing I could think of to distract him was to offer him the car. I had the title to the BMW in my pocket.

"Listen, bro, here's the title to my car. As soon as we get to Portland I'll sign this shit over to you. Let's just get out of here."

"There's nothing for me in Portland, homes," he replied. "You have a girlfriend and a job. I don't have shit, homes. My wife is all strung out and fucking for dope, homes. That's the mother to my kids. I feel like buckin' her in the head. Everything's turned to shit, homes, and I can't even see my kids."

I was desperately hoping Juan wouldn't pursue those thoughts. I could tell that he didn't want to go to Portland. I just couldn't take another trip into seclusion, mentally or physically.

I was all out of promises.

"Let's turn up here, homes" Juan told me. All my feelings of relief and anticipation were instantly extinguished. I really thought we were going to make it to Portland. When we had turned onto 395 and I saw that I-82 sign to Portland, I was giddy with excitement. Now those feelings were replaced with anger and disdain for this guy.

"C'mon, bro," I argued. "Look, we're already on the highway. Let's just keep going. You can have this whole fucking car when we get to P-town."

"Just fucking turn, esé. I need some fucking money, homes. You just want me to wonder around Portland with no money, homes?" Juan pointed the gun at my side.

"Say something, homes," he said mockingly. "I fucking dare you. Say one more thing. I swear to God. I run this fucking show. Now turn up here."

"Alright, bro, calm down," I responded. "Damn, I just miss my girl, ya know? I want to forget all about this trip and get home."

Carrie remained silent in the back with a blanket over her face.

We turned off the highway into an upper-middle-class neighborhood, passing a lot of new construction that was going on close to the highway. As we drove farther down this street, we came upon a cluster of well-built houses. This was a drastic change of scenery from the usual neighborhoods we had visited. Juan usually took us into places where the houses were more mobile than the cars.

As we drove, I could feel my anger taking over. I was gripping the wheel so tight that my knuckles were white. It was difficult not to just push the gas pedal to the floor and speed into a still object. Every part of me wanted to start screaming and try to wrestle the gun from Juan. But this wasn't an option. All I could do was grit my teeth and keep moving.

As we pushed on, Juan scanned each house. I burst out, "What the fuck are we doing, bro? Let's just go, man. We don't have enough gas to be driving around neighborhoods all day!" We had driven through the whole neighborhood by this time and it didn't seem like Juan knew where he was or what he was looking for.

"Do you think I fucking care about your gas or your fucking car, homes?" Juan responded. "How about I just end this shit right here, motherfucker? Matter of fact, just turn around here and park."

We had turned down a side street that ran the length of about four houses. A tall fence stood at the end of the road and blocked the view of the highway. The street had a gradual incline toward the fence, so as I turned around, the front of the car was pointing down slightly toward the intersection. I drove past the last house on the block and was heading back to the main road when Juan ordered me to pull to the curb.

"Stop here, esé. My aunt lives in that last house. I'm going to ask her for some money. You have money and I don't have shit, homes." Juan reached over and snatched the keys out of the ignition.

Carrie still hadn't moved, and her face was still concealed beneath a blanket. Apparently she had learned that any comments from her tended to result in death threats, so she remained silent during the loud exchange of words between Juan and me.

"Listen, homes, I'm going to see if she is home. If you try anything, you know what's gonna happen. I'll be right back."

I looked around at the houses and noticed a house with the garage door open. It was around 1:30 in the afternoon and people were out working in their yards and mulling around. Unfortunately, no one was standing outside on this street.

As Juan walked up to the house I started exploring my options. In the rearview mirror I saw Juan going up to the house. He was about 50 yards away from the car. The house with the garage door open was about 30 yards away. I could try running into the garage, shutting the door and hoping that the homeowners would listen to my cry for help and understand that there was a killer right next door.

But for that to work I would have to open my door, wake Carrie up, lift the front passenger seat up for her to get out, limp 30 yards to a stranger's garage, lock ourselves in, yell for help and hope for the best. Our only protection would be a garage door. It would have sealed not only our fate but also that of whoever was in the house. There was no doubt in my mind that Juan was a killer and could and would commit a murder without hesitation. So for me to try and escape in this scenario would be both suicidal and irresponsible.

Juan returned and leaned in the window. "I just wanted to make sure you weren't trying anything. She's home, so I'm going to ask her for some help."

"Well, go ask her, then," I shot back. "Damn, bro. How far do you think I could get with one leg and no keys?"

"Alright, I'll be right back," Juan said as he made his way back to the house.

The killing

I decided I would just lean my head back, close my eyes and pray. After all, it was broad daylight and we were in a nice neighborhood. What's the worst that could happen? Maybe this really was his aunt's house and he really was asking for help. In fact, it was the randomly selected home of 52-year-old Linda Moreno, her husband Loren, and their 17-year-old daughter, Danielle.

The quiet was shattered by the muffled sounds of what sounded like gunshots. Carrie immediately popped up from the backseat and peeled the blanket from her face.

"What was that? Were those gunshots?" she cried.

I was wide eyed. A feeling of doom and fear shot through me. "Aaahhh, it sounded like it."

We later learned Linda Moreno had been shot in the front of her head, between her eyes, and a second time in the back of the head behind her right ear. Danielle had been shot once in the back of the head. Kennewick police determined that five shots were fired in the home. One round was recovered from an exterior fence, one in a bathtub, two from Linda's body and one from Danielle's body.

I pushed the clutch in and the car started to roll forward but the small hill we were on wasn't steep enough to pop-start the car. Not having the keys would have prevented a successful pop-start anyway -- though at that moment, I was so paralyzed with fear that I forgot Juan had taken the key.

"Oh, my God, those *were* gunshots. What are going to do?" Carrie pleaded.

Just as I tried pop-starting the car, I saw Juan casually walking toward us. He was smiling. He held a purse in his hand as he made his way to the passenger-side door and did a little skip as he went for the door handle. Apparently he was happy.

Yet he immediately shouted, "Why was the car moving?"

"I fell asleep for a second there and took my foot off the brake," I replied. That was about the best answer I could come up with in my panicked state.

Carrie was sitting up with her hands clamping onto the passenger headrest and her head was in between the two front seats. She was frantic and looking in all directions. This was definitely not the time to question Juan or defy him in any way. Juan casually threw me the keys and told me to drive.

"Let's get going, homes. I think I pissed them off."

I took the keys and started the engine. Juan put the purse on the floor and took the gun out of his pocket. "Let's go, homes," he said again. I had a clear-cut decision to make: Drive or die.

I had paused for a moment trying to overcome the rush of terror that was preventing me from putting the car in gear. I pulled away from the curb and drove slowly to the intersection past the open garage. "Where is everybody? Am I imagining all this or what?" I thought.

Carrie was still leaning her head into the front of the car and started questioning Juan. "Oh, shit. What's that on your ear? Is that blood? Oh, my God, did you hurt someone?" Carrie said. I could tell that she was fighting back tears.

Juan was grinning and looked back at Carrie while rubbing his ear.

"You don't really think I'd hurt anyone, do you? You guys are my best friends in the world. I didn't hurt anyone. The dog wouldn't stop barking, so I might have got the dog a little bit."

I was expecting cops to swarm us any second. We made it back to 395 without incident. 395 is pretty flat and straight and when I pulled onto the highway there were no sirens or police vehicles anywhere.

"My aunt didn't want to help me, so I had to let off a few warning shots, that's all." Juan popped open the revolver's cylinder and replaced several spent cartridges.

I tried not to even look in his direction, let alone make eye contact with him. I wished Carrie would stop asking him questions too. Although Juan was now the calmest he had been since Carrie came into the picture, I could tell he was starting to get irritated with her questioning.

"Why do you want to know what happened? Are you gonna tell on me? Rojo, do you think she's going to tell on me?"

I could feel his stare on my face.

"No bro, she's not going to tell. There's nothing to tell, right? You said you didn't hurt anyone, so what's to tell?"

After watching Juan walk back to the car with that smirk on his face and the little skip at the end, I thought there's no way we were going to live to tell about this because this guy is undoubtedly psychotic. Someone who could shoot someone to death -- if that's what had happened -- and then laugh and skip is definitely unstable. These thoughts resonated in my mind as we drove farther from the Tri-Cities.

Though no one was asking, Juan kept repeating that he hadn't hurt anyone. At the same time he was digging through the purse. His story seemed to shift from one minute to the next.

"When I was talking to my aunt, her husband attacked me, so I had to lock them in the closet. He came out of the basement with a rifle, so I had to show him I wasn't playing. They're probably still locked in there. I might have gotten the dog a little on the way out, but everyone's alright."

I drove in a trance for the next three hours. Juan started telling us all kinds of things that I wasn't interested in hearing -- things that I'd had no idea were true of him.

"You're lucky you don't really know who I am or what I've done," he said. "I was on 'America's Most Wanted' for killing my mother-in-law and father in-law. They were molesting my kids, so I bucked 'em both in the head. I saw some pornographic pictures of my kids on their computer, so I took my oldest daughter with me one day and bucked 'em both in the face and in the head. My daughter and I left the house and her grandparents live right next door. Their grandpa came out and asked my daughter what happened. She told him those were just firecrackers and everything was alright. She's a little soldier, huh?"

"That's crazy, homes" I replied. It was difficult to respond to a far-out story like that. Up till now, Juan hadn't told us anything that would justify his paranoia. Now he was telling us about murders he had committed. In my mind that confirmed his intention to get rid of Carrie and me. His telling us those stories was sealing our fate.

From that point to the outskirts of Portland, Juan told us grandiose stories of his past. According to Juan, he not only held a high rank in the notorious 18th Street gang but was also well respected in the Mexican mafia. Juan told us that after he had executed his in-laws, his people secured his safe passage deep into Mexico. But, he said, his safety, transportation, new identity and income were predicated on his work for the mafia. He was employed by the mafia to be a "problem solver." He said that he "got rid of people's baggage."

According to Juan, the mafia had hired him to do numerous hits in various parts of Mexico. He also informed us that he had been sent as far as Chicago to terminate a problem. He told us of a huge reward for his capture. According to him, it was in the ballpark of $100,000.

I was inclined to dismiss these stories, but to totally disregard them would have been foolhardy. I figured that Juan, through his theatrics and stories, was trying not only physically to dictate our actions but also to put us into a mental state of submission. Perhaps he was making an effort to impress Carrie. The truth is that I really didn't know what he was doing or why he was doing it.

A sign for the Multnomah Falls came into view, which meant we were about 40 minutes outside Portland. This section of I-82 runs close to the river. You could throw a rock from your car window and it would splash into its deep waters . We exited the highway, winding down to the river.

Juan emptied the contents of the purse into a plastic bag. He handed Carrie the wallet from inside the purse and told her to take everything from inside it and put it into the bag. I saw her slip a driver's license into her back pocket.

When our eyes met, she gave me a look of desperation. I think we both believed our lives were over. I could see the hate in Carrie's eyes when she looked at Juan. Her withholding the license was her way of getting back at him, in my view. It would be a clue to who her killer had been once police connected it with whatever had happened in Kennewick.

We all walked close to the river. We filled the plastic bag half-full of rocks. Juan swung it around and chucked it into the river.

"Well guys, I'm all clear. There's no dirt on me now," Juan said with a smirk.

Except for the driver's license I said to myself.

This all seemed routine for Juan -- almost ceremonial. Now that I had slept a little and could actually put together a somewhat rational thought, I was giving Juan's stories a bit more credibility. Maybe this guy really was wanted. Maybe he actually was a hit man and had committed murder.

There were some indications he was well connected. There was the fact that his friends owned a car dealership that had meth-cooking taco trucks selling dope out of the lot. Then of course the phone calls from people ordering him to get rid of his baggage.

On the other hand, a lot of things didn't add up. If he was as connected as he said he was, why had I met him walking the streets of Portland with all of his belongings stuffed into a small backpack and selling small quantities of dope? Why was he so broke? I'm sure killing people brings in a decent wage.

Juan had said he'd been arrested for selling cocaine in downtown Portland. If he was also wanted for murder, then I'm sure Multnomah County (which encompasses Portland) would have held him for a little longer than a day.

If Juan had really killed his in-laws, wouldn't the police have his mother's house under some sort of surveillance? If he was so wanted, why were we able to drive around the Tri-Cities for days upon days, visit all his friends, drive through parks, parking lots and gas stations, go to grocery stores and rent a motel room in the same town he allegedly killed all these people? If there was a $100,000 reward for him, why hadn't anyone called him in? All these facts cast a shadow of doubt on Juan's stories.

Carrie and I had been with 'Psycho' for so long that we both started to identify with him a bit. We knew what set him off and tried to placate his unstable mind. Juan was so out of touch that I honestly believe he thought Carrie was his girlfriend and I was his best friend. I also believe that if he thought any different, our lives would have been ended long before.

Ever since the first trip into the secluded hills of Idaho, I had tried to moderate Juan's psychotic episodes. Playing off his twisted perceptions of reality was the only means of survival. If saying I was his best friend prevented him from pulling the trigger, then by all means I was his best friend.

The fact that I had only known him for a couple weeks didn't much matter. The fact that Carrie had been snatched up from southern Idaho and threatened with death seemed to slip Juan's mind.

Juan said to her over and over again, "You want to be with me, right? I didn't kidnap you?" Like he was trying to convince himself that everything was fine.

Carrie and I had to respond quickly and accurately. So we pretended like nothing had happened either. Every time he'd tell us a different story about what had happened at his aunt's house, we would just respond, "Oh really, that's OK. I'm sure everything is fine."

Juan looked happy as the plastic bag went sailing into the river. That made the whole episode more ominous. If he did hurt someone in that house, you'd never have guessed it from his behavior. As far as I knew, no one would ever live to tell anyone about what had happened. How could it be that easy to get away with murder?

The only thing that might arouse the authority's suspicion would be the driver's license in Carrie's back pocket. That's assuming her body would be found.

Back to the Blade

Trying not to show the despair infecting my spirit, I climbed back into the car and we resumed our drive to Portland. The sun had fallen below the tree line. I couldn't believe we were actually within 30 minutes of Portland. I-82 was empty, and we sailed along at 75 mph.

I believed showing any emotion would be construed as acknowledging Juan had done something bad in that house in Kennewick . Juan was always ending his stories with, “You don’t really think I would hurt someone, do you?”

Everything was a test with him. Every question had a hidden agenda. Although I was bursting with emotion, I couldn’t express it even slightly.

“I can trust you guys, right? You’re my friends, aren’t you?” he would say. We, of course, had to stay submissive and humbly reply with “Yes, you can trust us” in order to stay alive.

This type of submission and humbleness does not come easy for me. It’s not a natural response for a grown man to take orders such as this from another man. A natural response for a normal male would be, “Fuck you and kiss my ass.”

I’m sure someone on the outside of this situation would be quick to say, “I would have taken the gun from that son-of-bitch and beaten his fat ass.” I can assure you that given the facts and the reality of the situation, you would not have tried such a thing.

Granted, a normal person probably wouldn’t have agreed to give a stranger a ride across the United States for $1,500. Unfortunately, the addict in me accepted that proposition, and I was stuck in between life and death. It’s not until your family is threatened and you're forced to watch a near-execution that you have second thoughts about snatching a gun away from a bona fide killer.

As I've said, if Juan hadn't known where my family and girlfriend lived, and if he hadn't been threatening Carrie with death, I might have tried to kill him. But the odds against prevailing were too high.

We made it to downtown Portland around dusk. Burnside was of course my first stop. I still had a few dollars left from the $50 Sara had sent me. The thought of scoring some heroin had been reverberating in my mind for the last week. One of the most alluring assets of heroin is its ability to filter out grief, loss, trauma and anxiety. God knows my body craved it as well as my mind.

We drove up and down Burnside a couple times before we spotted a dealer. Juan did the negotiating. We parked on a side street. He handed me the balloon and I commenced cooking up the heroin. The euphoria that is produced and the relief that heroin provides is grand. Especially for an addict who has gone without and has suffered sleeplessness, cramps, diarrhea, exhaustion and anxiety attacks. Heroin makes the addict want to live for those few hours of ecstasy. Actually, being high is the only reason I wanted to live. It is such a self-destructive and self-loathing cycle.

"Alright, homes, we better get to your girlfriend's house before she thinks something's wrong," Juan said.

I pondered how to respond. Should I say, "Oh, no, we better not go there because you're highly unstable and perhaps you've even killed people and were and probably still are going to kill us"? Or do I pretend nothing ever happened and hope that I can find a way to defuse the situation?

Option One was probably not the way to go. Even though I would never have said those things to Juan, my slightest hesitation to go to Sara's house would have dangerously raised his suspicion. I was leaning more toward the second option. I felt Juan had calmed down a bit.

I believed in my heart that Juan wouldn't harm anyone at Sara's aunt's house. Her cousins were young, harmless and non-confrontational. Plus they had already met Juan. So the chances of them picking a fight with Juan or saying anything provoking to him were low. No one at that house knew what had happened these past few days, either, so there would be no cause for alarm.

I knew Sara was concerned and had a good idea that something was wrong, but she had no inkling of the trauma we had been through. This was a good thing. Sara can get pretty emotional in a stressful situation. If she knew of the bizarre and nefarious behavior Juan was capable of, she would have led him to believe that she was going to tell on him.

Sara had said she'd be at work until 9:00 p.m. It was roughly that time when we finished our business on Burnside. I was starting to experience the healing power of heroin. All the chaos and anxiety were banished from my mind. Life was once again worth living.

I knew when we pulled up and Sara saw Juan and Carrie in the car she wasn't going to be happy. Trying to explain why they were with me would also prove to be difficult.

I pulled to the curb in front of the building that Sara worked in. I saw the look of disapproval when she noticed Juan was still with me and Carrie was there.

I hastily exited the car to try intercepting a barrage of uncomfortable questions. Sara's frustration was understandable, considering I was only supposed to be gone six days and was supposed to have dropped Juan off in the Ozark Mountains. Not to mention that $1,500 I was supposed to have acquired for driving Juan cross-country. Now here I am with zero money, two weeks later, and I had to pawn the last bit of valuable stuff I owned for gas money.

I knew all this would not go over well with Sara. So I did my best to minimize these obvious problems and capitalize on the fact that she was lucky I even made it to Portland. As she approached the car, I managed to hobble over to her and embrace her on the sidewalk.

"What's going on, Mark? Who's that girl, and why is Juan still with you? I thought you were going to be alone," Sara said in a disappointed voice.

I hugged and kissed her with all my heart. "Baby, it's all really hard to explain right now. Things didn't go very well for us, and this is not a good time to be upset."

"Can't we take them somewhere and drop them off? I want to be alone with you. I mean, is that too much to ask?" Sara said.

I felt trapped. The windows were down in the car and I couldn't go into detail with Sara, though I wanted to. Juan's hard stare was boring a hole through me.

"Well, babe, they don't really have any place to go, and I promised if we got to Portland I would figure something out for them."

Sara had witnessed a small outbreak of Juan's anger a few weeks before, so I think she knew not to press the issue in front of him.

Juan got out of the car and said hello to Sara.

"I got him back to you in one piece. Sorry it took so long." Then he introduced Carrie. I had told Sara that Carrie was his new girlfriend. Carrie was drained of all energy and looked exhausted and sad, holding a blank stare. "Hihowareyou?" she said in a monotone.

Sara asked where she was from.

"I'm from Idaho."

"You're kind of a long way from home, aren't you?" Sara replied.

"Um, yeah. My aunt lives here in Oregon. I was hoping to see her while I was here," Carrie said.

All this was making me pretty uncomfortable. Carrie was a disheveled mess, her spirit clearly broken. I was giving Sara a wide-eyed look, hoping she would get the picture that a lot of questions could lead to something bad.

I started the car and we four headed toward southeast Portland. I kept Sara talking by asking her about her work and how her day was -- anything to keep from talking about how my trip went.

I was still disoriented and sleep deprived. My nerves were deadened by the heroin and the mind-blowing effects of being constantly threatened at gunpoint. Now that I was actually back in Portland with my girlfriend, all the recent events were like a nightmare. So when I spoke to Sara, my words were slow and soft. Though I was ecstatic to see Sara, it was hard to express any feeling because of my exhaustion.

As we approached Sara's aunt's house, I told her that I was going to call my boss and try going to work the next day. I figured that this was the only way to generate some money for Juan to get somewhere. I was talking to the entire group, in hopes of setting Juan's mind at ease.

I could tell he was starting to boil with frustration. He had no money, nowhere to go, a gun and a pocket full of bullets. He had exiled himself from his family and had allegedly killed his in-laws. His friends no longer wanted him around, and he had acquired a nasty meth problem. His behavior was not acceptable in the circle he was once allegedly in. Juan was clearly at a point in his life where suicide was a feasible means to an end.

I thought that if I promised to get him some money and offered him the car again, perhaps he would leave. Since there was no real plan established after we left the Tri-Cities, I felt like if I didn't come up with one, Juan wouldn't have any reason to go on and he would just end it all. By going to work, I was quite literally buying some time.

I knew my boss was pretty busy this time of year, so I was confident that he would have work for me. I conveyed my plan to everyone in detail.

"I'll call my boss when we get to Sara's and I'll line up some work for tomorrow. I should make $100, so that should be enough money for you guys to either get a hotel or gas money to get to Carrie's aunt's house."

That was the best idea I could think of. Suicide and murder seemed to be the only decisions Juan was capable of, so I figured if I offered him money and the car that would satisfy him for the night.

Unfortunately for Carrie, she was trapped in the role of Juan's girlfriend. I wished I could have pulled her aside and let her know that I was trying to keep her alive. Although it was hard for me not to place blame on her for triggering Juan's outbreaks. I knew it was far from her fault we were now faced with a life-and-death situation. Yet it was also true that her remarks repeatedly angered him, adding to the anxiety and tension we all felt.

Then again, if it weren't for my opiate addiction, we would have never met Carrie either, and I wouldn't have needed any more heroin if Juan hadn't thrown his shirt into my spoon. So placing blame was pointless. I was trying not to wallow in the problem and move toward a solution.

We pulled up to Sara's house close to 10:00 p.m. Her aunt was gone for the night. Sara's cousin Jason was the only one home. Her other cousin, Kathryn, was staying at a friend's.

Jason had a couple friends over and they were watching TV when we came in the house. Juan had met Jason before, so he needed no introduction. Jason said, "What's up?" and Juan introduced Carrie. It was an uncomfortable scene.

Sara had only been living there about six months and was a guest herself. Add three more people to an already delicate living situation and it's bound to cause a little friction. Unfortunately, I had no other option.

Jason was a nice kid trying to forge through his teens, a heavyset youngster still pretty dependent on his mom but certainly capable of achieving stability and success. He loved his cousin Sara and knew she was struggling with her addiction. His compassion led to his offering us shelter that night.

Once we were all sitting in front of the TV, I called my boss and long-time friend, John Smith. John is one of my closest friends -- probably my best friend. He stands about 6' 1", weighs about 240 lbs., and has short black hair parted to one side. He's a working-class guy who's managed to find stability in the midst of adversity, an old-fashioned, hard-working, truck-driving, beer-drinking American.

I told John I had made it back to Portland and was ready to go back to work. Even though my leg was still causing me a lot of pain, I had no choice but to go to work.

My boss gave me a specific time and place to meet him in the morning. I hung up the phone before he started asking me too many questions. I let everyone know I had to work early the next morning.

Sara came and sat on my lap. Carrie and Juan sat on the couch about six feet away. We were watching TV. I whispered to Sara that she should put it on the news. She of course questioned my request.

"Why? Oh, God, did something happen? You sure are acting funny."

"Please, girl, just be cool and turn on the news."

Sara found a news station. We all sat and watched in silence. I figured that if Juan had actually killed his aunt or his uncle or the dog, it would probably be on the news.

After a half-hour of news, there was no mention of any murders or robberies. Again I began to wonder if Juan was simply trying to scare us. Nevertheless, I knew that he had enough hate in his heart that he was at least suicidal if not homicidal. Therefore I had to proceed with constant and extreme caution.

I felt Juan was listening to me and believed I was going to help him. I certainly was doing my best to set his mind at ease and gain his trust.

With Sara's cousin Kathryn gone, Jason offered Juan and Carrie her room. Everyone was tired and I had to work at 7:00 a.m. the next day, so we decided it was time to retire.

Sara's room was directly across from Kathryn's and was barely big enough for a bed, but it was a room with a door. As we went to our separate rooms Juan looked in Sara's room and examined it before he turned to go into Kathryn's room. I could tell he was distrustful of the situation, but I think he knew I would never call the police on him while he was at my girlfriend's house. I believe he knew I was aware of the consequences if there was any sign of law enforcement or any strange behavior from any of us

If I had told Sara about any of the trips into the mountains, or the gunshots we heard in front of his aunt's house, she would have lost it. This of course would have sealed her fate, as well as that of everyone else within shooting distance.

That said, however, I saw a dramatic change in Juan's level of hostility since we had left the Tri-Cities. He was much calmer and didn't seem to want to kill everyone as much as before. His anger seemed to have subsided drastically.

At the same time, while he had appeared jubilant after he left his aunt's house, he was now showing clear signs of sorrow and frustration -- a man definitely on the brink of snapping. Usually when people stop talking and become withdrawn, they warrant close observation. From my experience, it's the quiet ones you have to watch out for.

Sara and I made sure Juan and Carrie were settled in before shutting the door to her bedroom. Jason and his friends were falling in and out of sleep when we retired. By this time it was past midnight and everyone was tired.

As I lay down on Sara's wide bed, I thanked God for letting me live. The comfort of a familiar setting is so much greater when you've gone through a traumatic and life-threatening event. While Sara undressed and prepared for bed I stared off into an abstract pattern in the ceiling paint. I lay there wondering how all this was possible.

I knew Sara was still upset about the presence of Juan and Carrie. So I snapped out of my trance and grabbed her by her hand.

"I'm so sorry, babe, for not coming through and bringing Juan back with me. But you have to trust me on this. I'm going to do everything I can to get rid of him, OK? But when we're with him we have to be cool. He is not a happy person and you've seen him get pissed already. So tomorrow I'll get him some money and hopefully we'll never have to see him again, OK?"

"Mark, honey, what the hell happened out there, and who is that girl?" she responded. "Juan never said he had a girlfriend. And why is he still with you? I don't understand."

"Baby, there's a lot you don't know about Juan and if I had my way he wouldn't be here right now, but things are not what they seem with this guy and tomorrow hopefully we won't ever see him again. Please don't ask him about the trip, OK? Trust me."

I rested my head between her breasts, and Sara ran my fingers through her hair. Good lord, it was good to be home.

Day 15
August 2, 2005
Portland, Oregon

The alarm woke me at 5:45 a.m. Time to get Sara to the methadone clinic and for me to get to work. The unsettling thought of no dope to wake up to set in as I stumbled across the room to silence the alarm. I made my way back to the tiny bed and Sara turned over, trying to ignore the reality of a new day.

I sat and searched my mind for a reason to live. The only motivation I could muster was the thought of getting enough money to satisfy Juan and having enough left over to buy some dope. My leg was still killing me, and my wound was starting to itch intensely.

I dug through some of my bags hoping to find a wrapper, spoon or cotton with some heroin residue on it, but to no avail. This would be another arduous day. Nose dripping and eyes watering, I scrambled around looking for my clothes. I would have to cope with work dope-sick and on an empty stomach.

I opened the door to Kathryn's room, and Juan was laying there awake with Carrie beside him. Her face was buried under the blankets and she appeared to still be sleeping.

"Are you ready, homes?" Juan asked me.

"Yeah, we should leave here in a few. So you guys should get ready," I replied.

Carrie poked her head out from the blankets and wiped the sleep from her eyes. I thought to myself, "What a nightmare this is. I have to bring this bullshit to an end. This is crazy." The look on her face inspired me to dedicate the day to ending this siege. It also reminded me yet again that there was a great deal at stake here: Carrie's two children, my family, my girlfriend, her family, Carrie's life and my life. Juan had told us he could easily have people erased from prison or anywhere else.

Trying to explain my predicament to a police dispatcher and have her take me seriously was also a major concern. If Juan really was the killer he claimed to be, then I had to be sure that if I did call the police he wouldn't know I had called them. If he thought in any way I had led to his apprehension, the results would be catastrophic.

I partially closed Kathryn's door and returned back to Sara's room. She was awake and rummaging through her makeshift closet for an outfit.

"Good morning, baby," I said to her, hugging her from behind.

"Hey, babe," she replied.

Hygiene is not top priority when you're strung out. When I had enough dope in my system, I'd take the time to shower, change clothes, brush my teeth and maybe eat something. But when you're without dope, you lose all motivation to tend to simple tasks. I was still winded from putting on my shoes, so I lay back down on the bed while Sara got ready.

Sara and Carrie had a few minutes to talk in private. Sara came back into the bedroom, closed the door and turned to me with a puzzled expression.

"Mark, that girl said she was in trouble and wanted me to call her mom or her aunt. She was crying. What's going on?"

"Babe, I told you that things are not what they seem. We need to just do what this guy says until we can get rid of him."

"Mark this is scary. I don't like this one bit. I wish you would tell me what's up."

I wished I could have told her, but Sara's remaining ignorant for the moment was important.

"Everything is going to be alright, OK, honey? Let's just be cool and get out of here," I told her.

It was around 6:20 a.m. when we took off. Juan and Carrie were in the back seat. Sara drove and I sat in the passenger seat. My addiction was provoking anxiety and my toes were curling up with frustration as we made our way to the methadone clinic. While the government kept Sara well, I sat dope-sick and miserable. Since I had no money to get any dope, I had to go to work. I was not mentally ready for a hard day of pumping concrete, let alone physically ready. There was no time to go to Burnside and try to buy some dope, either. I was hoping once I got to work and was away from Juan I could think of a plan. Time was running out, as was Juan's patience.

We pulled up to the methadone clinic and Sara hopped out. As soon as she disappeared into the clinic, Juan pulled out his aunt's purse from under the seat.

"We need to get rid of this. I'll be right back." He walked to a minimart trash can and stuffed the purse deep inside it.

Sara emerged from the clinic with a spring in her step. We sped off to meet John at the job site. Now it was 7:00 a.m. and we started to discuss the day's plan.

"You guys drop me off at work and take the car for the day," I said to Juan and Carrie. "I'll give you my boss's cell phone number and you call me in a few hours to see if I'm done yet," I explained.

"Listen, bro, I'm doing two jobs today, so I'll have $100 for you to work with. Just be cool for a few hours and call me. Here's John's number," I said. I had a business card with his number on it and passed it back to Juan.

"OK, homes, I'm trusting you. Don't disappoint me," Juan said as he took the card.

Sara shot me another concerned look after Juan said that. No words were spoken after that until we pulled onto the job site. I leaned over and kissed Sara goodbye. I hopped out of the car and waved as the beamer speed off.

I was pretty sure that at this point I was Juan's lifeline. I was sure he wouldn't harm Sara because I knew way too much about him. If he had taken her hostage, I could have blown the whistle on him. With no money and nowhere to go, it was in his best interest to wait for me.

I think he was seeing if I would come back. Sort of like a trial run. So I was taking this test very serious. Even though Carrie had annoyed me with her reckless remarks and haughty attitude, I still felt responsible for her.

John was starting to set up when I arrived at the job site. Pumping concrete is very laborious and I told John that my leg hadn't healed yet but that I would give it my best.

"So how was the trip?" he asked. "It didn't sound like things were going so well for you when you called me."

"No, things didn't go well at all," I replied. "You can't even imagine how bad things went, bro."

John was smart enough not to partake in the same self destructive addiction that led to his mother's death. His father, who is still alive, has also led a life of addiction. Then there's me, who has known John for twenty years and has been on the self-destructive path of heroin addiction most of that time.

So John is no stranger to the lifestyle of a heroin addict. He's also shy and passive-aggressive. It's hard for him to come right out and tell you what's bothering him. He's more likely to make little condescending remarks and give you the silent treatment when he's mad about something you did. He's not much of a talker. He's a doer.

Knowing John for this long, I know most of his idiosyncrasies, and if I were to come right out and tell him the predicament I was currently in and the magnitude of danger involved, he would more than likely want to involve the police. Or perhaps, since John owned a gun, he would want to devise a plan where we overpowered Juan. Neither of those ideas was appealing to me.

I tried to come up with a way to tell John what was happening, but I couldn't. Once we got busy working, I withdrew from all conversation and wallowed in dope-sick exhaustion. I didn't feel anyone could help me out of this one. I couldn't think of a way to even tell my best friend the horrors I had just been through. Even though Juan wasn't on the job site, I felt like he was watching.

Before I knew it, we were done. Pumping concrete usually doesn't last more than a couple of hours. The pump time runs $100 an hour, plus a set-up fee and $2.50 a yard, with a two-hour minimum. So the contractor wants us to be done in two hours. That gives us time to do up to three jobs a day. Unfortunately, midway through the job, our second appointment of the day was canceled. So this would be our only job of the day.

That wasn't the worst of it. John informed me he wouldn't be able to pay me until the next day. This was devastating news. No money, no dope and in the company of a killer.

In a way, I'm like John when it comes to speaking my mind. It's very difficult for me to come right out and ask for what I need. My pride always seems to get in the way. I'm quite familiar with the saying "A closed mouth doesn't get fed." I just don't put it to use very often. So instead of disclosing the wreckage of emotions I had bottled up, I sat in silence.

After we had finished up and got all the equipment cleaned, Carrie called John's cell phone. She gave me directions to a park in north Portland. John gave me a ride. While en route, I persuaded him to give me $10 for gas. Carrie had told me that the BMW was, as always, near empty.

John questioned my mood as we neared Carrie and Juan in the park.

"Is everything cool? You're kinda quiet," he said.

"Uh, yeah. I'm just tired, bro. It's been a rough month." I believe I was unconsciously trying to ask for help, though I couldn't seem to formulate the correct words. I stared out of the truck window with a myriad of emotions spinning around my head. No words, just a blank stare.

I tried to erase everything that was haunting my mind. I was hoping Juan would just disappear. Unfortunately, when we pulled into the park's parking lot, he and Carrie were leaning against the car.

I thought to myself, *Why am I purposefully putting myself back in harm's way? I must be totally out of my freaking mind.* Then I saw the tired, loathing facial expression Carrie sported and remembered why: to help her. There comes a point when human compassion and the desire to help a person in need exceed common sense as well as selfishness. This was way bigger than just me. By my selfish endeavors, I had unknowingly jeopardized more than a handful of innocent people. Now it was up to me to end the threat, but how? I'm no hostage negotiator, nor have I had any sort of training to deal with an armed killer.

One thing I knew was that I was still alive. So were Carrie and Juan. I believed that he was, and had been, listening to me thus far.

I also believed I held the best chance of defusing this situation. Bringing in an outsider at this point was likely to lead to deaths. It was unclear whose, but I knew for sure that one or more people would be dead if there were an unexpected police threat. That was my biggest fear. In the midst of a police chase or shootout, they would undoubtedly assume that I too was unwilling to cooperate and shoot me as well. There would be no time to explain my situation or role in all this.

All these too-familiar thoughts swirled through my mind as we approached my car. Waves of heat hovered over the asphalt. Both Carrie and Juan looked ill with heat stroke. Both were sweating and parched-looking.

John handed me the $10 and told me to call him later for directions to the next day's job site. He said he had a couple early jobs scheduled. Covered in dirt and concrete, I got out of the truck. John and Juan exchanged quick greetings before I shut the door.

Things looked tense as I approached. I was exhausted, and my clothes were still wet from spraying down the equipment. Even though it was blinding hot out, I was getting cold sweats, and my nose was a faucet of the dope-sick drips. Now I would have to explain that I had only $10 and that I wouldn't be getting paid until the next day.

"We're fucking starving, I've been wearing these clothes for who knows how long, we've been stuck in this toaster oven all morning and we're out of gas," Juan said in greeting.

"I got some money for gas, but that's about all I have right now," I replied. "One of our jobs got cancelled this morning so I only did one job. But I'm doing two jobs tomorrow, and they'll be cash jobs so I'll have plenty of money."

Juan was not very happy about this, and Carrie was so miserable she lacked the energy to even comment.

"Let's go get some gas for now, and we'll have to figure out what we're going to do from there," I said with as much enthusiasm as I could muster. "Sara doesn't get off work until 9:00, but we'll be able to get some food then."

It was hard not to focus on all the negativity surrounding us. Carrie was forced into complacency and visibly suffering from malnutrition, sleep deprivation and opiate withdrawal. All of us looked sickly, and Juan looked like he could die on the spot. His attitude and behavior seemed to welcome death. I knew the only way Juan was going to end this siege was to be killed.

It was hard not to feel a little sorry for him. He was obviously suffering from a mental disorder. At times he would be normal for hours at a time. But most of the time he was in a paranoid vortex of discontent. Though I felt sympathy, I was nowhere near ready to forgive him or abandon my effort to end the siege.

As we got into the BMW, I could feel Juan's anxiety building. His face was distorted with frustration. I knew I had to come up with some money before too long.

"Look, esé, I've been sweating in this fucking, dumb-ass shirt all day and I can't take this shit anymore. I don't know why the fuck I came to Portland. There ain't shit for me here." Juan pulled his button-up shirt open and buttons flew in all directions, mostly bouncing off the windshield. I suggested we pawn the little hand-held camcorder given to us as collateral by the punks we'd fronted dope to in Idaho.

If it had been up to me, I would have left the car, taken the bus downtown and spent the money on dope. Unfortunately, I wasn't running the show, and that wouldn't have gone over well with Juan or Carrie. So I pulled into the first gas station I saw and put $5 worth in the tank.

We hit 82nd Avenue, where a lot of pawn shops are located. Wherever a lot of crime takes place, a pawn shop isn't far off. After trying three different shops and three failed attempts, I decided that the camera was a lost cause. No one would accept it.

By this time it was late in the day, and hot. No air conditioner, no radio, no food.

I lived on the streets and suffered the harsh elements of the Northwest. I learned to adapt to the daily endeavors that the streets require. No food, no shelter and, worst of all, no dope was a daily problem. If these problems weren't solved, then you starved or fell prey to pneumonia in the relentless rainfall. But really, once you've familiarized yourself with the workings of the street, it's almost impossible to starve.

Most people are far too distracted by their addiction to worry about food and shelter. If there's one thing I know how to do on the streets, it's get money. But it's difficult having nothing again after having everything you need and being off the streets for a long time. It had been years since I had had to resort to my underhanded ways to survive.

The Nordstrom scam

Nordstrom had sustained my addiction for nearly ten years. When I lived on the streets I was what you call a booster. I would enter a store, preferably Nordstrom, and relieve them of high-priced garments. Nordstrom was my first choice of shoplifting targets, because it would give cash back without a receipt. Very few stores did that, and most of those that did were exploited so much that the policy was short lived. But it was well established at Nordstrom.

Higher-end stores usually don't put alarms on their garments because they have such an elaborate security system. When I was well (that is, high), I would put on a tie and slacks and take the role of a wealthy shopper. Youthful features, nice clothes and a spunky attitude usually makes you exempt from the scrutiny of security. Just in case there were alarms on the clothes I always carried a small pair of metal clippers to cut them off. If the store wouldn't give me cash back I would get a gift certificate for the amount of the item. I did this so often that I accrued a long list of "clients" who needed specific items for their kids, themselves or a friend. Many of those clients were shop owners themselves.

They paid 50¢ on the dollar, sometimes 75¢. They always wanted the strangest things, from coffee to Oil of Olay aging cream to daily vitamins. They would buy it from me and put it on their own shelves and resell it.

When I wasn't well, I would just go in and grab something close to the door. Or in desperate times I would take something off the shelf and bring it directly up to the counter and try returning it.

I acquired 15 shoplifting convictions and did a year in jail on the 15th one. It was a $25 Adidas sweatshirt that I did the year for -- hardly worth it. Even though I got away with it more than I got caught, my face was well known along the I-5 corridor. I was banned from Nordstrom for life, which made things difficult.

I had hit all the Nordstroms in Portland, but that had been several years ago. And I'd never been caught in any of the Portland Nordstroms before. So I mentioned the Nordstrom idea to Juan.

Juan knew about the Nordstrom scam. But he lacked the clothing and attitude to carry off returning items to that classy store. Stealing the item is only 70 percent of the job. Returning it takes a skillful and persistent voice of assertiveness. When you don't have a receipt, and you're dressed like a bum, your chances of them dipping into the register and giving you cash for a stolen item aren't very good. You have to be a portrait of a Nordstrom's shopper and speak with tact to win the cashier over. Then the manager as well.

Sometimes it's done by two different people -- the booster and the returner for it to work. It's actually quite an intricate process, but the cash makes up for it.

Unfortunately, visiting all those pawn shops and getting nowhere brought the weight of hopelessness crashing down on Juan. The Nordstrom thing didn't appeal to him. I was so dope-sick by this time that I couldn't even drive.

"Fuck this shit, homes. Just pull over. I'm gonna drive. I can't do this anymore," Juan said.

I pulled over, put the car in neutral and got out. Juan came over to the driver's side and took over. Carrie quietly asked, "Can I just call my mom and let her know I'm OK please?"

Juan ignored her but shot her a callous look in the mirror. He leaned over to me and whispered, "See, homes, she's gonna tell on me, so we're gonna take a little trip. We're gonna visit my old Boy Scout campgrounds."

The Boy Scout campgrounds

At this point I had no energy to even devise an argument against his plan.

Juan took us to the Sandy River, another secluded area that was heavily wooded, with houses few and far between. This is the kind of place where people have summer cottages and a lot of land.

Juan started reminiscing about when he was younger and his parents had a summer home up here and he would go to Boy Scout camp along the Sandy River. He told me that a lot of these houses were empty and that some people leave a car in the garage with the keys near-by.

"Listen, homes, I'm gonna find a house and steal a car. I'll take the girl with me and you can get back to your life," he said. "This is too chaotic for me, and these voices keep telling me to do you, and I don't want to have to do that. You need to get away from me while you can."

That sounded good, though I knew he would change his mind in a few minutes, so I just agreed. After we drove for about a half hour Juan turned off the road and down a driveway. The driveway was lay-ered with years of fallen pine needles. It didn't look as though it was used very often. Huge evergreen, pine and hemlocks towered over it, blocking out the sun.

Juan drove about a 100 yards before we came to a clearing. A low-budget country-style house came into view. It was two stories and in need of some cosmetic repairs. The grass was tall enough to reach the bottom-floor windows.

"It doesn't look like anyone has been here for a while," I said.

"Yeah, but there might be a car around here I can steal," Juan replied.

"I just wish you would take me home," Carrie said.

Juan looked at me and winked. "Oh, I'm gonna take you home, don't you worry," Juan replied condescendingly.

He got out of the car, casually pulled the gun half-way out of his pocket and checked the cylinders. He slid it back into his pocket and told me to get out of the car.

"Here we go again" I thought. I figured that if Juan didn't find a car, he would kill us for sure.

Carrie was all too familiar with this scene and spoke up with a teary but assertive statement. “I’m not getting out of this car, and if you try to make me, I’ll scream so loud they’ll hear me in Portland.”

Juan motioned me away from Carrie. I figured as soon as I reached him he would shoot me twice in the head, just as he'd been telling us he would for the past few days.

“Listen, esé, you got to get her out of the car," he whispered in my ear. " I think she trusts you. Then I’ll do the rest. No one will ever find her up here. You can go your way, and I can go back to Mexico.”

And there I was in a treacherous situation again. If I didn't do as he said, I'd immediately lose what little trust I had gained. Then I'd be the enemy and all would be lost. If I did do as he ordered, she'd be killed and I'd surely be next to die.

Either way, I had to say something. Silence was the enemy. It was obvious that Juan really did hear voices and that if there were no other voices around, he would start doing what the voices in his head told him, which was to kill us.

“We better make sure there’s no one around before you start shooting off the gun,” I said with confidence. I was trying to buy some time at this point. As usual I didn’t really have a plan other than to stay alive.

A house was roughly 20 feet away from my car. “These people could show up at any time, bro," I said to him. "Maybe we should find a different spot. Plus she isn’t going to get out of that car for any reason.”

“I can’t keep doing this, esé," Juan replied. "I’m losing my fucking mind. I know she’s going to tell on me. You probably are, too. I gotta do this shit now, homes.”

Juan started for the car door. “Look, girl, I’m not gonna hurt you. Just get out of the car.” He opened the door and pulled the seat forward.

“I’ll scream. Don’t touch me. Please!" Carrie said. "I just want to go home. Please don’t do this,” she pleaded as she scooted to the other side of the car.

Juan looked at me. “Look, homes, I don’t want to fuck up your car with blood, so you better help me get her out of there,” he whispered.

“Bro, we’ve been here for too long. I think we should just find a different place,” I suggested. We had been there for close to ten minutes already.

Juan looked around and slammed his hands on the roof of the car. "Fuck, esé! I can't keep doing this. I wanna just buck myself in the head and get this over with."

"Just take it easy," I reassured him. " I'll drive, you just relax and we'll find a better place, alright?" I didn't want to go as far as saying "I know how you feel" or something cliché like that. I knew his temper was quick and blinding, so I felt it best to just offer different options.

It made a world of difference what words I chose to use. Saying the wrong thing at a time as tense as this could be fatal. Juan was starting to trust me and I was doing everything possible not to break the trust I had been building. I felt it best to incorporate Carrie in the circle of trust as best I could.

"Listen, bro, you can trust her. You two should just go to Mexico and get away from it all. I mean, some pretty bizarre stuff has happened this last week, and I think we all need to get a good night's sleep. She's been cooperating as best she can. She's just scared."

Juan sat and seemed to ponder my words.

"Besides," I continued, "we don't have enough gas to be driving around this mountain all night.

I could only guess how Carrie was feeling while these quiet and insidious conversations were going on. She probably felt like I was on Juan's side and that I was conspiring to kill her. It wouldn't be until it was all over that we could compare our thoughts on these events.

He and I piled back into the car and backed out of the driveway. I still had $5 that I was hoping to buy some much needed heroin with, but we needed it for gas. We had driven around aimlessly for so long that the gas gauge was well into the red.

Fortunately for Carrie and me, running out of gas I think was the deciding factor in Juan's not shooting us in those secluded woods. If he had opted to kill us at that spot, his getaway car would have run out of gas only a few miles from the crime scene.

We had passed a small convenience store before we turned off onto the dark driveway. I spent my last $5 on gas. I felt like squirting gas on Juan and setting him on fire. But even after all the terror, pain and suffering this man had inflicted on Carrie and me, I couldn't bring myself to commit murder.

Boosting for time

It was impossible to assess what was going on in Juan's mind, but it was easy to see how out of touch with reality he was. I believe Juan had his mind set to kill himself, and whoever was near him at the time of his meltdown would be a target as well.

Still, every time he took us into a secluded area and then left it, I felt maybe he was getting better. Maybe someone could help him with the constant barrage of voices he was contending with.

The sun was fading as we wound our way back down the mountain. I found myself shaking my head at the fact that I was driving a killer around, a truly disturbed agent of brutality.

We still had a couple of hours to kill before Sara got off work. At this point I had to be assertive or die trying.

"I'm going to Nordstrom's and boosting something, and when Sara gets off work I'll have her return it," I told Juan and Carrie. This was the only solution I could come up with to get some money. I knew Juan wasn't too fond of the idea but I assured him that all he had to do was sit in the car. I would take care of the rest.

When you're trapped in the maze of addiction, you tend to develop a self-centered attitude and usually look out for what's best for you. This characteristic made it difficult to appease Juan. I was forced to cater to the perpetual psychotic outbreaks he displayed. Rather than try overpowering this gun-brandishing homicidal gangbanger, I thought it more advantageous to talk him down.

Since the first trip to one of Juan's "death camps," I used the only defense I had -- my voice. Now I felt that was losing its effect.

It was obvious that Juan came from money. His lifestyle revolved around major drug transactions that brought in substantial amounts of cash. Now he was penniless and homeless. His friends weren't willing to help him out anymore due to his fugitive status. So I offered him cash and my car to move on.

In no way did I want him to think I wasn't on his team. Neither did Carrie. We were two people acting for their lives and the safety of their families. The reality of death was so clear that both Carrie and I had to become superficial friends with our captor.

Money and drugs were short-term necessities for Juan -- drugs to help suppress the atrocities he claimed to have committed, and money to buy more. I took it upon myself to act in this time of desperation.

As I made my way back to Portland, I found myself reflecting back to the previous days. Man, did this guy really shoot his own in-laws? Was he really a hit man?

And most of all, what happened in that house in the Tri-Cities? Was that really his aunt's house? I would say probably not. I believe that the frustration from no killing, betraying his friends and vice-versa, not being able to see his kids, the burden of homicide, the chanting voices inside his head and the sorrow of being utterly alone had pushed him to kill.

I think Juan knew he was living his last days. I remember him saying, “My homies will know who did this” after we had gotten back on the freeway after leaving Kennewick following the home invasion. Since he had failed to execute us, he had to show his friends that he was no "bitch" -- that he was a true killer.

Every time we left one of Juan’s "death camps" he would be boiling over with frustration and say, “I guess I’m just a 300-pound bitch.” I’m sure he thought his homies were thinking that, and by killing someone he would reclaim his reputation.

My situation was dismal. Now I had to infiltrate a department store, boost a high-priced item and then have Sara return it. In a way, I hoped I would get caught just to separate myself from Juan and the constant threat of death.

But that would leave Carrie alone to die, and I would be the direct cause of any brutality against my family. I couldn’t live with either of those results. So I had to pull this off and get this guy some money, fast.

As we approached the city I got that familiar jittery feeling in my stomach. I’ve always been intrigued by the city and had become one with its streets. Going to commit a boost made me think back to when I was consumed by the lifestyle of street hustler, living from fix to fix and heist to heist. The strange people I would meet every day and the intricate stories of despair that each person was trying to shoot, smoke, snort or drink away. Life on the streets was an addiction for me as well. The daily regimen of boosting and selling became a way of life and a means to survival.

Fraternizing with prostitutes was part of the game. A lot of moms, daughters and sisters wore down their soles walking the ho stroll. I become friends with some of them. A woman’s power to nurture is never lost completely, and I tended to trigger that emotion and then feed off of it. It was never really a sex thing with me. Heroin tends to drain your libido anyway. Some of my best running partners were prostitutes. They made excellent returners. But just like with anything on the street, things change, people die or disappear or end up in prison.

No two days were the same for me on the street, and every person I met had their own ways to survive. I learned their tricks and used them when my ways didn’t work. I’ve run with, done dope with and committed crimes with people from every walk of life. A lawyer who lost his license to practice because of a nasty heroin addiction and found himself estranged from his wife and kids and living in a dope-infested motel. An ex-body builder who exhausted every doctor in Seattle for pain killer prescriptions and turned to heroin to kill the pain. (He was a good boosting asset because he was so big that the security guards never wanted to try apprehending him.)

Then there was the grunge scene, with a lot of rising stars who used heroin to curb the stresses of stardom. Drugs became their main occupation. All the fame and fortune in the world couldn't save them. Meanwhile, here I sat with no status, and somehow I was still alive. Why, I couldn't say.

My life up to this point had been a bout of unsuccessful ventures. Now it was hanging in an ominous balance. I could feel my fight or flight mechanisms kicking in, and I wanted to live. I dreamed of having a family and taking care of a beautiful wife and trying to guide my children in the right direction. I still had so many things I wanted to do. I wanted to teach my kids the same things my dad taught me.

Seeing a gun pushed into the back of someone's head and watching the fear and helplessness jolt through their body is devastating. So is listening to the sound of a human being pleading for her life and the flow of tears falling from a dirty face. A human life, breathing, heart beating, blood flowing, emotions keen and aware.

All this ending with one swift movement. Truly mind-boggling. Not only was I about to witness a murder, but I was watching the prologue to my death. This is what was about to happen to me. Two shots in the head is what Juan kept telling us he was going to do.

"I buck 'em in the head two times and they fall real fast and I just casually walk away," he would say.

All these thoughts were flooding my mind as I tried to mentally prepare for this boost. We pulled up to Nordstrom in the heart of downtown Portland's Pioneer Square. I found a parking place nearby and changed into my best outfit, which was pretty crappy after being stuffed in my small suitcase for weeks. I slicked my red hair back with some cheap gel and told Juan and Carrie I would be right back.

Just like I had done a hundred times before, I made my way to the entrance of Nordstrom. My nerves were shot. My legs were throbbing; my adrenaline pumping.

People passed me by as I approached the store, totally oblivious to my cause, totally unaware that a killer was sitting only a few feet away.

I had to keep my composure. I had to focus. I had to live. I had to pull this off.

I walked in and put on my game face. I was a happy shopper. A true Nordstrom stock holder. This is my store, my environment. I went directly to women's swimwear. Again, I would rely on my charisma to get me through.

I approached a young and spunky female salesperson straight away. She was dressed professionally, but her smile and friendliness made her approachable. Nordstrom's personnel are always so gregarious and helpful. I love this store.

I made up a story about going on a Caribbean cruise with my girlfriend, who'd just had a baby. I handed her a suit to put on hold for me, and as she turned I grabbed another suit, hanger and all, and crammed it down my pants. I covered up the slight bulge from the hanger with my shirt and gave her a fake name to hold my suit under.

Concealing the item is one of the most stressful parts of a boost. You have to boost it without attracting the attention of the many shoppers that usually surround you, the cashiers, the reputable security that impersonates casual shoppers and the ultimate enemy, the eye in the sky. Even if no one is around when you slip an item in your bag or down your pants or even put the item on, you have the cameras to contend with. There have been many times when I thought I had gotten away with a theft only to be tackled after I left the store.

I made it. My heart was pounding, and beads of sweat had gathered on my eyebrows as I weaved my way back to the car. I found it difficult to swallow, difficult to breath. But it was over. I had created enough space between myself and the scene of the crime that I knew I was safe.

I saw Juan in the passenger seat keeping a vigilant watch. I could only imagine what kind of demons were infecting his mind. His eyes were hostile and penetrating. I'm sure the weight of holding two people against their will and killing your wife's parents put some scary images in his head. Then knowing that you're literally being hunted by multiple law enforcement agencies, from America's Most Wanted to the locals, could carry a heavy burden as well. Looking into his eyes, I could see despair and uncertainty. It was unsettling to have to rejoin him.

Carrie was, as usual, in the back seat sitting with lost eyes and a sad face. Flocks of people walked past my car -- shoppers, tourists, students and business folk coming and going. But not one of them could be called on to help me out of this.

As I opened the driver's side door, I prayed that some kind of opportunity would present itself. An opportunity to end this siege without someone being killed. I prayed for a safe way out.

I opened the car door and got in. The hanger made it hard to sit, so I withdraw the bathing suit and threw it in the back.

Before I tossed it, I gave a quick glance at the price: $114. The reason I went to women's swimwear is because a woman (my girlfriend) would be returning it. It's good to know who is going to be returning the item before you steal it. That way you have a story to go with the person and the item.

Not just anyone can walk in and talk the cashier into forking over a couple of hundred dollars in cash without a receipt. My ex-girlfriend and I had mastered the art of boosting and returning. One day she would go into the store and boost and I would dress up in my suit and tie and return the item or usually it was several items. Then, the next day, I would do the boosting and she would return.

This went on for years until neither of us was allowed in the store. We had exhausted that scam to the point of incarceration. If I was caught in Nordstrom's one more time, I would be charged with burglary. This had kept me out of the store for good, since burglary is a felony and my felony record had been on an expansion plan for quite some time. I stopped boosting. This situation, however, forced me out of retirement.

It was getting close to 9:00 p.m., so I told Juan we would go to Sara's building.

"See, everything's going to be alright. I told you I'd pull it off. Now we'll get some food, do the return, get the cash, get some dope, and you can drop us off at Sara's and take the car," I said with relief.

For a heroin addict, just knowing you're going to get well puts your mind at ease and takes the intensity of your sickness down a few notches.

A moment of clarity and a glimmer of hope washed over me as I drove to Sara's work on Fifth Ave. She worked at a small Italian sandwich shop. The pay was hardly sufficient to live on, though I was proud of her accomplishments since she had moved to Portland. I could see her spreading her wings and becoming a woman. She was learning how to live and commute in the city. She took her responsibilities seriously and worked hard. Watching someone you love maneuver through life's obstacle course with a full tank of ambition provides fuel for your own tank, which is what Sara did for me. She gave me a sound reason to keep on keeping on.

I parked the car just outside Sara's work and informed Juan and Carrie that I would be a few minutes. "Sara gets off in about 10 minutes, so I'll go in and order us some food. Hopefully it's not too busy and we'll be right out," I told them.

"I'm starving, so don't be taking too long. I don't want to have to cause a scene in front of your girlfriend's work," Juan told me with calculated calm.

By this time I had heard Juan's death speech so many times that I responded half-way through his threats, "Yeah, yeah, yeah, bro, I know." I knew he was serious. It's just that after hearing the same thing over and over again, I couldn't help being a little short with him.

A trickle of people were coming and going out of the entrance to Sara's work. It was quitting time. I was anxious to see Sara. Even though I couldn't tell her the details of my situation, it was comforting to see her and even more so to be held by her and to hear her say she loved me. When I was with her, I felt alive. I could feel my spirit rising out of its slumber and craving life. The hostile environment of Juan's world seemed to block every ray of hope and only gave way to misery and death.

I left the car and started for the entrance. Every fragment of my being wanted to run and never come back -- to leave Carrie and Juan far behind and forget all that had transpired. But I couldn't. I couldn't leave Carrie alone to be tortured and killed. I was her only lifeline. I knew I would have to bring closure to this mess.

I tried to push all these ominous thoughts out of my head as I made my way down the escalator. The food court was pretty bare. I spotted Sara as soon as my feet hit solid ground. She had her little visor on and her hair pulled back in a pony tail.

After I watched her for a few seconds, our eyes met and we exchanged smiles. Life is truly blissful when you have someone to share it with. We still had that shine in our relationship. Our love was in full swing and we were always happy to see each other.

"Hey baby. You look so cute in your little visor. Are you almost done?" I asked.

"Yeah, I just have to finish cleaning up. Are you hungry?" she replied with compassion in her voice.

"Yeah, I'm starving. I still have Juan and Carrie in the car. I didn't get paid today and it's a bad situation. I had to go to Nordstrom and boost a fucking bathing suit to try and get some money for this dude. Plus I'm totally fucking sick and ready to lose my mind," I said with frustration.

"Baby, why do you still have them with you? I want to spend some time alone with you."

Again, I wished I could just spill out the wretched emotions I had built up inside me. All I could do is stuff them deeper. It was difficult not to lash out and say hurtful things in an even more hurtful tone. I kept my frustration at bay the best I could, but Sara could tell that I was on the verge of a meltdown.

"Well, I guess I better make something for all of us," she said.

"Yeah, they're starving too. Hopefully that will ease the tension a bit. But we have to hurry -- Nordstrom closes at 9:30, and we have to try returning that bathing suit. Then we'll be able to get well and give some money to Juan so he can go wherever he wants to go."

Sara started putting together some pasta and chicken while I paced the food court. A small fountain with a wishing pond surrounded by tropical plants sat directly in the middle. I was so broke I didn't even have a penny to make a much-needed wish with.

I couldn't have Sara return the bathing suit to the same store I just stole it from. We would have to go to Lloyd Center Mall to do the return, which was about ten minutes away. Sara put food in to some disposable containers. I glanced up at the clock on the wall: 9:05.

We hurried up the escalator and out the door. Carrie and Juan were sitting impatiently in the back seat. Sara took shotgun position, and I handed the food back to Juan. "We gotta hall ass to the mall to return this shit," I said.

I was weaving in and out of traffic, trying to jockey for position with sweaty palms and aching muscles. I flew through lights and over bridges towards the mall. Now I was a junky with a purpose and a plan.

I was only a few minutes away from getting well. A junky's whole reason for living is to get well. Letting the drug absorb all the pain, all the hurt and misery that dwells in the user's mind.

I pulled into the mall parking lot at a good 50 mph. I raced to the front door only to watch a heart-wrenching scene: a Nordstrom employee locking the door.

My world shattered. I felt like someone had just stuck an ice pick deep into my heart. It's difficult to describe the dismay and complete devastation that a heroin addict experiences when your path to wellness is blocked. You wish you could just die right there on the spot. All the precious energy you just spent to get well is washed away in the blink of an eye.

As I sat there in the parking lot, I took inventory of my soul. How could things get any worse? Not only were my plans crippled but now I had to tell Juan something reassuring. I believe if my girlfriend hadn't been with us, I would have encouraged Juan to just shoot us and get it over with. I was well past my breaking point. I was tired of taking orders, tired of being sick, tired of living all together.

I hated showing Sara how dependant I was on heroin, even though she already knew. It's still embarrassing and degrading to reveal how bad off I really was, how strung out and dependent on this shit I was.

I had been doing so good for so long and now I was back to less than zero. At this point nothing else really mattered. I had to do something. I had to get well. I had to submerge my problems in a spoon full of dope. The anxiety was boiling over inside me. I felt like my life had exceeded it's course. Unfortunately no matter how much I wanted to just lie down and die, I had to do something.

I decided I would swallow the little shattered pride I had left and try talking Sara into parting with her last $20. She had just gotten paid but after sending me that Western Union, paying her rent and buying gas to get to work and the methadone clinic, she only had $20 left and two weeks until she got another paycheck. I felt like an ass even having to ask for the Western Union, but desperate situations require desperate measures. I had to start my plan.

"Babe, look. I need to borrow that $20 or I'm not going to make it to work tomorrow. I can't stay up all night sweating and wishing I were dead. I need to work or we won't have any money to make it through the week. Plus Juan and Carrie need to get home. I'll replace the money tomorrow, I promise," I said while resting my spun-out head on her lap.

"Mark, that's all the money I have, and we're almost out of gas," she replied. "I need to get to the clinic in the morning and you have to get to work. We need that money," she said while running her fingers gently over my head and through my hair.

"I still have this bathing suit, too ,and that's a hundred and something dollars. We'll return that first chance we get tomorrow, but I'm not doing shit until I get well," I said with a tired voice.

"Well, you know I'm going to give it to you, but we're going to be in a bad situation tomorrow if your job is somewhere far and we have to make sure I get to the clinic in the morning," Sara replied with both disappointment and understanding.

I felt like the stuff that builds up around the drain in a public restroom. But now that I had $20, I could feel the sickness retreating already.

"You got a good girlfriend, homes," Juan said. "She takes care of you. You should be happy you have someone that loves you like that."

I believe Juan could see that I was that determined to get him some money -- that I was going to work, even stealing shit to try helping him. He looked as beat down as I felt. I think he realized that I was doing everything I could, and that put his paranoia in remission, which was my goal. If I could build up his trust enough to keep letting me go to work, I believed I could somehow get Carrie away from him as well. Juan's character was almost passive when Sara was with us but, at the same time, I knew what he was capable of in a matter of seconds.

It was close to 10:00 p.m., and Burnside slows down the later it gets. Carrie and Juan were pretty quiet as I left the mall parking lot. The street lights were gleaming and the air was still resonated with heat from the sun. Everyone looked tired and defeated from a long day of chaos. Me, I was back on my path to being well and anything else was irrelevant to me. Even though I would have to share a small bit of heroin with three other people and be sick by morning, I was still feeling pretty tranquil.

I hit the Blade, looking for a familiar face or any Mexican for that matter. After a few drive by's I spotted Drew. Juan saw him as well. He sold us $30 worth of heroin for $20.

Juan, Sara and I all hopped back in the car. I sped off toward a secluded area with determination and relief. Finally it was time to get well. I parked a few blocks away from the Blade and dug out my instruments.

I quickly brewed up the small piece of tar [heroin] with precision and more or less evenly split the brown liquid among us. Everyone was finished with theirs while I poked and prodded around for a vein. I finally managed to draw blood from my ankle and slowly push my medicine in. Serenity at last. I sat back in my seat and let the drug take its course. With every passing second my anxiety, pain and frustration diminished to the point of Zen.

Now it was close to 11:00 p.m. and time to sleep. Sara's aunt was back, so there was no way we could stay there. If I'd been alone I would have a good chance of being able to sneak in. Sara was tired and I didn't want to burden her with my problem. Nor did I want Juan to think I was trying to ditch him So I suggested that we take Sara home and then figure out where the rest of us would sleep when we got to south-east Portland.

Not being able to tell Sara the true story continued to be difficult. It was hard to justify my decisions and my determination to keep Juan and Carrie with me. Whenever Sara and I were alone, she displayed her anger of their constant presence.

"Mark, why don't you just drop them off downtown where you found them?" she would say. I wished it were that easy, but that wasn't an option.

Sara loved me and would always communicate her concern for me. One of those concerns was that I spread myself thin by helping my friends, especially when I was dealing heroin. I ended up fronting so much product out that I would sometimes lose more money than I would make. "Mark, you need to learn how to say no to your friends" she would say. But it's difficult to watch your friends suffer from withdrawal.

I believe that she thought I was just trying to help Juan. Not with dope, but trying to help him find a place to stay. Little did she know that I was actually fighting for my life and the lives of my loved ones, hers included.

We drove through Portland's street towards the south-east part of the city, where Sara's aunt lived. I couldn't think of any good remedy to my problem. I kept thinking that Juan actually did kill someone in that house in the Tri-Cities -- that he only took a purse with a few dollars in it in exchange for a life or lives.

"Sorry bro, it looks like we have to sleep in the car again," I told Juan and Carrie. "I'll have some money tomorrow and hopefully this will be the last night of this shit."

"Fuck it, homes," Juan replied. "I got my girl and we're all gonna stick together, right? If you want to sleep with your girl, you can. I can trust you, right, homes? We're going to be parked right outside. I don't think you would want to jeopardize anyone here by doing something crazy. You know I'm ready for anything, homes. I'm going out like a soldier, and I'll make all six of these bullets count and have plenty more to use if I live that long," Juan said with a serious look.

Oh, that's great, bro. Thanks for reminding me, I thought.

"Yeah, babe, sneak in and sleep with me," Sara said. "I'll go see if my aunt is awake. She's probably sleeping. I'll come back out in a bit when it's clear."

Carrie was already wrapping up in a blanket and trying to find comfort in an uncomfortable setting. Through Juan's clouded perception of reality he managed to say the words "I trust you." This pushed me to make the decision to ask for help.

This whole hostage thing had to be stopped even though I knew in my heart that someone would get killed. More than likely all three of us would be shot either by Juan's bullets or bullets from some law enforcement agency. Regardless of the outcome, Juan had to be stopped, and if all three of us had to die, then so be it.

I couldn't take it anymore, and I knew Carrie felt the same. She was in many ways worse off than me. She couldn't even leave his side. The rancid smell that lofted from his dangling flesh was unforgettable. The constant threats whispered into her ear must have driven her nearly insane.

We all sat in the darkness waiting for Sara to return. I tried not to think about my dismal fortune. I had to find a way out. *Tomorrow . . . tomorrow I'll make a move,* I said to myself. I have to let someone into my world. I have to get some help. I can't resolve this on my own.

After 10 minutes, Sara came creeping up in her PJs. "Babe, everyone's asleep, so let's go get some sleep," she said.

"Are you guys gonna be alright?" I asked. I felt uncomfortable leaving the car but Juan seemed at ease. I'm sure the heroin had a lot to do with that. It was comforting to see him relaxed a bit rather than his normal hostile self.

Juan seemed to be trusting me more and more with each passing day. Other than the short time I was at work this would be the only time I was not sitting side by side with Juan. For Juan to let me sleep that far away from him was a big step. The first night he came into Sara's room and checked it out before retiring into the adjacent room. Now he was trusting me to go into the house and sleep.

A window of opportunity seemed to be slowly opening for me. Now I just had to figure out what I would do with this little bit of newly developed trust. There would be no second chances here and to think that if I made one mistake death would be the result. Not only for me, but for anyone who happened to be around Juan when a confrontation arose.

"Alright, bro, we're going to get some sleep," I told Juan as I got out of the car.

"Leave the keys, homes, just in case, ya know?" Juan replied.

I threw him the keys and bade him farewell. Part of me hoped he would take off in the middle of the night and I would never see him again, but I knew that was unlikely.

I wrapped my one arm around Sara and she leaned into me as we made our way to the house. The smell of her hair wandered into my nose and triggered a feeling of comfort. Women are, in my mind, healers, nurturers and creators of divine intervention. Women could also be an advocate for the devil, but I find myself loving them just the same. Sara was my mental healer and I felt human with her in my arms.

We quietly entered the house and made our way to Sara's tiny bedroom. It was late and the house was silent. Sara's bed was barely big enough for one person. However, we made due and it was far more comfortable then the car. It was nice to be alone with her and be able to enjoy each other to the fullest.

As soon as the door closed we meshed together with a titanic build-up of passion. Sara and I always made love like it was our first time. Gazing into her eyes made me forget about the miserable life I chose and the pressing issues on my mind. As I held my glance, I tried to send her mental messages of distress.

"Hey I'm alone, scared and want to just die. Please help me, baby. I need you. I want you and wish I could tell you what's happening" I put all those feelings into a slow methodical kiss. As my emotions spilled over I leaned into her ear and told her that I loved her and I was sorry for being what I was.

We gently and purposefully peeled off each other's clothes. Sara and I communicated with our bodies well. We knew exactly how to push each other into ecstasy. Sara's naked body was hard and well defined. I touched her with intimate care as she wrapped me up between her thighs. We made love like we were the last people on Earth.

It was rhythmic and soothing. The climax came slowly, but sleep then fell upon us quickly. We drifted into unconsciousness on a small bed in a small room. Two people in love, oblivious to everything but the warmth of our bodies. Unfortunately this would be the last time we would ever reach rapture together. The dark days that lay ahead would effectively shatter many lives and every relationship I held dear.

Day 16

August 3-4, 2005
Portland, Oregon

A draft from Sara's window snapped me out of a short slumber. I woke up cold and naked. The early stages of withdrawal were already under way. The clock read 5:30 a.m. Another four hours of sleep under my belt, which brought my grand total up to about fifteen hours for the past fifteen days.

I looked down at Sara and ran my fingers across her face. I quietly whispered, "This is the day. I gotta do something, baby."

She was still sound asleep. With heavy eyes I looked upon Sara's youthful features. A sleeping beauty indeed. I snuggled up behind her and tried to absorb some much needed warmth. My dope-sick body was ice cold and my muscles ached. Every minute that ticked by brought on another wave of defeat. I didn't want to get up and face the realities that lay ahead. I wanted to be free. Free from my addiction, free from suffering, degradation and deceit. Most of all, I wanted to be free from Juan's morbid grasp. I had to push on. I had to get up and end this nightmare.

The minutes kept marching on, and my will to live was retreating. I had to get dressed and call John. I had to get Sara to the clinic and most of all, I had to get help.

It was now close to 6:00 a.m., and I was late. I sprang up and got dressed with irritation already brewing.

"This is fucked. I'm fucked. We're all fucked," I said to myself. I slipped my shoes on and went to check on Juan. I could feel the tension rising as I popped my head out of the door. *Is this guy still gonna be there, or did he take Carrie off into seclusion to make good on his death threats?* I wondered.

I saw my red BMW parked in the same spot as I had left it. Juan must have heard me approaching, because he was looking right at me. I came up on the passenger side and he unlocked the door.

"What's up, homes? Are we leaving? I'm fucking hungry," Juan said.

"Yeah, I have to call my boss real quick and find out where we're working today and Sara's gotta go to the clinic, so I'll be right back. I just wanted to make sure you were awake and ready," I replied.

I called my boss, John Smith, and got directions to the job site. Fortunately it was close by. As Sara got ready I tried to pump my confidence up.

OK, this is the day. I'm gonna confide in my best friend to help me come up with a solution to this mayhem. I'll tell him what I know about Juan and have him check the computer and see if this guy really is who he says he is. I mean, come on -- America's Most Wanted, hit man, mafioso? This all seemed 20th Century Fox shit to me.

I couldn't take the chance of trying to call his bluff. I had to know exactly who I was dealing with. Even though every part of me knew that this guy was crazy and, in my eyes, capable of murder. I still didn't know any facts about Juan or his past. I couldn't just call 9-1-1 and say, "Yeah, hi, I'm with this fat Mexican named Juan who offered me over $1,000 to give him a ride to the Ozark Mountains. We met a girl in Idaho and he decided to kidnap her and turned both of us into hostages.

"He has also been threatening to have my family killed, me killed and to kill himself, but not before killing any police officers that try to apprehend him. So if you could try not to shoot the girl or the red-headed guy in the car when Juan starts shooting at you guys, that would be cool. Thanks, and have a good day."

That's quite a story to comprehend. It was hard even for me to believe. For a dispatcher to take me as seriously as the situation required seemed unlikely. I needed a person of sound mind to give me the time to explain the situation. That person would have to be John, my boss and life-long friend.

Sara got ready pretty quick and I was as ready as I could be with feelings of dread and ambivalence weighing heavy on my mind. Sara and myself marched on to the car. Juan was standing outside the car pacing back and forth when we approached.

Juan asked to borrow a shirt of mine, as his was filthy. I didn't have many clean clothes and was reluctant to let him borrow anything. But I felt it best to comply. Juan took off the soiled shirt he was wearing and grabbed the clean shirt out of my hand.

As he stood there shirtless, I noticed the name "Moran" tattooed across his back. He also had a small "18th St." tattoo, along with a picture of a buffalo and a girl on his arm.

All his tattoos were amateur and looked like he had got them when he was younger. The one that caught my attention was the name "Moran" on his back. A lot of people tattoo their last name on their back, and that was a huge clue that his name wasn't Juan Martinez. I had never really believed that was his name. That was also another important deterrent from not calling the police. I didn't even know this dude's real name.

I've never been inclined to call the police for any reason at any time, though I didn't believe that this situation could go on much longer without some sort of intervention by the cops. So if a call was made to the authorities, I felt that having a real name to give them would trigger the proper response and they would take the call seriously.

I started to go over what I would say to John. Now that I had a name, maybe together we could find out who this guy Juan really was. I needed access to a computer, and John is computer savvy enough to research the proper web sites to find something about Juan, starting with America's Most Wanted.

Since my job site was closer then the methadone clinic I decided to just go directly to the meeting spot. Sara, Juan and Carrie could figure how to make the rest of the morning work without me. Sara, just like the day before, had to go to the clinic, then to work.

The drive to the meeting spot, which was McDonald's on Sunnyside Blvd., was short and uneventful. We arrived around 7:00 am. John was already there.

"Alright, baby, have Juan and Carrie bring you to the clinic, and then they can take you to work and drop you off. I'll pick you up tonight when you get off work. I should have some money for us by then," I told her.

"OK, babe. Have a good day at work, and I'll see you tonight," she responded. There was a hint of hesitation in her voice, so I felt it best to embrace her a bit more than usual.

"I love you, baby. And I promise things will get better. Sorry things aren't going very good right now but we'll keep working and get our own place and be happy," I told her. I wanted to say more to her, but I was already pushing the envelope. My every word was being scrutinized by Juan, and he already thought Carrie and I were plotting against him. I didn't want him to get the impression that Sara knew anything about him or what had happened.

After saying my goodbyes to Sara. I turned to Juan. "Alright, bro. you guys call me in a few hours on John's cell phone, and by then I'll know what time I'm getting off work. Maybe in the meantime, you guys can return that bathing suit."

"You know I ain't got no ID, homes," Juan responded. "The cops got that when I got arrested downtown a few months ago. I fucking missed my court date and probably have a warrant on that name. So I'm not going to show my face in a fucking mall, esé."

"Alright, bro, relax, I'll take care of it. Just call me in a bit," I told him.

This exchange confirmed that his name wasn't really Juan Martinez. When he'd mentioned missing court, I remembered him showing me a ticket he had gotten. Apparently he had been arrested a couple months before I met him. According to Juan, he was arrested for possession of cocaine and booked into the Multnomah County Jail, in downtown Portland. I recall him saying how lucky he was -- the police had booked and then released him to the streets within 24 hours.

"I thought I was booked for sure after they ran my fingerprints," he had told me. "I was even trying to find away to kill myself while I was in my cell, but then they just let me go."

If that was true, then he couldn't have been on "America's Most Wanted," "Crime Stoppers" and wanted by the US Marshals, as he had claimed. The police would have never have let him go.

John and I arrived at the door to McDonald's at the same time. I was determined to come right out and tell him of my dilemma.

"We have to talk. I don't know how I get myself into these ridiculous situations but, I need your help," I told John. I felt like such a first-class loser and my self-worth level was less than zero. Looking like a starving transient didn't make me feel very confident either. Nonetheless, I still had to muster up the courage to tell my story.

We ordered a couple of sandwiches and sat down. We sat at a table next to the front door and had a good view of the parking lot. I was so nervous and paranoid that Juan was watching me that I needed to keep a watch over all exits and all activity in the parking lot.

"What's up, man? You've been acting weird lately," John asked me.

I had already opened the door to my problem, so I had to lead him all the way through. Amazingly enough, I just came right out with.

Telling John the story

"Dude, I think this guy I'm with is wanted for murder. I think he might have even killed someone when I was with him. He told me that he killed his in-laws because he thought that they molested his kids. You wouldn't believe what I've been through in the past few days. I mean, this dude is beyond crazy, and that girl that's with us is from fucking Idaho! He totally kidnapped her, bro, plus he's got a gun and a pocket full of bullets. I don't know what to do. I don't even know how to describe the amount of insanity that this dude put me through, but I have to do something.

"I need you to look this guy up on the internet. I think his real name is Moran. So when you go home today, get on the computer and go to 'America's Most Wanted' and enter the name 'Moran.' I don't know if this dude is fabricating all these stories, but I do know that he's been holding me and that girl hostage."

I rattled all this off with animated body language and my words spilled out like water breaking a levee. I had been wanting to tell somebody this story for almost a week now.

John was shocked at the brief summary of events I had told him. He seemed confused. I didn't want to go into great detail about the events prior to the "aunt"'s house. I needed John to know that I was dead serious about this guy. I also needed him to know that the girl who was with us was going to be killed and it was only a matter of time before she was dead. I felt it best to just tell John the basic facts that hopefully would show up on the internet.

We finished up our McMuffins and I studied the parking lot for any abnormal activity. I could tell John was indecisive about what I had told him and I just left him to his thoughts. We got into John's truck and made our way to the job site.

"Only you could get involved in a fucked-up situation like that, dude," he said. "I think you are probably the unluckiest person I've ever known."

"Yeah, that's probably true. I seem to attract trouble like no other," I replied.

The job site was only a few miles from McDonald's so there wasn't a lot more said on the way. I told John that Juan or Carrie would be calling sometime that morning to find out when I'd be getting off work. I also said I'd been telling Juan I was going to give him money to move on.

"I've been building up his trust these past two days, but not having any money is a real stressful situation," I told John while we were waiting for the concrete truck. "On the other hand, I can't just give him money because he'll take that girl with him and kill her. So once you find out if this guy really is who he says he is, we'll have to figure it out from there."

"Dude, I don't have any money on me right now. You'll have to wait until tomorrow," John told me. This of course wasn't good. Now, once again, I would have to tell Juan the bad news and I knew he would be getting suspicious by this time. I didn't want to come back empty-handed, so I more or less begged John to stop by a cash machine after work. I don't think he was totally sold on this whole murderer thing yet. So he was reluctant to give me money, knowing I spent 90 percent of my money on drugs.

John was far from supportive of my way of life and tried his best to deter me from self-destructive behavior. This wasn't a good time for him to be in that frame of mind. Still, not handing over a large sum of money to Juan was probably best.

I felt helpless trying to get Carrie out of this ordeal. Money was the only way to prolong our lives. I still had the bathing suit. I hoped that would discourage Juan's ambitions to get rid of us.

We finished pumping out the concrete and started cleaning up. I told John that he could drop me back off at McDonald's.

"Why don't you just leave them, dude?" John asked.

"Are you serious, bro? This dude knows where my Pops lives, and Sara. I even stopped by my mom's work in Tacoma. He knows way too much about me. This dude is crazy enough to hunt my whole family down!"

It proved difficult to convey the imminent danger to an outsider. He hadn't seen Juan in action. In addition, it was hard for him to take me seriously, as a direct result of the long river of deceit I had been successfully floating down for most of my life. I have been lying to get what I want for as long as I can remember. Lies fueled my addiction, and many of my relationships were infected with deception. It was quite possible John thought I had conjured up this extravagant story to get some money.

This is one result of addiction: no trust. It seems that I've spent half my life destroying everything around me, and I'll be spending the rest trying to rebuild it.

Even though I could tell John was a little skeptical about my story, I knew he would still help me. I knew he would do a full investigation on the name "Moran."

Around 1:00 p.m., we pulled into the McDonald's parking lot. There was a Washington Mutual Bank in the same parking lot and John pulled up to the ATM. I could sense that he was a little irritated by me dropping this colossal problem in his lap. Who could blame him?

After John got the money from the ATM, he hopped back in the truck. "Here you go. Here's $10. I'll look this dude up tonight. Just call me either later on or in the morning. I think I have an early-morning job scheduled," John told me.

There was a brief moment of silence before I reached for the door handle. I didn't really want to get out of the truck. I wish I could have just left that parking lot and never looked back. After my brief hesitation, I grabbed the handle and jumped out.

Juan and Carrie were parked close to the entrance. Back to the madness I went. Carrie was in the driver's seat and Juan was sitting shotgun. They both looked pretty sickly.

I was so physically drained it was hard to put one foot in front of the other. My leg was starting to heal, but working on it, even though I was doing minuscule tasks, was still a tremendous discomfort.

I decided to just get in the back. I was thoroughly disgusted with my current situation and the perpetual presence of Juan. Unfortunately I couldn't just sit in the back and stew in my misery. I had to start weaving a lie about why I didn't have the hundreds of dollars I promised to deliver.

"Like I said on the phone, the contractor didn't have any cash on him, so John gave me ten bucks for now and said he would have to wait until tomorrow to pay me. So I'll have to go and return this bathing suit. That will get us through the night. With that hundred bucks and the couple hundred I'll get tomorrow, that should be enough for you to get to where you're going," I told Juan.

I made it sound like it was all a sure thing. After all, I was playing the role of my life. There was no room for error.

We were reliving the prior day almost to perfection: another $10, no dope, no place to go. But this day held a little more hope -- by talking to John, I had opened a door that might bring closure to the chaos.

Sara didn't get off work for several more hours, and a feeling of despair encapsulated us all.

"Well, what the fuck are we going to do now, homes?" Juan said. He was obviously irritated and started talking to the imaginary enemies in his head. "Fucking just leave me alone. I'll take care of this shit!" he yelled out before I could answer his question.

It's hard to talk to someone who is having an argument with himself. "Look, bro, I'll get this bathing suit returned as soon as Sara gets off and we'll have some money."

I told Carrie to pull into a gas station so we wouldn't run out of gas. I got out and put five dollars in. Carrie didn't want to drive anymore so we switched spots. I decided to drive downtown to Sara's work and try getting something to eat.

I parked along the sidewalk just outside Sara's building. She packaged up some chicken Alfredo for us and promised to be ready to leave by 8:45 p.m. to do the return.

We stayed parked along the curb long enough to eat. Carrie wanted a cigarette, so we decided to spend the remaining $5 on a pack of smokes. We made a quick trip up the street to a small convenience store. I hopped out and bought some cigs and we all smoked liked it was our last cigarette.

Silence swirled into the smoke as we sat and watched all the passersby.

"We could go to Nordstroms and get a box and a Nordstrom bag to put the bathing suit in. It always looks better when the item is all wrapped up," I suggested. Everyone agreed, and we made our way to Nordstrom.

This mission went smoothly, and we now had a presentable item to return. We decided to find a parking lot and just wait until Sara got off work. I found a fairly empty parking lot not too far from Sara's work. I parked, and Juan and I leaned our seats back. Carrie wrapped up in her blanket and lay down in the back. I was the first to pass into a state of unconsciousness.

Before I knew it, the clock read 8:00 p.m. I dropped my seat up and rubbed my eyes. Juan was bright eyed and chain smoking when I awoke. Carrie was still lying dormant in the back seat.

The intensity of the situation had diminished a bit. No yelling or threats with the gun displayed for several hours. I was actually having feelings of hope and I could sense a bit of confidence taking hold. Still, I knew death was ready to pounce at any time. I could only hope Juan either would shoot me in the back of the head so I wouldn't see it coming or would deliver a body shot that I could survive. By this time I was ready for either one. Well, as ready as one could be for such an event.

Sara finished cleaning up and met me with a deep kiss.

"All ready," she said.

"I still got Psycho with me, but this will be the last night with him. I promise. We'll do this return and get a hotel or something. Tomorrow I'll get paid and they'll be on their way." I said with confidence. I just hoped that story was true. There were no guarantees when it came to Juan.

When we reached the mall, I coached Sara on the particulars of the return and what to say. I had wrapped the bathing suit up with tissue and put it in a fancy Nordstrom box and then put the box in a Nordstrom bag.

"Alright, good luck. And don't take no for an answer," I told her.

Sara got out and disappeared into the mall. Juan, Carrie and I waited with anticipation. If everything went smoothly, we would finally have some money, which meant dope, gas and a place to stay. In that exact order, too.

After ten minutes, Sara emerged without the bag. No bag equals money. Sara sported a big smile.

"Worked like a charm, almost $120," she said while getting in the car. She handed me the money, and I told her to drive to Burnside.

It was getting late, and The Blade was dead. I would have to venture into the bowels of the city, which is always a dangerous mission. Interacting with the savage street dwellers and the hardcore addicts who make their homes under the I-5 bridge is always a last resort. A lot of people never return from under the bridge. You're not only susceptible to a robbery, but you could very easily be stabbed or shot for as little as $5.

At this point I didn't care and forged on. I told Sara to stay behind but she insisted on coming with. I gave Juan $70 and took the rest with me.

The first obstacle to overcome was a 10-foot fence. Then, you have to parallel I-5 for about 200 yards until you come to a steep drop-off. As you look down you can make out a dirt path that winds down and under the freeway.

I went first. You have to squat down and slide on the heels of your shoes for about five feet. Then the dirt becomes a little more loose and easier to plant your feet in. I did this and turned to guide Sara down.

I had to constantly flick a lighter to see where the ground was. It was pitch black and the farther under the bridge we went, the darker it got.

The smell of extreme living hits you straight away. The musty stench of urine is overpowering. Beer bottles, used cookers, old syringes and tattered clothes were scattered on the rotting dirt.

People had constructed cardboard condos for a sense of privacy. These structures were nestled directly under the concrete that supported the freeway so you had to actually bend down to avoid hitting your head.

As I neared the biggest condo, I gave a quick whistle.

"Hola. It's Rojo. I'm friends with Drew. He said "Romero" was down here. I need two blacks and a white [two 20-pieces of heroin, and two-tenths of a gram of cocaine, respectively]," I said cautiously.

The darkness swallowed us, and it was so quiet we could hear the rats scurrying around hunting for food.

"Qué onda [what's up], Rojo? Who's with you, homes?" a voice called out from behind a cardboard wall.

"Oh, it's my novia [girlfriend], Sara. She's cool," I told the voice.

"So you're friends with Drew?" said the voice. A wide-eyed Mexican poked his head out and shined a flashlight on Sara and me.

"How much money you got, homes?" he asked.

"$40. You have both?" I replied.

"Give the money to my hina," he said.

I could barely make out the Mexican's face. The reflection of the flashlight gave me a quick glimpse of a long-haired, dark-skinned and visibly strung-out man. Then a skeleton of a woman emerged from behind the cardboard, clearly a victim of too many drugs and not enough food. Her face was pasty white and her eyes were sunk in.

"Here's two blacks and a white," she said. I handed her the money. I quickly opened up the balloons to make sure they were selling me the real thing. After I had confirmation on the product, we made our way out of darkness and back to the lights of the freeway. Cars flew by, paying no attention to us or the dark world that lay just beneath them.

Sara and I made our way back up the path, over the fence and straight to the car. Any kind of healing my leg had been doing was undone. Blood spotted the back of my pants where my wound was. I was determined to get well, get Juan his coke and get to a hotel. Nothing else mattered.

Carrie and Juan were still sitting in the back seat. Juan was looking around with paranoid eyes.

"Let's get out of here, homes. This place is hot."

Sara had to go home and change, so we made our way toward south-east Portland. On the way to Sara's aunt's house, Juan started to fix up his cocaine. Sara got upset and said something to Juan that would intensify the situation.

"Hey, don't be doing that shit yet. We're about to pull up to my aunt's," Sara told him.

We were still at least five miles away from her house. I believe Sara didn't want him doing the dope without her getting her fair share.

Just like any addict. she wanted to fix as soon as possible, and since she was driving, she couldn't fix. So she didn't want anyone else to -- which was understandable but not reasonable at this point.

I wanted to fix as well but didn't want the argument that would accompany it, so I decided to wait. I could tell Juan was pissed that she told him he couldn't do his shot. He put his coke away with a sigh of irritation.

Minutes later we pulled up to Sara's aunt's. She wasn't even home, which brought another sigh from Juan. Sara ran in, changed and was back in a flash. We drove up the street and all four of us indulged in a much-needed shot -- Juan of cocaine , the rest of us heroin.

As soon as we finished up, Juan started to unravel.

"Alright, I'm fucking driving, this is my show. I ain't gonna have no girl telling me what the fuck I can and can't do. We're going to my cousin's in Troutdale, and all you motherfuckers are gonna see what I'm about. You get in the back and keep your mouth shut," he told Sara.

As soon as Sara saw the hate in his eyes and heard the anger in his voice, she broke. I mean completely lost all composure. Carrie and I were used to Juan's threats and deranged outbreaks. Sara wasn't.

We switched positions. Juan took control in the driver's seat. I took shotgun, and Sara got in back with Carrie. Sara was crying loudly and uncontrollably.

"Please stop crying. He doesn't like it when you cry. It pisses him off and he'll hurt us," Carrie whispered to Sara.

"It's gonna be alright, baby," I said.

"Dude, you better shut her up," Juan said.

Sara was so hysterical that she was hyperventilating. Juan pulled the gun out, holding it in one hand while gripping the steering wheel with the other.

"Dude, shut her up right now or I'll pull over right now and start buckin'
motherfuckers in the head."

Juan was yelling. Sara was freaking out and Carrie was pleading for her to stop.

"Just pull over, bro. Let me talk to her," I said.

Juan jerked the car into a Taco Bell parking lot at about 50 mph and slammed on the brakes.

"Get the fuck out, homes! Do something with her before I do!" he shouted.

Sara couldn't stop crying. I flipped the seat up, grabbed her hand and pulled her out. Juan was rocking back and forth, chanting.

"Baby, I swear to God, please stop crying, please. You already know this dude is unstable. We just need to get through tonight and we'll be rid of him," I said. I held her tight against my chest and held the back of her head and stroked her hair. I tried everything I could to console her. Finally, after five minutes of sobbing the tears slowed down and her breathing went back to normal.

"Why is he so upset with me? What did I do? I just want us all to get along. Is that too much to ask?" Sara asked me.

"Look, baby, we need to just try doing whatever this dude wants. You have no idea who we're dealing with. It doesn't matter what you say to this guy. He's subject to snap at anytime over anything. It's not your fault."

I walked her back to the car with my arm around her. I told Carrie to get in the front so I could keep Sara calm.

Going to Troutdale?

"Is she done crying, homes? Because we're taking a little trip," Juan said as we got back into the car. I could see Sara was about to lose it again, so I quickly wrapped her up in my arms.

"What's he mean we're going on a little trip?" she whispered.

"Nothing. We're alright. We'll get a room and get some sleep," I assured her.

Juan was driving erratically and I could see the frustration in his eyes.

"Dude, it's getting late. We should just get a room and call it a night," I said.

"Oh, yeah, we're gonna call it a night alright, bro," he replied. "One you won't forget."

I figured I'd let him cool down for a few before I started any further negotiations with him. We drove toward Troutdale for about 10 minutes before I tried to talk him out of taking us into that area's secluded woods.

"Look, bro. I'll be getting a couple of hundred dollars in the morning. Let's just sit this out until tomorrow. We'll get a cheap room and lay it down for awhile. You haven't slept in a bed for a long time. Let's just get a good night's sleep for once."

"How about I just fucking buck myself in the head? How about that, huh?" Juan said.

"No, let's not do that, bro. Tomorrow will be a better day," I told him.

"Alright. You fucking drive, because I'll ram this car into a fucking wall in about two seconds if you don't shut up. I'm fucking dead, homes. Don't you understand? My life's over and you guys are gonna tell on me if I let you live. I don't know what the fuck I'm doing any more."

Juan pulled over and we switched seats. He put the gun back into his pocket and rested his head against the window. I took off to find a hotel. It was close to midnight by this time and emotions were high. We needed to find a hotel fast.

I spotted a Day's Inn off of 82nd Avenue. We pulled in, and Sara and I got out to rent the room. Juan handed me the money out the window. It was close to $60 for a room with two beds. There wasn't a lot of conversation going on after Sara's meltdown and Juan's threats. Everyone was pretty drained and ready for bed. We all fell asleep fast with hardly a word spoken.

Day 17
August 5, 2005
Portland, Oregon - Vancouver, Washington

6:00 a.m. The wake-up call roused us all out of a deep sleep. I felt stronger. Like something epic was going to happen that day. Something tragic. I had a knot in my stomach and my mood was melancholy. I tried to shake it off while I got ready to call John. I was totally nervous and almost didn't want to pick up the phone.

"Well, I gotta call my boss and find out where we're working today," I said.

I had to make Juan aware of who I was calling to avoid any confrontation. He already thought we were plotting against him, and a random phone call could provoke a homicide.

"Alright, homes, find out if he's got our money," Juan replied.

I picked up the phone with a deep sigh, like it was the last phone call I'd ever make. John picked up on the second ring.

John: "Hello?"

Me: "What's up?"

John: "Dude, where are you?"

Me: "I'm at a hotel."

John: "You need to get over here right now!"

Me: "Alright, it will take me about a half hour."

John: "Just hurry and don't bring that dude with you."

Me: Ah . . . well, I kinda have no choice, bro."

John: "Well, don't park anywhere near my house."

Me: "Alright, I'll see you in a bit."

John's voice was a bit frantic, and I could tell something was really wrong. John never sounds scared like that. At 6' and 240 pounds, not too much frightens him. So I hung up even more disturbed than before I made the call.

John had obviously learned that on Friday, July 9, 2004, James T. Moran (aka Juan Martinez) had murdered Glenn Dale Carr, 57, and his wife, Debra Jolene Carr, 50, at their home in Kennewick, Washington. The deceased couple were Juan's four children's maternal grandparents. The children were unharmed.

Juan was staring at me during the whole conversation, which made me think that he was on to me. But he didn't really seem to be suspicious.

"Everything cool, homes?" he asked.

"Yeah. I have to meet him in Vancouver, do a quick job and then get my money," I told him.

We dropped Sara off at her aunt's house and got on the freeway north to Vancouver. I-205 was busy with commuters. I turned off the freeway and started closing in on John's house. After ten minutes of driving we arrived in rural Brush Prairie, Washington, just across the Columbia River from Portland, Oregon. This is where John, his two kids and wife reside. They have a nice rambler-style house toward the end of a quarter-mile, freshly paved road.

I parked in front of a dense tree line that blocked off Juan's view of John's street. When I parked, I made it seem like John's house was just on the other side of the trees. I was praying Juan didn't start questioning why I parked there. Thankfully he didn't.

"Try and get some money for us right now, homes," Juan said.

"Alright, I'll see what I can do," I replied.

I got out of the car with a sense of apprehension. That early morning walk to John's seemed to last forever. As I approached his driveway I saw him in the garage with a shotgun in his hand. He was pacing back and forth just inside the garage door with fear in his eyes. John was looking in all directions when I came into his line of sight.

"Dude, where's he at?" John asked me frantically.

"He's parked at the end of the street behind the trees," I replied.

"Dude, he better not have seen where you went. I can't believe you brought him near my house! Do you know what that dude's done? He's a fucking killer, bro. He's wanted for killing his own in-laws and kidnapping his kids!"

John showed me a print-out from "America's Most Wanted." Juan was the 8th most wanted man in the nation.

> James Moran is wanted for the brutal double murder of his in-laws, the Carrs. In July, 2004 the Carrs were shot to death in their home in Kennewick, WA. Moran then kidnapped his children and an amber alert was issued. James Moran has been on the lam for more than a year. Reports have been made that he was spotted in Arkansas earlier this year.

Even though I already had a pretty good idea that what Juan told me was true, I was still shocked. To see these horrendous actions recited on a major media program and printed in black and white was mind bending. Now all those stories Juan had told me were talking on a whole new meaning.

"If I see that dude, I'm shooting him," John said.

"No, bro, then you'll be fucked," I replied.

"Well, we have to call this number -- 1-800-CRIME-TV," John told me.

"Dude, he's going to kill that girl if he sees any type of law enforcement near him. This dude is certifiably crazy. I don't think the police even know how dangerous this guy is. He's not going to be arrested. He's gonna take out as many people as he can and then kill himself. I swear to God, he's serious about not going to prison."

"Well, do you know where he's going? We'll follow him and call that number when he pulls over,." John suggested.

"Alright. Give me like $10 and I'll go give it to him and tell him I'm getting a couple of hundred bucks in a couple of hours," I replied.

John gave me the $10 and I set out on my mission. I got back to the car and Juan and Carrie were sitting in the front. Juan was behind the wheel with the car running.

"OK, I talked to my boss and we're going to pick up the money. Here's $10 for some gas and smokes. You guys just call John's cell number in an hour or so."

"Alright, homes, we're going to Wal-Mart to try and use this card. We'll call you in a bit," Juan said. It was a gift card he'd taken from the wallet inside the purse he'd stolen during the brief visit to his aunt's house, if that's really whose house it had been.

My heart was racing. It was difficult to wrap my mind around the fact that I was talking to a killer -- someone wanted for shooting his wife's parents to death. Someone who probably did kill someone in that house in Kennewick. How I was still alive was almost inconceivable to me.

I parted with Juan and Carrie for the last time. I walked back to John's house. John had put the shotgun away and was warming up his truck when I came back.

Calling "America's Most Wanted"

"Alright, bro. They're going to Wal-Mart and leaving right now," I told him.

"Get in. Let's go!" John replied.

I hopped in his lifted Tahoe truck and we began our reconnaissance mission. It felt like a scene out of a movie. If Juan saw us following him, I believed he would definitely start shooting.

I was frightened as we pulled out of the driveway, and I could sense that John was too. I had witnessed firsthand what Juan was capable of, and though John had read what Juan had done, I don't think he realized how disturbed this dude really was. John was more aggressive toward the situation than I was.

We came to the end of John's road and looked both ways. No sight of Juan.

"Which Wal-Mart did he say he was going to?" John asked me.

"Uh . . . the closest one, probably," I replied.

We turned right and pulled out on Highway 500. Still no sign of the red BMW.

"I guess we already lost 'em," John said.

I was relieved. I surely didn't want to be the one to confront him or even be in the area when the cops closed in on him.

"Dude, you're gonna have to do the right thing and call that number," John told me.

This is something I dreaded. I knew I would be putting an unstoppable ball in motion. Once that call was made, the chances of Carrie's surviving would be slim. But I couldn't keep going on like this. I had to do something, and this was my only option.

"Alright, let's find a pay phone," I said.

John pulled into a small convenience store.

"OK, I guess this is it. I'll be right back," I told John.

I've never called the police for anything, ever, so it felt awkward to say the least.

"This is crazy," I thought to myself as I approached the pay phone. I picked up the receiver and dialed 1-800-CRIME-TV.

Dispatcher: "Hello, Crime TV."

Me: "Ah, yeah, I'm calling in regards to the fugitive James Moran."

Dispatcher: "OK, what state are you in?"

Me: "Washington."

Dispatcher: "And you said the name was James Moran?"

Me: "Yes. He's wanted for a double homicide in Kennewick, Washington."

Dispatcher: "How do you know it's him? Is there something personal you can tell me about the fugitive?"

Me: "Well, he's had me and this girl held hostage for the past week. He has a gun and a pocket full of bullets and he's taken us to these death camps and almost killed both of us. He's threatened to kill our families if we tell on him. He's taken us into the mountains and dragged the girl out and put the gun to her head but someone came by and he didn't pull the trigger. He even took us to a pig farm and was going to shoot us and feed us to the pigs. This dude is totally crazy and he still has the girl and they're at Wal-Mart in Vancouver, Washington, right now."

Dispatcher: "Slow down, sir. Now can you give me a description of the fugitive, like tattoos or scars that would identify this guy?"

Me: "Yeah, he has a tattoo across his back that says 'Moran.' He also has a tattoo of a girl and a buffalo on his arm. He's pretty big, probably 240 pounds but he used to be even bigger like 350 pounds. He's lost a lot of weight."

Dispatcher: "So are you being held hostage right now?"

Me: "No. See, I built up his trust enough for him to let me go and get him some money. I'm supposed to bring him back the money in a little bit. The girl is still with him, though, and if he sees any police around him he's going to kill the girl and then himself. So you can't just pull up on him. You're gonna have to surprise him."

Dispatcher: "OK, so he's at a Wal-Mart in Vancouver, Washington, you said?"

Me: "Yeah, he told me he was going to Wal-Mart to get some smokes."

Dispatcher: “OK, so what you’re saying is that you escaped this guy and he still has the girl hostage?”

Me: “Yeah. Plus I think he killed someone in the Tri-Cities a few days ago. We pulled up to a house where he said his aunt lived. He went in and I heard gunshots. Have you heard of any murders in the Tri-Cities?”

Dispatcher: “No, I haven’t.”

Me: “Well, are you going to sneak up on this guy?”

Dispatcher: “Well, sir, I’ll have someone check on it. Thanks for the call.”

Me: “What do you mean you’ll have someone check on it? This guy is a killer and we don’t have much time. That girl is gonna get killed. It doesn’t sound like you are taking this very seriously.”

Dispatcher: “Sir, calm down. We get a lot of prank calls here and you sound pretty confused right now, so we’ll take it from here. Have a nice day.”

CLICK.

Me: “Hello? . . . Helllloooo? What the fuck!”

I held the receiver in my hand for a few seconds, then stared at it in disbelief. I knew they wouldn’t take me seriously. I was disgusted. I walked back to the truck slowly. I opened the door and just kind of stood there.

“Well? What happened are they coming?”

“Dude, they hung up on me. I don’t think they believed me at all,” I said.

“Shut the fuck up. What do you mean you don’t think they believed you? Did you tell them you know this dude and it's the same dude on 'AMW'?” John asked.

“Yeah."

"I guess we could call 9-1-1,” John suggested.

“No, dude! They’ll be all gung ho and that girl will get killed in the crossfire, or Moran will shoot her. We don’t even know exactly where he’s at. Maybe we should wait 'til they call. Then at least we’ll know where they’re at.”

“Let’s go to Wal-Mart and see if we can find them,” John said.

My biggest concern was trying to save Carrie’s life. I knew that this situation was on the brink of disaster. I also knew from Juan’s actions that people were going to die when he was confronted. At the very least he would shoot himself. I just couldn’t imagine Carrie making it out alive unless the cops snuck up on him and took him out before he realized what was going down. Any other way would bring bloodshed.

John and I drove to the closest Wal-Mart, but there was no sign of my car. We searched the parking lot with extreme caution. I didn't want to just run into them and try to explain why we were in the same parking lot at the same time as he was.

After driving around the perimeter of the parking lot a few times we decided to check Vancouver's other Wal-Mart. As we entered the parking lot I was looking not only for the red BMW, but also for FBI agents, US Marshals or any kind of law enforcement in the parking lot. I figured my call would have at least generated a call to the local authorities.

But there was no sign of either Juan or the authorities. Now I was sure my first call had been disregarded. John and I sat in an adjacent parking lot while keeping a watchful eye for any signs of my car. After an hour passed, we decided to move on. John and I didn't even see a security guard, let alone the army of federal agents I was expecting to see.

We pulled back out onto an arterial and started driving without direction. John and I scanned every parking lot and side street looking for the fugitive and his captor. After about an hour of searching, the phone rang. I took the liberty of answering it. I heard Carrie's voice on the other end.

Carrie: "Hey, is Mark there?"

Me: "Yeah, this is me. Where are you guys?"

Carrie: "We're at a Burger King right off of I-5"

Me: "There's a few Burger Kings right off the freeway. Can you see anything else around you, like some other stores or buildings?"

Carrie: "Uh, yeah. There's a Shilo Inn and a Super 8 next to me."

Me: "OK, I know which one you're at. Just give me like 45 minutes or so. I got the money. We just have to finish cleaning up."

Carrie: " OK. Try and hurry. We're hungry, and this sucks sitting here."

Me: "OK, everything's gonna be alright, and I'll see you in a bit, OK?"

Carrie: "Alright. See ya."

I hung up feeling sad. Carrie's voice was drained of all energy. I wished I could have told her that I was on her side and trying to extract her from the situation. But there was no way of letting her know our plan without jeopardizing it. I believe she wouldn't have favored our calling 9-1-1, as she was the one sitting in front of the barrel of a gun.

Now that I was outside the immediate range of Juan's gun, I was more willing to try the police. I obviously wasn't capable of resolving anything on my own, and for this situation to end, lethal force would be necessary.

"This is it, bro. They're at the Burger King next to the Shilo Inn right off the freeway," I told John.

"Let's do a drive-by and check out the scene," John replied.

I started to fidget. A sense of impending doom started working its way through me. The closer we got, the more I started to unravel. I felt sick.

I saw the Shilo sign protruding into the sky high above any other sign. We took the exit and Burger King came into view within seconds. I immediately slid down in my seat and gave a quick glance towards the parking lot.

"Oh, shit. There they are!" I blurted out.

John was looking over and spotted the BMW at the same time.

"Yep. That's your car," John said.

We crept by the Burger King and tried blending in with the few cars that were around us. The parking lot was virtually empty.

"Alright, bro, what are we going to do now?" I said.

"Dude you're gonna have to call 9-1-1, because obviously America's Most Wanted isn't going to do anything," John said.

About 200 yards past the Burger King was a convenience store. We drove over I-5 and into the parking lot of the store. I sat in the passenger seat with my hands tightly clasped together, swaying back and forth.

"Man, this call is going to change my life forever," I said.

I looked over at John, shook my head and opened the door.

"This is gonna suck, bro. I don't think she's gonna make it," I said to John.

I was kind of hoping John would just say, "Never mind. Let's just get out of here." But that wasn't going to happen. We were too committed at this point, and I needed to end it.

I lit a smoke and took a long pull.

"This may very well be my last cigarette," I thought. I felt like Carrie was in the electric chair and I was making the call to the executioner to flip the switch.

The pay phone was located off to the right of the front door to the convenient store. Only a few patrons were shopping inside. The traffic on the street was starting to pick up a bit as I grabbed for the receiver.

My view of the Burger King parking lot was partially obscured by a thin tree line. I-5 separated the store and Burger King, so I could barely see what was going on. Still, I felt like Juan could see me so I buried my head deep in the pay phone.

Calling 9-1-1

I pushed the numbers 9-1-1.

Here we go again, I thought. I'm going to speak calmly and slowly. I knew Juan had been making his mental preparations for this moment for a good year so I knew he was ready. But were the cops ready to meet James Moran?

The phone rang two or three times before a male operator answered:

Operator: "9-1-1. State the nature of your emergency."

Me: "I need to report a hostage situation in progress. I've already called America's Most Wanted. Did you hear anything about the call on the fugitive James Moran?"

Operator: "No, what's going on and where are you?

Me: "I'm across the street from the Burger King off Mill Plain road right next to the freeway. My friend is being held hostage by James Moran. He's got a gun and a pocket full of bullets."

Operator: "What's he driving?"

Me: "A red 325i BMW. It's sitting right in the middle of the parking lot. You guys need to sneak up on this guy because he's going to kill the girl and try to kill whoever approaches him. Then he'll kill himself."

Operator: "How do you know this man? Are you a hostage?"

Me: "I'm not right now but my friend is. I got away. I was giving this guy a ride and he -- well, let's just say he freaked out and things got out of hand. I even think he might have killed someone in the Tri-Cities. Have you heard of any murders in the Tri-Cities in the past few days?"

Operator: "No, there's been no murders."

Me: "Are you sure?"

Operator: "Yeah, there's been no reports of a murder."

Me: "That's good. I thought for sure he had killed somebody."

Operator: "OK, sir. Can you hold the line, please?"

Me: "Ah, yeah."

I put the phone down and lit another cigarette. I couldn't believe he put me on hold. I paced back and forth in front of the pay phone. Apparently the dispatcher called Burger King and asked if anyone there owned a red BMW. in the meantime, Juan and Carrie had gotten out of the car and gone into the Burger King. Juan was in the line when the call came in.

While Juan was looking at the menu, Carrie tried pulling one of the employees into the bathroom. At that very moment the Burger King employee who took the call got on the intercom, "Does anyone here own a red BMW?"

Juan, obviously shocked, walked up to the counter and told him, "I own a red BMW. Why, what's going on?"

The cashier told him, "Oh, someone called looking for you."

Juan turned around and saw Carrie trying to drag the employee into the bathroom. That didn't go over well. Juan grabbed Carrie, and they made a hasty departure.

I saw several patrol cars fly by me toward the Burger King. I was thinking, "Oh, shit, here we go. There goes my car and the girl, and he's going to kill everyone around him and probably kill himself."

I dropped the phone and ran to the corner to see what was going on. I saw my car exiting the parking lot. I ran back to the phone to ask the dispatcher what was going on. He told me to calm down and that they had everything under control.

From the looks of it, they didn't have anything under control. I left the phone once again, just in time to see Carrie jump out of the car. Now the chase was coming toward me.

The Clark County Sheriff deputy's patrol car directly behind my car smashed into the back of the BMW, spinning it around and killing the motor. Then another patrol car smashed into the driver's side door, shattering glass in all directions. Juan was pinned up against the divider on the I-5 on-ramp, with cops surrounding the car. He was caught.

With a sinister grin, he raised the gun to his head and pulled the trigger. Rather than a shower of blood and brain matter, as a larger gun might have produced, the shot issued only smoke from the wound site. His head simply jerked as police swarmed the car and he slumped over.

He was airlifted to Oregon Health & Science University in Portland. James T. Moran, known to me better as Juan Martinez, died the next day.

Part 3
Arrested

Chapter 1

At this point I wasn't sure whether Carrie had been shot or had been injured by jumping out of the car. The scene was tumultuous. Police cars were scattered all over. I couldn't even see my car any more. Officers had surrounded it and had blocked off all the streets leading to the crash site. I-5 was totally shut down and traffic was starting to back up in all directions.

I stood in the convenience store parking lot with a look of disbelief. I looked in awe at the chaos that encompassed me. I walked back to the pay phone.

Me: "Hello! Are you still there?"

Dispatcher: "Yes. I need you to go over to the Burger King parking lot and tell one of the officers that you're the 9-1-1 caller. Can you do that for me?"

Me: "Uh, yeah, I guess. Is James dead?"

Dispatcher: "We don't have confirmation on that yet, sir. We just need you to go to the parking lot, please, sir."

Me: "Alright."

With both relief and anxiety, I hung up and made my way to John's truck. I jumped in and told John that I needed to go to the Burger King parking lot. John made it pretty clear that he wasn't too excited about driving into the epicenter of chaos. But we made our way through the roadblock to the parking lot.

John pulled up to the back of Burger King and realized just what serious a situation this was.

"Alright, man, I'm out of here. This is crazy," John said.

I hopped out and walked directly into the tidal wave of cops, black Navigators, grey Ford Tauruses and curious onlookers. I took a quick look behind me ,and John was already gone.

I awkwardly approached a uniformed offer.

"Hey, I'm the 9-1-1 caller."

Before I could say another word I found myself being twirled around, handcuffed and stuffed into the back of a patrol car.

"This is for your own safety, sir," the cop told me. Strangely enough, I didn't feel any safer.

I noticed Carrie standing in front of a patrol car about 20 feet away with a cigarette in one hand and a Burger King cup in the other. She looked frazzled and disoriented as she apparently described the events that had just unfolded to another officer.

"Excuse me, sir, but why am I handcuffed? I'm the one who called. That's my friend over there. She's not handcuffed."

"Well, sir, we're trying to get a handle on what's going on here."

The cop turned and started talking on his radio. He shut the door on me so I couldn't hear what he was saying. I sat in the back of the patrol car and watched the parking lot being transformed into a media circus. Black Explorers, cop cars and media trucks were trying to bully their way into the lot. Reporters with their zealous cameramen stormed the scene like looters in a riot. Like an angry ant hill, people were running in every direction.

Finally the officer let me out of the car and uncuffed me.

"Alright, sir, there are some agents who want to talk to you. From what I've gathered from your friend and the background of this James Moran fella, you guys have been through a lot. Agent Alexander is over there in the black Explorer."

As I walked toward him I shot a glance over at Carrie. She had obviously been crying and was, like me, in shock. We caught each other's eye and held a brief stare filled with compassion and disbelief. We both just shook our heads at one another. No words were needed to interpret the mutual feeling of relief we felt. The moment was shattered by the swarming amount of activity in the parking lot. It would be hours before I saw Carrie again.

I kept walking toward the detective, still taking in the surrealism of the situation. A news helicopter flew overhead as the detective greeted me.

"Mr. Tucker, I'm Agent Alexander, of the FBI. We're going to take you to the Major Crimes Unit to ask you some questions." We shook hands and I agreed to go with him.

As we got into his car, I heard the agent talking to a dispatcher. Apparently the US Marshals were also on the scene. Because Carrie was from Idaho, kidnapping across state lines was involved, so the FBI wanted to be present while we were being interviewed.

Carrie and I were put in separate vehicles. She rode in one of the black Explorers and I rode in a Taurus. The State Patrol had the I-5 onramp blocked off and traffic was being re-routed. Cars were backed up for miles. Fortunately we had a police escort. The officers turned on their lights and we were granted passage right through the middle of the hornets' nest of traffic.

After 15 minutes of maneuvering through cars and trucks, we made it to Vancouver's North Precinct. Uniformed officers with S.W.A.T. gear were going into the police station. One officer in particular was walking into the building at the same time as me. Sweat was dripping from his forehead and it looked as though he had been jogging in full body armor. He had obviously been involved in the brief standoff with Juan. He gave me a nod and said, "Hey, good job. Consider yourself lucky you're still alive, young man."

Agent Alexander guided me through a short labyrinth of hallways. We passed several offices marked with various names of detectives. Finally we came to a door marked "Interview Room."

"Alright, Mr. Tucker. Have a seat in here and we'll get started," the agent said.

I sat and started to analyze my surroundings. This wasn't my first experience with the whole interrogation thing. My first trip to the precinct had been for an alleged burglary when I was 13 years old. The police, the jail and the intimidating detectives with their interrogation techniques were enough to get me to sign all my rights away and tell on myself.

Since then, I've learned to keep my mouth shut. The most important Miranda right is to remain silent. Anything you say *can* and *will* be used against you in a court of law.

But this situation seemed different to me. This was an FBI agent, and the atmosphere was much more serious. I had just experienced a catastrophic amount of insanity and was still shell-shocked from it all. But since both dispatchers had told me no one had been murdered in the Tri-Cities, I was second-guessing the events of that day.

The agent came back into the room with a uniformed officer, a woman in her mid-40's. She was blond, spunky and very cordial.

"This is Officer Sornberg. She's going to sit in on the interview," the agent said.

The agent started in on his questioning. The questions were casual and relaxed in tone. He just let me tell my story. I was relaxed in my responses, because I was exhausted and a bit leery of the agent's motives. I was just trying to be as helpful as possible.

I thought I was doing the right thing by telling them about the incident in the Tri-Cities. Not in a million years did I think that I would ever be implicated in a crime. So I just kept rambling on with my story. I definitely gave the pair the short version of the tale. I felt like I had given them the highlights and that that would be sufficient. They obviously hadn't heard of any murders -- if they had, I was sure the focus of his questioning would have been on the Tri-Cities.

The pair's reaction to my story was nonchalant. It gave me the impression that they didn't really believe me. At the time I didn't realized how bizarre my story must have sounded to the average Joe. I made the mistake of assuming that it wouldn't fall under such extreme scrutiny. Since Carrie and I were separated, there would be no way to collaborate such a tale. So I just took for granted that they would believe us and we would be on our way.

Carrie was interrogated separately by the same officers.

Chapter 2

After Carrie and I had endured our separate interviews with the homicide detectives and FBI agents, we were thoroughly tapped, and we were starving. The officials offered to take us out to dinner.

"Are we under arrest or what?" I asked before replying to the offer.

"You're not under arrest, but you're not really free to go, either," he replied.

"Oh, that's great," I thought.

But the detective reassured us that we were heroes, that dinner was on them and that they were going to put us up for the night.

"You two saved the day," he told us. "They've been looking for this Moran fella for more than a year."

Again, Carrie and I were put into separate vehicles. I rode with Alexander and Carrie rode with another Vancouver homicide detective. As we made our way toward downtown Vancouver, I sifted through my thoughts and the blurry events of the day. I could barely remember what happened the day before. It was strange. My brain was refusing me passage into the past, like it had a built in defense mechanism temporarily blinding me from the traumatizing events that had recently befallen me.

Hardly any words were spoke between the detective and myself during the short trip to the city center. After about ten minutes we arrived at McDonald's. I was so famished it felt like my body was feeding on itself to sustain consciousness.

We arrived first. Carrie and her escort pulled up a minute later. Shortly thereafter a third Taurus pulled up with the homicide commander along with a female detective. We all placed individual orders. Again, there was little conversation. I wished it was just Carrie and myself. I had so much to talk to her about. So many things I wanted to ask her.

Like what was she thinking when Juan pulled her out and put the gun to her head? What was Juan always whispering to her? How did she feel when we left the casino, or went to the pig farm, or about the incident with Gocho?

So many catastrophic events had happened, yet we were still alive. That to me was the most amazing thing of all. Unfortunately the detectives deterred any conversation between us. The detectives avoided asking us anything further about the incident. We all ate and they discussed where they were going to put us up for the night.

I was thinking, *Man, these guys are going all out. What a change this is for me. I'm usually being tackled, chased and handcuffed by the police. Now they're buying me dinner and putting me in a hotel. They even bought us cigarettes.*

The detectives had Carrie and me somewhat separated the whole time. They discouraged us from talking, which made me suspicious and a bit irritated, though I was too tired, sick and miserable to argue.

We finished eating and the detectives conversed about this and that. Agent Alexander and I walked back to his car. Carrie and her escort got in their Taurus. The homicide commander led the way out of the parking lot and toward downtown Vancouver.

After a short jaunt down I-5, we exited at the City Center. The Columbia River separates Washington from Oregon, and city lights from Jansen Beach and Vancouver illuminated the water with electric colors. We paralleled the river west, maneuvering through traffic lights.

As I looked up, I saw the Red Lion hotel come into view and Alexander pulled into the parking lot.

Damn! The Red Lion, I thought. These guys are really going crazy with it. The Red Lion sits right on the river and has the best view of the city, the river and everything else a tourist would be interested in seeing. Definitely one of the nicest hotels Vancouver has to offer, if not the nicest. Needless to say, I couldn't help but to feel a little special.

The ambience was upper class. Everyone was dressed in a suit or gown, but Carrie and I looked liked we had just escaped from a refugee camp. We all sat in the middle of the lobby. I sank into a big oversized couch and Carrie sat directly across from me in an identical couch.

The detectives discussed the sleeping arrangements. The captain delegated job assignments for the night as I sat and watched civilians walk in and out of the lobby.

What a strange day, I thought to myself.

Carrie was nestled in the corner of the couch with her head cocked to the side and resting in the palm of her hand. The events of the day seemed so far from reality that I had pushed them out of my mind and was ready to just sleep, sleep, sleep.

A few minutes passed and Carrie kept telling the detectives that she wanted to call her mom and that she just wanted to go home. Meanwhile, another detective came over with two key cards for two separate rooms.

The detective handed the key cards to two other detectives and pointed them in the direction of our rooms. I felt like I had cinder blocks strapped to my feet as I followed a skinny, dark-haired detective down a hallway and up a flight of carpeted stairs.

Carrie and her armed escort branched off to another section of the hotel. Obviously we wouldn't be sharing a room. Apparently the detectives really didn't want us communicating in any way.

We reached a door and the detectives swiped the card through a slot next to the door latch. The room was nice: plush carpet, king size bed, coffee maker, Play Station and a decent view.

I fell on the massive bed like I'd just been knocked out by George Foreman. I crashed onto the fluffy pillows and firm mattress. Finally -- a bed. A huge, comfortable bed.

The detective sat in a chair in the corner of the room and began to read a magazine.

"So . . . I guess you'll be staying with me, then, huh?" I asked.

"Yeah, it's for your own safety," he replied.

Man, have I heard that before. That's usually the first sign of being fucked. I was too tired to give him one of my classic smart-ass rebuttals. I fell asleep nearly instantly, and before I knew it, sun was finding its way through the blinds and creating abstract patterns across the room.

"Time to get up, Mr. Tucker," a voice said. "You've got time to take a shower, and then we're going to be heading down to the Major Crimes Unit. The Kennewick police department is coming from the Tri-Cities to talk to you."

The clock read 7:50 a.m. I could have slept for another week. I managed to crawl out of bed and into the shower. My mood was foul. No dope to wake up to. My leg was still throbbing and I was under the watchful eye of a homicide detective. Not exactly the ingredients I would use to create a fun day.

With no signs of Carrie, I was escorted to a Sherriff's car in front of the hotel. A middle-aged blonde female was driving. She had three stripes on her sleeve, symbolizing the rank of sergeant.

"Good morning. I heard you had quite a day yesterday," she said after I had gotten in the car.

"Yeah, it was pretty crazy."

"You're lucky you're alive. That guy sounded like a real psycho."

"That he was."

"I hear that you're the one who called 9-1-1."

"Yeah, it was either that or let him kill the girl and me and whoever else pissed him off."

"So you're pretty much a hero, then."

"Yeah, I guess I am," I responded.

We were interrupted by her cell phone. It was one of her kids. I listened to her trying to police a problem between two kids. In a way it was calming to hear a mother consoling her children. Just a reminder that life was still normal for some people and their lives weren't infested with lies, crime, murder and the genuine wickedness that surrounds drugs and the people that use them. She was friendly with me and put my mind at ease as we made our way to the Major Crimes Unit.

The sun was bright and fighting off the morning chill as we passed the courthouse and pulled into the Major Crimes building, which was above the Coroner's office. At first I thought I was going to have to identify the body when I saw the coroner's sign.

Two detectives came down the stairs to meet us. The female sergeant let me out and the detectives greeted me and escorted me up the stairs and into the building. It was barely 9:00 a.m. at this point.

The building was rather small and only held about six separate little offices. Desks and computers took precedence in the building.

"We have a few hours to kill. The Kennewick police department are on their way, so you can just hang out in here."

Alexander led me into a room with two desks facing each other with a small path between them, two dry eraser boards hung on the wall along with patches from every Sheriff's department in Washington neatly pinned on a cork board. A TV sat off to the side with a rack of VHS tapes marked "State Patrol Crash Scenes, Traffic Stops, and DUI Stops."

"I'm just supposed to sit in here?"

"Well, yeah. I know it's going to be a bit boring, but Kennewick should be here shortly."

"Can I at least watch one of these tapes?" I walked over to the rack and pulled out the crash scene tape.

"Yeah, I suppose so," the detective said. "I've got some work to do, so just let me know if you need anything."

I asked him where Carrie was. He told me she was in another room. I hadn't seen her since last night and was curious about her whereabouts.

"Did you guys let her call her mom?"

"She's taken care of," the detective assured me.

I pushed play on the VCR and it began showing the aftermath of horrific car crashes. The camera showed mangled cars wrapped around telephone poles, crashed into embankments and head on collisions. It was pretty grotesque and wasn't really what I wanted to be watching after the trip I had just endured. After about a half hour of seeing that kind of carnage I stopped the tape and curled up on the floor. I was still totally exhausted and needed about two more days of sleep to even begin to think straight.

Around 11:00 a.m., one of the detectives came in to check on me.

"You want to go smoke?"

"Yeah, sure." I got up with carpet imprints on the side of my face and some drool creeping down my chin.

"Man, this is bullshit. Can I call my girlfriend? She's probably freaking out."

"We'll see what we can do." Standard cop answer.

As we made our way outside, I saw Carrie in a small interview room. I recognized the FBI agent from the day before sitting in the room with her. The office was teaming with activity. Detectives were everywhere.

"So I guess Kennewick is here?"

"Yeah, they just arrived. They're going to interview Carrie first, and then they'll interview you."

We exited the building and lit up. I tried to pick Alexander's brain for information about what was going on and when I would be able to go home. What was going on with my car? Was Juan dead? But he wasn't really letting me know anything.

We finished up our smokes and went back inside. We passed by the interview room where Carrie was. Three detectives from Kennewick and the FBI agent were sitting around her with the look of anticipation on their faces.

It would be two more hours before I would be in her shoes, reliving all the bizarre events of the trip. I went back to my piece of carpet and lay back down.

Finally I was summoned to the interview room. Detectives Carter and Gregory from the Kennewick Homicide Unit were there to conduct the interview. They read me my Miranda rights. Anyone with a criminal lifestyle knows never to agree to waiving these rights.

"Anything you say can and will be used against you in a court of law" is a very real statement. Although I knew better to sign my Miranda rights away, I believed I would only be helping the police to better understand what transpired on my trip and the level of insanity Juan had displayed. I figured it couldn't hurt to tell them what had happened.

The furthest thing from my mind was that I would ever be implicated in anything that Juan had done. Never in a million years did I think I would ever be arrested and sent to prison for calling 9-1-1 on a schizophrenic killer, especially after having my life threatened countless times, being held at gunpoint and ordered to drive all over the Northwest.

Chapter 3

As I began to describe the chain of events to the detectives, my muscles started cramping and my nose and eyes started watering from opiate withdrawal. I was agitated and didn't realize I was leaving big chunks of the story out -- chunks that would probably would have made a huge difference in my future.

With every word I spoke, my frustration grew. I wanted to get up and leave. I was giving them the short version of events and wanted nothing more than to go back to sleep. My mind was foggy, and trying to explain a fourteen-day siege to two homicide detective was painstaking. I kept having to go back through the story because I would forget a whole section. What was important in my mind was the fact that two dispatchers -- one from "America's Most Wanted" and one from 9-1-1 -- had assured me no one had been murdered. I felt like since Juan shot himself, this interview was just procedural.

After about two hours of interrogation, I got to the part of the story when we stopped at Juan's aunt's house. This was clearly the interview's focal point. My nerves began to scramble as the detectives turned up the intensity of their questioning. Though I was told that there had been no murders committed in the last week, the detectives were giving me a different impression.

"So Mr. Tucker, explain to us what happened at James's aunt's house," the younger of the two detectives said.

At this point, my alarms were going off. *Don't fall into the "nice cop" trap. End the interview and request that counsel be present,* I thought.

But here again, I knew I hadn't committed a crime, so what could it hurt to tell them what happened? Unfortunately, like a rookie, I fell into the trap. I was unaware of the magnitude of this interrogation and the ramifications it would have for me.

I was worried about participating in the interview in my condition. With the absurd amount of drugs I had ingested in the past two weeks and the effects of withdrawing from heroin, my mind was far from sharp. With much irritation and frustration, I explained my version of the that day's events. My memory was foggy and incomplete. I tried to talk slowly and purposefully, but the anxiety of the original situation was bringing fear and indignation into my voice.

"After we picked up the Western Union from my girlfriend, we got something to eat and finally got back on the highway going toward Portland. Shortly after we got on the highway, Juan --"

"You mean James?" the detective interrupted.

"Yeah, James ordered me to turn off the highway. He was mumbling about not having any money of his own and was starting to freak out a bit. I told him he could have the money I had but he didn't want it.

"We entered a nice residential neighborhood and he told me to drive slow. He seemed to be checking out every house as we drove around. I kept saying to him, 'Dude, let's just go to Portland. I can get money there.'

"He finally got so pissed off at me he just told me to pull over. We had turned down a dead-end road and I had already turned the car around and was facing the street we had originally turned off. He threatened me, saying he'd kill me if I tried anything when he left the car. I kept assuring him that I wasn't going to try anything and that I just wanted to get to Portland and back to my girlfriend."

"What was Carrie doing this whole time?" the detective asked.

"She was lying down in the back with a blanket over her head."

"OK, continue."

"So he got out of the car and walked up to a house that sat at the end of the street, on and behind the passenger side of the car. Out of my rearview mirror I saw him walk up the driveway to the house. A fence blocked my view of the front door, but before I knew it he was walking back to the car.

"He leaned his head in the car and told me she was home so I said, 'So ask her for help.' He replied, 'I was just making sure you weren't trying anything.' Again I assured him I wasn't.

"He turned and walked back to the house. Then, as I was sitting there, I heard several muffled explosions. Then suddenly I saw Juan in my rearview mirror. He was skipping down the sidewalk with a purse in his hands."

"Now what was Carrie doing?" a detective asked.

"After I heard the explosions, she pulled the blanket up and away from her face and asked me if those were gun shots, but I wasn't sure so I told her I didn't know."

"OK. Then what happened?" one of the detectives urged.

"I panicked and pushed the clutch in and tried to jump-start the car, but it didn't work. Before I knew it, Juan was getting in the passenger seat and told me to drive."

The two detectives were listening with intense looks on their faces. I didn't want to continue but pushed on. I just wanted to lie down and rest. I more or less skimmed through the rest of the story.

I lacked the energy to think or remember all the details of the day in question or any other day for that matter. It had been 14 days of unfiltered degradation. Out of those 14 days, which equals 336 hours, I had slept maybe 20 hours tops. So I had been awake for a little over 300 hours. Now call me crazy, but I believe anyone who's just exposed himself to that much abuse would have trouble remembering each day and the events that transpired therein.

With a deep and drawn-out sigh, I continued. I told the detectives how Juan had riffled through the purse and found a small amount of cash, credit cards and other miscellaneous items. I also told them that we had stopped for gas, cigarettes and a pop. At this point I was starting to shut down and needed a break.

"I need a smoke," I told them.

They stopped recording and we went out to smoke. I remember thinking to myself, *These guys didn't solve anything. If it weren't for the testimonies of Carrie and me, they wouldn't have known that James Moran was in Kennewick at all, let alone at that house.*

As we left the interview room, another detective emerged from a cubicle. "Hey, guys, they just pronounced James Moran dead."

One detective with me stayed behind as the younger one and I went out to smoke. Apparently Juan had lived through the night, and the doctors had just released his time of death. It was around 2:00 p.m.

When I finished up my smoke, we went back into the office. As I walked back toward the interview room, I saw Carrie on the ground in the fetal position. She was crying and shaking her head, saying, "I don't know what's going on. They said I'm under arrest. I don't understand."

I was ushered into the room before I could respond.

"What's going on with her?" I asked.

The cops finally leveled with me, after hours of keeping me in the dark.

"Well, we have a problem, Mr. Tucker. See, that house you stopped by -- two people were murdered. A mother and daughter were shot to death. The father had to come home to his whole family murdered."

Chapter 4

My head sank and my eyes filled with tears as I tried to absorb the reality of the homicide. Up to this point I hadn't actually known -- just suspected -- that Juan had killed anyone at that house. I felt like the detectives had laid a trap and I walked right into it. I had given them enough information to formally charge me with rendering criminal assistance in the first degree.

"Mr. Tucker you've been extremely helpful to us. But the fact is that you benefited in the proceeds of the robbery. James put gas in your car and bought cigarettes for all of you. And you drank some of the soda he bought. Therefore you're guilty of benefiting from the robbery."

I was still in shock about the murders and didn't realize that I was being arrested. Anger, sadness, indignation and a strong feeling of betrayal swirled through my mind as I tried to hold back a complete nervous breakdown.

"Are you saying I'm under arrest?"

"This man came home to his whole family murdered."

"What's that got to do with me?" I protested.

"You drove him. But we can make this easier on you and probably let you go if you tell us Carrie was in the house. We have an eyewitness who says he saw two people leave that house."

This was an obvious fabrication and another trap. "Carrie and I never left the car. There was never enough time to leave," I said. I was blinded by anger at this point and stopped cooperating.

I was led to another room, where the Chief Deputy Prosecutor was waiting to telephonically arraign me. He was young and sharply dressed. He wore his black hair short. His demeanor was that of an aristocrat, confident to the point of arrogance. A man who lived his life one conviction at a time.

With documents already typed up and neatly laid out on a desk he put the phone on speaker and was on the record with Judge Earl Hampton, of Benton County. I pled not guilty and had no counsel present.

No reward

As to the purported $100,000 reward, I never came close to getting it. There was talk of it when I was at the Red Lion, but after that, the talk died away. My lawyer, Kevin Holt, later inquired into the matter, but "America's Most Wanted" denied I had ever called. The dispatcher who had taken my call later called Holt and acknowledged that I had in fact called. Still, I never got any of the money. The whole thing just faded away.

After I was arraigned by Benton County, I was stripped of all my clothes and put into an ill-fitting blue two-piece outfit that looked like hospital scrubs. We were led across the street to the Clark County Jail. (Vancouver is in Clark County.) We were booked in and dragged in front of a camera. Our pictures were taken and would be plastered all over the newspapers, the TV and even America's Most Wanted.

Carrie and I were taken to Benton County jail in a vehicle that resembles a dog-catcher's truck.

As I walked into my arraignment hearing -- a perfunctory first meeting with the judge, to set or reset bail -- the courtroom for the Superior Court of Benton County (Washington) was overflowing with people. Judge J. R. Merchant was presiding.

As I took my seat, I felt angry, penetrating eyes zeroing in on me. People in the audience were holding up pictures of people I'd never seen. TV cameras followed me all the way to my seat and focused in on me. As I looked around the courtroom, I was met with hateful stares, shaking heads and teary eyes.

Among the more than 50 spectators were the husband and father of the mother-daughter pair Juan had killed in Kennewick, friends of that pair, and members of Juan's late in-law's family, the Carrs.

At that hearing, I was represented by a public defender filling in for the PD who would be my attorney from that point, Kevin Holt. He informed me that first-degree rendering criminal assistance is a Class C felony in Washington state. The judge in the case had set my bail at $50,000, which my attorney said was high for a Class C felony. "But this is a high-profile case," he said.

A detective had told me I'd be freed pending trial -- on my own personal recognizance, or PR, in legal parlance -- because I had led authorities to Moran.

"I'll say something to the judge, but I'm pretty sure he lied to you," the PD said.

The judge called *State v. Tucker*, docket number 05-1-01031-6. All eyes were on me as I made my uncomfortable way to the defense table from the jury box where all the defendants were seated awaiting arraignment. While I was walking toward the table, I had to pass directly in front of the spectators. They shoved their signs and pictures high in the air and toward my face. Their hatred rained down on me.

After a perfunctory discussion, bail remained at $50,000 because I had a lengthy record (six felony convictions and 30 misdemeanor convictions) and no ties to the Tri-Cities area. I was returned to my cell -- Pod 204, which would be my home for many months to come.

My PIN, needed to use the jail's phones, didn't work for weeks, so I had no contact with my family. My court-appointed lawyer still hadn't shown up to interview me after two weeks of waiting, and I couldn't call him. I wasn't familiar with how the court system worked with such serious charges as the ones I was facing, so a lot of inmates counseled me. I was pretty famous within the jail, because the case had been highly publicized on TV. My celebrity brought me offers of help.

"Trouble," a federal inmate from 20th Street Crips out of Long Beach, California, counseled me on my speedy-trial rights. He also told me that if I don't get a paid lawyer I would surely lose in a trial.

Three weeks went by, and still no sign of my lawyer. The mental strain of not knowing what was going to happen to me was driving me crazy.

I did get a couple of visitors -- one from the Tri-City Herald newspaper and another from KNDU News. I gave brief interviews, but I was afraid of incriminating myself, so I held back. The interviews at least had the effect of causing Holt to make an appearance at the jail to do some interviewing. Holt introduced me to his private investigator.

"What the hell do you think you're doing talking to the media? You're making our job harder every time you talk to those people. We'll never win this case if you keep opening your mouth," Holt's private investigator said.

"Since you want to tell your story to everyone, why don't you tell me what happened?" Holt added.

My initial impulse was to tell them to fuck off, but I needed help and Holt was my only option, so I held my temper and began to tell my story in its entirety.

Since I had been locked up, many situations I had blocked out had risen to the surface. The pig farm, the shooting range, the sturgeon hole, and the fact that I had a badly injured leg were just a few things I had left out of my initial interviews.

I made the mistake of assuming they and others would understand and believe my story. Now that I have had more time to reflect, I know it was unreasonable to assume that my lawyer, private investigator, family members and most of all the victims of James Moran would automatically understand why I drove when he told me to drive and jumped when he told me to jump.

These people weren't there in the car with us and will never know the terror that was visited upon Carrie and me. That's a fact that took me years to come to terms with.

During this interview and many others, I displayed a cocky and frustrated demeanor, which probably made it even more difficult for people to understand what happened or even want to hear what I had to say.

After about two hours, we wrapped up the interview. Both Holt and Scudder once again told me to stop talking to the media. I promised I would. I went back to my cell dazed and confused. I was relieved that Holt had finally come to see me, but it seemed he wasn't too gung ho about taking on my case.

I knew nothing about the law, so I made it my goal to educate myself. Since there was no law library available, I had to hit up the inmates with paid lawyers. Their lawyers would send in case logs and court procedures. Most of those inmates were accused of federal crimes, so the information wasn't totally relevant. Still, for the next 30 days I read up on all the law I could -- mostly arraignment procedures, court rules, speedy-trial rights and jury trial rules. I also obtained the RCW (Revised Code of Washington) on rendering criminal assistance.

There was no doubt in my mind that I was innocent of rendering criminal assistance. Unfortunately, the law has many loopholes and grey area. I had no money for a paid lawyer rather than the public defender.

Holt was well known in the Tri-Cities and had a pretty good reputation, but money makes a world of difference in our justice system and unfortunately I didn't have any. So Holt had to fight this battle on a tight budget. Another point for the prosecution.

By this time my PIN for the phone was working. I called my Pops, and he had heard the story on the news. Another penalty of living the life of an addict is that you have exhausted all your resources, especially your family. Trust is the first thing an addict destroys. The truth eludes us and is replaced with intricate lies. So in a time of need, it's difficult to find help.

Phone calls were limited to 15 minutes, and it was impossible to explain my complicated situation in that time. Each call cost more than $10, so I couldn't keep calling back. My Pops has always been there for me, and this time was no different. But he was in his 70's and could not pay for a defense lawyer.

Then I called my mom. Same scenario. Trust, broken and abused. My life of self-destruction had destroyed our relationship. Her willingness to believe my story was strained by my muddy past. I reluctantly asked her to help bail me out, but she was unwilling.

County jail time drags on. Pinochle, pushups and laps around the dayroom are about all you can do to keep your sanity.

My 60th day in custody was approaching. In Washington, the state must try a defendant within 60 days of arrest unless he signs a waiver, which I refused to do. I believe that Holt was deliberately not communicating with me so that I would fire him. If you fire your lawyer, your 60-day speedy-trial rights are automatically revoked and you're stuck in the county jail for another 60 days, giving the prosecution more time to build a case.

I did file a formal complaint with the bar association. I was also brought into the judge's chambers to discuss the lack of assistance I was receiving. While in the judge's chambers, Holt tried to withdraw from the case. But the judge wouldn't let him do that, and my trial date remained the same.

About a week before my trial date, I received a letter from King County Superior Court. It was a warrant for possession of heroin -- a charge I thought had been dismissed. I thought wrong.

This was another blow. It would add a felony point to my record. That meant if I lost my trial, the judge could give me a maximum sentence of 60 months (five years).

A day before my trial was scheduled, I was called to court. The usual crowd was present: the media, the victims and my lawyer. I took a seat in the jury box. Holt came over and asked me once again to sign a speedy-trial waver. Again I declined.

"Alright, then, Mr. Tucker," Holt said, "I think they're going to let you go today on a PR [personal recognizance, trusting the defendant will return for trial]."

"They're gonna let me go?" I replied. I was taken aback by his comment, but at the same time relieved. Maybe they were going to drop the charge altogether.

My name was called and I approached the bench. The original prosecutor was absent. In his place was the chief prosecutor, Andy Miller. I felt nervous. It's not too often that the chief prosecutor shows his face in the courtroom, let alone gets up and speaks on the state's behalf.

"The state feels that Mr. Tucker was the key instrument in the apprehension of James Moran," Miller said. "Due to his cooperation, the state is willing to release Mr. Tucker on his own recognizance." I was released this way at least twice.

As Miller spoke, I turned to look at the audience. I was thinking, "See, I'm the one that brought this whole thing to an end. I'm not the bad guy here." I signed some papers and was given a new court date.

I still had that charge to face in King County, so I wasn't released to the streets. I had to wait for transport west to Seattle -- an eight-hour trek across the state in shackles. But at least I was going to familiar territory. It would be a week-long wait until the next chain bus rolled out.

With good time (I got sentenced to nine months but followed the rules well, so I got one-third off my sentence), I served six months in King County and was shipped back to Benton County. It was June 2006 by the time I was being booked back into Benton County jail, and it was like I never left. All the officers there knew me and my case well. I was shuffled through the booking process quickly, given my bed roll and escorted upstairs to the lock-down pod. My new home was 13A Upper.

The other inmates surveyed me as I walked down the hall. Most of them recognized me from the news, and the ones who didn't would know me by the morning.

The intake pod is set up a bit different than the open bay pods. You're locked down for 21 hours a day in your cell. You get out for 30 minutes three times a day to eat, plus 1.5 hours for showers, phones and recreation per day. Six a.m. came and breakfast was being served

I went to court after breakfast and was greeted by my lawyer, Holt. There was a film crew and the father/husband of the women Juan had killed in Kennewick. He never missed any of my court appearances. I wished I could tell him my side of the story. He has never heard it. My heart went out to him and all the other people who fell prey to Juan's madness.

The judge set another court date a month out. I felt like time was on the State's side and they intended to use up every minute of the clock. It would be late December or early January before the case would be heard by a jury.

I watched the whole summer go by through windows obscured with metal bars and wire mesh. I had no access to a law library and very seldom saw my lawyer.

In the fall, Holt hired a forensic psychiatrist named Jay Jackman. He had graduated from Stanford University and had both a law degree and a medical degree. He came to do an evaluation on me. The State wanted to see if I was malingering (faking a mental illness) or embellishing the events that had transpired. Jackman heard my whole story and made a diagnosis of my mental state.

He used the DSM-4 -- Diagnostic and Statistical Manual, the standard mental-health diagnosis instrument -- to make his diagnosis and prognosis. He diagnosed post-acute stress disorder, post-traumatic stress disorder, chronic depression, and social anxiety. He also made mention to the Stockholm syndrome.

This was all news to me. The only thing I knew I had was late-stage alcoholism and drug addiction. I had never heard of those other ailments.

Jackman was adamant about these conditions and prescribed me something for the night terrors and anxiety. I had recurring nightmares of James pointing the gun at my head and pulling the trigger. I saw dead people in different stages of decomposition. I heard Carrie screaming for her life and running through the desert. I thought all the Mexicans in the pod were plotting against me, seeking retribution for telling on their homie.

It wasn't all just fantasy. I actually was jumped in the jail's DOC (Department of Corrections) pod by a couple of 18th Street gang members. This is where all the people that have been to prison or were on their way were put. Inmates who were violent and had been sanctioned also usually did 30 days in the DOC pod. The gangbangers said I had told on their “Big Homie” (an O.G., or original member of a gang).

The incident happened at breakfast. This is the only time that all the inmates are out of their cells at once. I was on the upper tier and had made my way down into the day room and got in line for chow. When the lower doors came open, two younger Hispanics called me over to their cell. I was a bit hesitant but didn't want to look like I was scared so I walked a few feet closer to their door.

While all my attention was focused on them, someone pushed me from behind into their cell. Before I knew it I was receiving a barrage of punches to the head and body. My adrenalin kicked in and I started swinging back. I made contact several times but missed a few times, hitting the concrete wall.

I remember getting punched in the cheek, and I went into a kind of controlled rage. I managed to get one of them to the floor. I got my arm around his neck and wrenched as hard as I could. His homie was still landing punches to my face.

I dropped my head behind the head of the one I had in the choke hold to try and defend against the punches. A few more seconds went by and the guy who pushed me into the cell poked his head in and warned the guards were coming.

If the police get involved they bring in the "goon squad" (several large officers armed with mace) who don't ask any questions. They just start spraying. The rule is to keep as quiet as possible and fight in stealth or you get a "dry snitch" jacket (reputation). A dry snitch being the guy who gets loud and inadvertently alerts the police to the occurrence.

So we handled our business and left the cell single-file like nothing had happened. This is the way it is for the ones who fight for what they believe in and maintain "the code." I knew I had done the right thing by calling the police on Juan, and they felt justified in standing up for their dead homie. The pod officer gave us a suspicious look as we grabbed our trays. He hadn't seen anything but knew something had happened.

Months went by. Summer tuned to fall. I had been locked up since August 4, 2005, with the exception of the two months I was out on a personal recognizance. Now it was October 2006, and I was about to help pick my jury. I had never been to trial before and was unfamiliar with how the process worked. I always took plea bargains.

Part 4
Trial

Chapter 1

This first trial, in Benton County, which began Oct. 9, 2006, ended after one day when my attorneys moved to relocate the trial out of Benton County because I couldn't get a fair trial there. Of 30 prospective jurors questioned, the court excused 14, mostly because they admitted knowing something about the case or had already formed an opinion about my guilt or innocence. I was still being held in Benton County jail on $50,000 bail.

My trial was moved a few counties away, to Spokane County. Jury selection in the second trial began Nov. 20, 2006. Opening statements were set for Nov. 27. My courtroom attorney was public defender Kevin Holt. I couldn't afford a private attorney.

The change in venue meant several more months before we could get the trial on a docket in another county and more time stuck in the paralyzing unknown -- not knowing my fate and sitting in a cell wondering, " Is my family safe, is my dad going to live through his triple-bypass surgery, am I going to prison, am I getting out, will the surviving victims ever hear the whole story?"

I sat in my cell for another sixty days, pacing and pondering my future. Finally I was given a solid trial date in Spokane. It was late December 2006 when I was transported to Spokane. One newspaper ran an article about me before the trial. It read in part, "Mark Tucker, the alleged accomplice in the brutal slayings of the two women in Kennewick, will be going to trial." This article made me look so guilty that when I was booked into the Spokane County jail, the classification officer put me in the super-maximum area on the fifth floor. I was given a white jumpsuit and handcuffed.

The guard said that was standard procedure with inmates charged with murder. I advised him that if he consulted my charging papers he would see I wasn't charged with murder.

"Until I'm told otherwise, you're going to the fifth floor," he said.

I knew better to try arguing the point, so I complied and was moved to the maximum security floor. It was set up with single-man cells, with 23 hours in your cell and one hour out. They handcuffed you and escorted you to the shower, locked you in and you have to stick your cuffed hands out of the feeding slot in the door so they could uncuff you.

Holt came to talk to me later that night and I told him where they had put me. He was shocked. Apparently he said something to the guards, because I was transferred off that floor the next day.

The jury selection started on a Monday, and it was the same routine as in Benton County. The room filled up with potential jurors and the elimination process began. The procedure lasted about two hours. The youngest juror was in his late 40's and the oldest was 78. The prosecution eliminated any liberal people that I thought would be open to my story. In my mind I had already lost.

The next day would bring opening arguments. The prosecution used PowerPoint presentations to help make their case. Benton County's prosecution team was beefed up pretty well for the trial. Scott Johnson was their chief deputy prosecutor, and there were several others sitting at the table as well. The state did not hold anything back. They put on a good show that day and the next two days after that. Among the witnesses the State called to the stand were my by-now ex-girlfriend, Sara; my lifelong friend, John Smith; my father, William Tucker; Carrie Blackford; and many of the detectives on the case. (Sara had just stopped talking to me. We never discussed what had gone wrong. Suddenly, and without words, the relationship was over.)

The strangest witness was Magania, Carrie's baby's dad's brother, who back in July 2005 had sold a quarter ounce of meth for me and then tried to get the money back. I saw him in the hallway the first morning I was on my way to the court room. I remember totally freaking out because I thought he was an undercover cop there to testify against me for the meth deal. Everyone I just mentioned was actually in the hallway, with the exception of my Pops, But Magania was the one who stuck out the most.

Being escorted down that hallway handcuffed and feeling like I was walking to the electric chair, I looked around for a friendly face. I made eye contact with John to try getting some assurance that everything was going to be alright. He saw me and said, "You're gonna be outta here in no time ,buddy." A bit of relief passed over me as the two court officers opened the doors to the courtroom.

The prosecution side of the courtroom was packed. My side was empty. Another blow to my mental condition. I was feeling like the loneliest man in the world as I sat down next to my lawyer. One of the co-investigators, Kathy B., was also sitting at my table. She acknowledged my fear and grasped my hand with a motherly look of empathy. “We're going to do fine, Mr. Tucker, don’t worry."

.“Yeah, right," I replied. "This is going to be long day, Mrs. B.”

The big issues at trial were whether I had met the relevant elements of the offense of rendering criminal assistance. Even if I met all those elements, if the jury found that I was under "duress," it would have to find me not guilty of rendering criminal assistance. That's because duress is a complete defense to the offense of rendering criminal assistance.

Washington law (RCW 9A.76.050) defines rendering criminal assistance as follows:

A person "renders criminal assistance" if, with intent to prevent, hinder, or delay the apprehension or prosecution of another person who he or she knows has committed a crime or juvenile offense or is being sought by law enforcement officials for the commission of a crime or juvenile offense or has escaped from a detention facility, he or she:
(1) Harbors or conceals such person; or
(2) Warns such person of impending discovery or apprehension;
or
(3) Provides such person with money, transportation, disguise, or other means of avoiding discovery or apprehension;
or
(4) Prevents or obstructs, by use of force, deception, or threat, anyone from performing an act that might aid in the discovery or apprehension of such person;
or
(5) Conceals, alters, or destroys any physical evidence that might aid in the discovery or apprehension of such person;
or
(6) Provides such person with a weapon.

It is a first-degree offense when the assistance is rendered in pursuit of a murder or another class A felony.

I tried to remain hopeful, upbeat and genuine. I knew that I wasn’t guilty and that whatever happened, whatever the outcome might be, I did everything I could do to end the situation without multiple deaths occurring, including my own.

Chapter 2

The day wore on as witnesses answered questions from both the prosecution and the defense. The prosecution used a 72" screen with a sophisticated PowerPoint presentation to present the details of their case. The screen was so big it blocked out the defense table. I objected because I couldn't even see what the jury was watching. The judge finally called a short recess so I could be moved to see what everyone was watching.

Soon the stand was taken by all the detectives who had interviewed me, my friend John, Sara, several people I had never seen before who were involved in assessing Juan's crime scene, and Carrie's step-dad, who was a municipal judge in Pocatello.

Before Carrie herself took the stand, the prosecution did an excellent job of discrediting her. This is why her step-dad was flown all the way from southern Idaho: to let the jury know that Carrie had lied in the past.

To my surprise and relief, that is also why the Mexican drug dealer Magania was there. The prosecution flew him all the way from Pocatello to ask him two questions. "Has Carrie lied to get what she wanted?" The answer was "Yes."

"Do you find it difficult to trust what she says?" Again the answer was "Yes."

"Thank you, Mr. Magania. You may step down," the prosecution ended.

I was relieved to know that he wasn't taking the stand against me. This Mexican gangbanger, who had almost shot me and had told me he had been to prison several times, was now telling the jury how dishonest Carrie was. It didn't make sense to me, but then, a lot of things during the trial didn't make sense.

As the prosecution dragged on, I found myself asking Holt, "What does this have to do with me?" Almost everything that was being presented was about Juan. The weapon he used to kill two innocent women was shown to the jury, bullets that he had in his pocket, what he had taken from the house. The 9-1-1 call from one of the victims was played for the jury. All these items were directly linked to Juan, not me. I was supposedly being charged for rendering criminal assistance.

It was clear to me -- and I think to everyone -- that I was taking Juan's place on trial. The only glimmer of hope I had would be when Carrie finally took the stand. Yet somehow I knew that she wasn't going to be able to deliver effective testimony. She was too emotionally invested in the events that had transpired to paint a clear picture for the jury.

After watching Scott Johnson's tactics, I knew that he would draw first blood and pour salt on her wounds.

It was a painful scene to watch as he badgered her with condescending questions. She could not finish a sentence without breaking down.

"I can't understand why I am even here. Do you know what that piece of shit did to me? I couldn't leave, he knew where my kids lived and told me he was going to kill them," she managed to say. Then she would start crying so badly that the jury would have to be excused. The jury was excused four times in less than a half hour of testimony.

One thing she did manage to say was, "If it wasn't for Mark I would have been killed." Not that that really helped, but she still managed to say it. She was asked to step down and was escorted out after that statement.

When my friend John was called to the stand, Johnson once again provoked him with his questioning. John, you'll recall, was with me when I had called America's Most Wanted. He was also the one who had found out that Juan Martinez was really James Moran. The morning I called him was when I saw the name "Moran" on his back. That's when John had found him on the "AMW" web site. I never knew until that moment that Juan Martinez was also James Moran. He was also the one who was with me when I called 9-1-1 and told the dispatcher what was going on.

Matthew Nass, one of Sara's cousins, testified Juan and Carrie had been gone from the house for two hours and that I knew he was gone. During closing arguments, prosecutor Angelica McGaha made the point that I never told the authorities, Nass or Sara what was happening, even during that two-hour period of relative freedom.

McGaha also made much of the fact that I didn't tell John Smith about the gunshots I heard in Kennewick or about Juan's coming out of the murder house with a purse. She also cited testimony that I sped away from the murder house at top speed and multiple opportunities he said I had to inform authorities that I was being held hostage.

She said I had had the keys to the BMW during the Kennewick murders and so could have driven away. That was false. I never had the keys in my possession. My lawyer never objected to McGaha's false assertion.

McGaha denied I had suffered at all, making me out to be a greedy drug-user who hung out for the ride so that I could improve the story in this book.

When it was time for us to present our side of the case, Holt argued that duress meant a threat not just to my life but to someone else's -- Carrie's, for example. He conceded I knew about the murder, as the law required him to do if he wanted to use duress as a defense.

"Mark's knowledge about something happening in that house is equal to his knowledge of the murder," Holt said.

So he, too, was still wondering why I was on trial and had a resentment against the way the situation was being handled. After a few questions he was asked to step down and was deemed a hostile witness. The prosecution was scoring major points, and the defense seemed silent and non-combative.

What little glimmer of hope I had that the jury would find me not guilty was extinguished in those three days. The spirit I had held onto in the 18 months I had sat in county jail waiting was gone in the whimpering of Carrie's broken testimony.

"Well, maybe when it's our turn to present our case, things will get better," I told Kathy, who always sat right next to me during the proceedings.

"Yes, don't worry. Kevin will do a good job. You're in good hands," she assured me.

I felt like Holt wasn't objecting enough or paying close enough attention to what was going on -- especially when I had to interrupt the proceedings to see what was being watched. I felt we were just going through the motions to get an official guilty verdict from the jury.

Court usually ended around 4:00 in the afternoon. The jury was excused, the court officers put the cuffs back on me and I was escorted back to changing rooms. I put my county blues back on and was sent back to the cell.

The inmates in my cell always asked me how it went. "So how'd your lawyer do today, Red?" asked J-Swiss, a Gangster Disciple (GD) from Philly.

"A little like yesterday, Swiss -- shitty. I don't even know why we're dragging this on." I told him.

"Yeah, Red, you're getting railroaded for sure, but from the sound of it you're lucky to be alive," he said, trying to find the positive in it all.

I tried to remain hopeful as I tossed and turned the night away. At 6:45 a.m. I got breakfast in a sack, with 10 minutes to eat and be ready for court. Today would be the conclusion of the prosecution's case and the beginning of our defense.

Dressed in some hand-me-down clothes an inmate had given me, I was cuffed again and brought to the courtroom. I only had one witness to call: Jay Jackman. This was the forensic psychologist who had interviewed me in Benton County Jail. We planned on mainly telling my story through him, hoping the jury would interpret it better than coming from me.

He took the stand around 9:00 am Thursday morning, Holt began to ask him about his credentials. It took 10 minutes to tell the jury all of his qualifications. A graduate of Stanford University, he had passed the bar exam and had an M.D. degree too. It was actually too much. It was too impressive and gave the impression that he was a paid witness, even though I was an indigent inmate without one dollar on my inmate account.

The questions were endless, as were the objections. Sidebar after sidebar, we finally made it to lunch time. Jackman's voice was perfectly pitched, consoling and very calm. As he told my story and gave the jury a description of my mental health conditions, the courtroom was serene and silent. This was my best day so far.

The prosecution also keyed in on Jackman's lengthy qualifications. Johnson was really exploiting this element. “So Mr. Jackman, you’re a lawyer, a psychologist [sic] and a forensic specialist? Is there anything you don’t do?” he asked sarcastically. Again, very effective. He basically discredited our star witness. During the cross-examination he told Jackman that he sounded like a dime-store novelist.

Finally Jackman was asked to step down. He had spent several hours on the stand and never once lost his temper. A very professional and keynote witness for the drowning defense.

I kept studying the jury looking for a friendly face, a face that was silently saying, “He’s not guilty of helping this fugitive escape prosecution.” I thought the woman in the second row, juror number 7, had that type of look, but of course nothing is for sure in these matters.

I tried to look calm, sympathetic and confident while sitting at the defense table day after day. The jury is constantly staring over at the table looking for clues or body language that might help them make their decision. It was like we were in the world series of poker.

Tomorrow I would be taking the stand. A very risky choice, but Holt suggested I take the stand so the jury could get to know me. I was nervous but felt I could make a good impression and let the jury know what horrors I had been subjected to. Holt and Kathy tried to coach me as best as they could, but I knew the prosecution would do its best to discredit me and bring up my past.

This was our last resort and I planned on just being honest and trying not to let my emotions, anger in particular, cloud my responses. I figured the truth would set me free.

I went back to my cell with mixed emotions. I was feeling a bit excited because I knew that this whole thing was coming to an end. Good or bad, it didn't really matter just as long as it was over. I could find relief in that. I was feeling scared and alone as well. No one would ever really know how bad it was for Carrie and me except for us. It seemed pointless to even try describing the situation to people with no comprehension of the world I lived in. But I was sure going to try.

Friday was upon us. It was my big day. "Just be yourself and tell the jury what happened," I was telling myself. I was doing anything I could do to stay calm. The only advantage I had was that I knew the prosecution was going to try baiting me into becoming angry and looking guilty.

The jury was summoned, and Holt called me to the stand. I told myself, "Stay calm and look confident but not too confident; look pleasant but not happy; look humble but not too humble."

The questions began and the objections started. Every time I would start to tell the story the prosecution would object.

"Objection. The defendant cannot sit there and tell us a story. He has to stick with the question," Johnson would shout out.

The constant needling was very effective. My story was broken and hard to follow. There were so many crucial parts that were left out. Each time I would try to fill in the blanks and explain why this or that happened, the prosecution would object. It got to the point where I just wanted to give up and leave the stand.

Finally I got through it. It was a long and counterproductive event that could have been done better if the right questions were asked. I felt Holt did his best. Still, my testimony did not make things better, as I had hoped.

As a reader you have heard the whole story. As a juror, you would have heard a quarter of what happened. This lack of facts in this case would be a pivotal point for the jury.

There was not enough time to fit in closing arguments and a deliberation that day, so I would be spending another long weekend in the Spokane County Jail. The closing arguments and deliberation would be held over till Monday.

Two full days of worry of the worst kind. No sleep, and my hair started falling out in patches. My anxiety was making me physically ill, and I couldn't eat. I felt like I was strung out again and there was no cure. Only the verdict could bring me relief -- or perhaps more resentment.

I was trying not to marinate in self-pity and fear that weekend. Finally the weekend ended and it was time to face a jury of my peers. There was no one on the jury from the same decade as me, let alone my age.

I dressed in street clothes once again. I felt a glimmer of hope that maybe I wouldn't have to take them off this time. I was so sick of wearing clothes that weren't mine -- hard plastic slippers, and who knows how many people had worn the underwear I had to put on.

I had gotten to know the two officers who escorted me to the courtroom every morning and asked them what they thought, since they had to sit through the whole trial.

"You're lucky to be alive," one of them said. "I think you were just at the wrong place at the wrong time, but who knows? The jury might let you go."

America's Most Wanted was there, along with some local newspaper reporters. As always, the prosecution side of the court room was full and my side was empty.

It was time for closing arguments. I noticed a Walmart bag on our table with some magic markers in it. There was also a giant note pad with blank white paper laying on the table.

The jury entered the room, and it was go time. The jury was told what stage we were in and what was about to happen. The prosecution had its projector and a computer with a PowerPoint presentation to make its final points. It took them about an hour to get through the well orchestrated presentation. It was quite impressive.

During closing arguments, the state pointed out that by employing the duress defense, I was essentially agreeing that I was guilty of rendering criminal assistance but that I should not be convicted because I had a complete defense. The State agreed it still had to prove rendering criminal assistance beyond a reasonable doubt, but it focused during closing arguments on attacking my duress defense. Not surprisingly, my own attorney focused during closing arguments on supporting that defense.

The State relied most heavily on the section of the duress-defense statute that says, "The defense of duress is not available if the defendant intentionally or recklessly placed himself in a situation where it was probable that he would be subject to duress." Tucker "had plenty of time to figure out, 'How am I going to get away from this person?'"

Angelica McGaha, a deputy prosecuting attorney, argued to the jury on December 5, 2006: "It is only him that is responsible for putting himself in that car with James Moran."

McGaha defined recklessness as "knowing and disregarding a substantial risk that a wrongful act may occur, and the disregard of such risk is a gross deviation from conduct a reasonable person would exercise in the same situation." She asked rhetorically, "would a reasonable person stay in that car" with Moran? "Would a reasonable person have asked for help?" She concluded, "A reasonable person would not put themselves [sic] in this position."

Then it was our turn. My lawyer was short and had a very distinct voice that you either resonated with or cringed at. I was a cringer, though again I am sure he was doing his best.

He set up an easel and placed the white paper pad on it. Then he grabbed the magic markers and began to draw out our closing argument's topics.

"To say that Mark, when he agreed to give this individual a ride, somehow makes him responsible for this whole event is ludicrous," Holt argued. "James Moran took advantage of two people who had an addiction. And because of that addiction, he was able to manipulate them and control them."

He continued, "Is Mark a hero? I think Mark was trying to survive." At a certain point in the trip, "Carrie and Mark believe that everything has changed and they are no longer free to go." After the murders occurred, "There's so much information out there they are trying to process, it's difficult to see what they can and cannot believe. . . . "

"It's very important that you limit this case down to exactly what it is: transportation from 2:23 in the afternoon to their arrival in Portland August 1. From the time they were murdered in Kennewick until the time he called 911 is 74 hours. That's a pretty fast turnaround in law enforcement. That's faster resolution than we have on most TV shows."

Mark asked John Smith to check out Moran online even earlier than that, bringing the total time elapsed after the murder to less than 48 hours, Holt argued.

"What we really have to decide is simply this: was it reasonable for Mark to refuse to drive from the Moreno home to Portland on August 1, 2005?" If they hadn't, he continued, "we'd never know who murdered the Morenos, and there would be several unsolved murders in Oregon where they find a red-headed young male and a young female."

The State, as usual, had the last chance to speak to the jury before it retired to deliberate.

"For counsel to have the audacity to paint Mark Tucker as a hero is almost too much," Johnson said. "That man's no hero, and he's not the victim. This is not a case in which your verdict will be difficult. If he truly believed he was a hostage, as he said, he had time and time again to put an end to it, but he didn't. And why? Because he was greedy, narcissistic and a dope fiend. This was going to be his chance to make money. That's what the evidence shows."

At this point I really wanted to just stand up and say "You know what, folks? We're just going to forfeit. Clearly we are not going to win, and this is now far beyond the ridiculous stage. Magic markers, people, that's how were doin' it. I know you are all impressed by my lawyer's stick figures but we're just going to throw in the towel."

Obviously I refrained from carrying out my thoughts, but it was difficult to watch as this presentation unfolded. After Holt's stellar performance, the jury was given instructions.

The instructions to my jury -- the only law they are supposed to consider -- summarized that statute as follows:

Instruction No. 7. A person commits the crime of rendering criminal assistance in the first degree when, with intent to prevent, hinder or delay the apprehension or prosecution of a person who he knows has committed or is being sought for murder in the first degree and/or robbery in the first degree, he provides such person with transportation.

The court then restated in a separate instruction the requirements for conviction:

Instruction No. 12. To convict the defendant of the crime of rendering criminal assistance in the first degree, each of the following elements of the crime must be proved beyond a reasonable doubt:

1, that on or about the 1st day of August, 2005, the defendant rendered assistance to another person by, (a), providing that person transportation;

2, that the person to whom the defendant rendered assistance had committed or was being sought by law enforcement officials for murder in the first degree and/or robbery in the first degree;

3, that the defendant knew that the person had committed or was being sought for that crime;

4, that the defendant acted with intent to prevent, hinder or delay the apprehension or prosecution of that person; and

5, that the said act or acts occurred in the State of Washington.

If you find from the evidence that each of these elements has been proved beyond a reasonable doubt, then it will be your duty to return a verdict of guilty.

Finally, the court told the jury about the defense of duress. It instructed them:

Instruction No. 14. Duress is a defense to a criminal charge if:

(a), the defendant participated in the crime under compulsion by another who by threat or use of force created an apprehension in the mind of the defendant that in case of refusal, the defendant or another person would be liable to immediate death or immediate grievous bodily injury; and

(b), such apprehension was reasonable upon the part of the defendant; and

(c), the defendant would not have participated in the crime except for the duress involved.

The defense of duress is not available if the defendant intentionally or recklessly placed himself in a situation in which it was probable that he would be subject to duress.

The burden is on the defendant to prove the defense of duress by a preponderance of the evidence. "Preponderance of the evidence" means that you must be persuaded considering all of the evidence in the case that it is more probably true than not.

Of greatest interest to the jury would be whether I had had the requisite intent to prevent or delay Juan's apprehension and whether -- or when -- I knew he had committed a crime. Apart from those questions, was I under duress, so that conviction was legally impermissible? (I learned later that Miller had initially considered charging me and Carrie with murder but lacked sufficient evidence.)

Chapter 3

I was escorted to a concrete room with no chair and no bench. It was about 5' x 5', much smaller than a normal cell. There I stood and then sat and then paced the three steps it took to get to the other side. The committee in my head went back and forth.

“You're going to prison. No, you’ll be getting out today. I have five felonies, which makes my sentencing range 18-24 months, and I’ve already done that, so either way, guilty or not, I'll be getting out." My thoughts were bouncing around like a pinball.

After about three hours, the officer unlocked the door and told me the jury had come to a decision. "Thank God!" I said as he put the cuffs back on me. We made our way back to the courtroom, and my anxiety level shot back into the danger zone.

I took a seat next to Holt. He looked a bit nervous as well. The judge summoned the jury and they walked in the room one by one. I tried to make eye contact with each one but they all had their heads down. Not a good sign. It is said that if a juror makes eye contact with you then the chances are they are going to have a not guilty verdict. No one even looked in my direction. People have been trying to read juries for as long as the system has been in existence, but I would have bet all my chips on "guilty."

The judge asked the delegated spokesman if they had reached a verdict. "Yes, we have, your honor," he responded and gave the bailiff the paper.

The judge read it and asked juror number one, "How do you find the defendant?" Juror number one was a female, and she stood with a bit of hesitation. My toes began to curl and the courtroom fell silent. "Guilty," she said.

That word reverberated through my head and my heart sank. The other side let out a little "whoop whoop." It was over. Each juror stood and said "guilty." I had to hear that word 12 times. Each time it sent a chill down my spine.

The jury had deliberated just over three hours in deciding, on January 18, 2007, that I was guilty of rendering criminal assistance by helping Moran carry out the murders of Linda and Danielle Moreno.

After that was done, the prosecution stood and said, "Now we will move into the sentencing stage." Another jury-instruction pamphlet was passed out to all the jurors and they began to read them as the prosecution explained what was to be done now.

"We feel that the nature of the crime and Mr. Tucker's past criminal history warrants an exceptional sentence. We the state feel that Mr. Tucker should be given the maximum sentence. His sentencing guidelines only have a range of 18 to 24 months, which he has already spent in custody, so as it stands he would be released right after this trial."

"We appreciate the jury's time, and I know this isn't normal procedure, but we would ask the jury to deliberate one last time on this matter" Johnson humbly requested.

The jury was excused once again and I was cuffed and brought back into the dungeon. This time the jury was only out for about an hour. Again not a good sign. Confusion and anger swirled around in my head as I took my seat next to my lawyer. I was praying for a reprieve on this one but there was another softer voice in my head that was ready for the worst and ready to go to prison.

Just as I suspected, the jury voted for an exceptional sentence. This meant that I could be given the maximum sentence the state could impose for a Class C felony -- 60 months in prison and a $10,000 fine.

The sentencing date was set over for late January of 2007, and I was on my way back to Benton County Jail. I had a good three weeks to sit in the jail before I had to face the judge one more time.

I knew that if I hadn't been strung out on heroin, homeless and broke, I would have never accepted a sketchy proposition like the trip to the Ozarks. I made a self-centered choice for an empty promise. I never got any money and ended up paying for most of the trip myself. I almost lost my life and put my family in harm's way. There was no excuse for making such a foolish choice.

I do know I did my best to bring Juan's terror to an end. I had no control over his actions, and when you're staring down the barrel of a cocked gun, things seem to change. Especially when the guy holding it has no problem pulling the trigger.

Given Juan's history, along with the evidence presented from both the defense and prosecution, it's clear that he was fully capable of murder. I was not confident enough to forcefully try disarming him. Nor was I willing to run off and leave Carrie to die. If I had chosen that route, and he wasn't killed by the police and didn't kill himself, I knew the threats he had made about my family would have been carried out.

Those three weeks went by slow and methodically. I was put in the DOC (Department of Corrections) pod, locked down in a single-man cell 21 hours a day. This is when I spent hours writing and reflecting. I finished a lot of this book in that time.

I prepared a short speech for the court. I ended up throwing it away, though. I knew there were no words that could ease the minds of Juan's victims. My ego really wanted to let the court know that I couldn't have prevented any murders and I did my best to bring the whole thing to an end. How could I have helped Juan avoid prosecution if I'm the one who brought the police to him?

The sentencing guidelines prescribed 29 months as the maximum for rendering criminal assistance. But the jury had decided that my past convictions should be considered in the sentencing decision, something that normally wouldn't happen except that I had so many of them.

That raised the permissible sentencing range to a minimum of four years, three months and a maximum of five years. Judge Robert G. Swisher, of the Benton (Washington) County Superior Court -- the same judge who had presided at my trial -- chose the maximum sentence, as requested by the prosecutors.

I was sentenced to 60 months in the state penitentiary, with a $62,000 "special-cost" fine and 24 months of community custody upon release. Then the judge asked if I had anything to say.

My words were slow and humble. I briefly expressed my sympathy for the loss and took responsibility for accepting Juan's offer. And just like that, it was over.

The judge signed the judgment and I was escorted back to my cell and was on my way to prison. Almost two years of wondering what my fate would be. Pacing in a cell, walking endless circles around the day room, writing, reading and stressing. This chapter was finally over. Now I would be exposed to another kind of stress, a new cell, and a new day room to pace the years away in.

You know you've been upgraded to a whole new level of security when the guards are now holding AR-15 assault rifles while you walk to the bus from the jail to the penitentiary. Ankles handcuffed, wrists cuffed together to a chain strapped around your waist fastened with a master lock. You have to walk like a penguin or the cuffs on your ankles will dig into your ankle and you'll fall.

You're not allowed to take any personal items with you on the chain bus. No pictures, no letters, no papers. So of course I was immediately asked to get rid of the 200 pages of this book that I had brought with me.

"Mr. Tucker, you can't take all this shit. What are you thinking?" the guard asked me.

"Oh, no, sir. See, this is my appeal, and these are all notes from my trial," I said frantically, knowing he was about to throw away almost two years of writing. The guard started reading some of the pages and threw them in my property bag.

"Sounds like a bunch of shit to me, Tucker, but I'll let you have it when you get to Shelton." That was a close call but the book survived.

Six grueling hours shackled and cold, we traveled over the cascade mountains back to my side of the state to the receiving units (R-units) in Shelton , Washington, where we were stripped again and given grey jumpsuits, a sack lunch and a prison I.D. My new identity was inmate 711171, a guest of Washington State Department of Corrections.

They lined us up like cattle and moved us through the process. It was packed and chaotic. Most everyone was tattooed from head to toe and affiliated with a gang. The tattoos gave distinct clues of what "set" (gang or neighborhood) they were from. The prison guards yelled at everyone to quiet down so they could give out our new addresses.

I was sent to R-3 along with several other inmates. We were all dispersed to different areas of the lower receiving units (the lower R's). I spent about a month in the lower R's and then transferred to the upper R's. I spent eleven weeks in R-5 and awaited my classification.

This was actually worse than county, and the time in my cell was chipping away at my sanity. The highlight of my R-unit experience was when I was walking to chow one day and from behind me I heard, "Dude! that's him. I swear it's him."

I turned to the person, preparing for a fight.

"Hey, is your name Mark Tucker?" the guy asked me.

"Yeah, what's up?" I asked, wondering where this was going.

"Ah, man, John Walsh put you on blast last night. You didn't watch 'America's Most Wanted'? " he asked, shaking his head in disbelief.

"No. What happened?" I said as my ego started jumping up and down, jockeying for center stage.

"They were talking about how you drove the getaway car in a murder and claimed that you were a hostage. It was the 'ten minutes of shame,' bro," he told me. "They had some actor playing you. He didn't look anything like you, though."

"Wow, yeah, that was me." I paused trying put together how they were able to re-enact something they never witnessed. "That sucks that they said they weren't going to air anything. I refused to sign their contract but I guess they did it anyway."

"Yeah they did you dirty. They made it look like you helped big time!" he finished as we parted ways to different housing units.

Salt on the wound, I thought to myself. It didn't even matter anymore, but I still felt like I was getting raked over broken glass.

Chapter 4

Finally, I was classified to my mother institution (your first prison), Airway Heights, which is just outside of Spokane, Washington. Just when I started to get into a routine, they yarded me up and shipped me back across the mountains to the same county I had my trial in.

This place was huge and way newer looking than the R-units. I went through the same routine as at Shelton. Stripped, given another prison I.D. but no jumpsuit this time. They actually gave me clothes. It looked like they had just cut some legs out of a cardboard box but they were better than the orange jumpsuit.

I was assigned to the long-term minimum unit (L-unit). As you get off the bus you're screened by the prison classification. The high-profile inmates know who you are and what you're there for. The biggest thing is if you're a north sider or a south sider. These are the biggest Mexican gangs up there. Put simply, they hate each other and it's "on site," meaning no matter where you are, when you see an opposing gang member, you're fighting right there, right then.

I don't want to get into prison life too much, but I can tell you that, in a blink of an eye, a life can be taken, along with dignity, respect and sanity. It's a hard life and this was my first time down. I was fearful of the unknown and walked with caution.

One thing I knew I had to do was go straight to the "shot caller" for the 18th Street Gang, the "key holder" (the leader who has final say in all missions). It wouldn't be too long before they knew I was there. I knew they would want to deal with me straightaway. I just wasn't sure if they wanted to kill me or just beat me into oblivion. I told on their homeboy "The Grizz," and I was sure they wanted retribution.

I'm not a tough guy, but I had to make my stand and handle the situation or walk the mainline (when general movement occurs within the prison) in fear. You get tested in your first couple days. If you fail and get a "jacket" (a label) of being soft, you're going to live a miserable existence.

After I had gone through orientation I was "paper checked"(a request to see your charges) by a neutral, well respected "white boy"(no gang affiliation but will side with the whites), who asked to see my judgment and sentence (J&S). This is a list of every felony you've ever been charged with, including the one you're in on. This is a sure way for someone to see if all your crimes are "solid" (no sex crimes or weird charges). Mine were all drug crimes except for the current charge.

But this person heard that I had told on somebody and got them killed. I had collected all the newspaper articles about my charge in case these circumstances arose. I explained my situation and he agreed I had done the right thing.

I also told him my plan to go to the 18th Street Gang shot-caller and tell him who I was and what happened. Roach, the white boy who had paper-checked me, told me that a guy named Crow "held the keys to the car" (was the leader of the gang, or keyholder) and that he would be in the "big yard" (outside recreation area) that afternoon.

Everything in prison is a hierarchy. The entire prison is divided up into territory, including even showers, phones and tables. Each territory belongs to a different gang.

No attacks can be carried out or drug deals made without the proper protocol. If they're in a gang, blacks don't associate with whites unless given permission -- segregation and racial profiling are still alive and well in prison. All murders and attacks must be cleared with the keyholder.

This was my time. I was ready to fight for my life. If this was my day to die, so be it. I had been through too much to stop living now. It is much better to die on your feet than to live a life of quiet desperation. I had no back up, I didn't know anybody and didn't really care. I was so motivated by fear that it didn't make much difference if I was alone or not.

"L-unit! Big yard!" a voice boomed through the intercom. My heart raced as I pushed through the hundreds of inmates rushing for the field. There was a giant wall that stood about 18 feet tall and 50 feet wide that everyone played hand ball on. This is where the south siders hung out. I approached a fairly large group of Hispanics, tattooed and wearing creased shorts and white socks that went up to their knees. I saw "18th Street" tattooed on a couple of their backs.

"Well, this is it" I said out loud. I swallowed hard and moved into their area.

There are always a couple "soldiers" (younger gang members) "keeping point" (on the look-out for guards or any threats). One thing about prison: your awareness needs to be at an all-time high. Every day you're walking with wolves, and you can't let your guard down for one second or you can wind up dead or maimed and not even see it coming.

I was immediately surrounded and a circle started to form around me when I got too close.

"What's up, homes? You lost or something?" his voice was confrontational and alerted some of the O.G.'s of the gang.

Now they came over to see what was up.

"What's up, white boy? You need somethin' or what?" the older one asked as he positioned himself right in front of me. Tattoos of clowns and gang graffiti covered his whole body all the way around his neck and up to his face. I looked at him with all the confidence I could muster.

"Yeah, my name is Mark Tucker. I was the one who was with Grizz when he shot himself." I said scanning my surroundings waiting to be attacked from all sides. Gang members usually come at you four or five deep. No movement came, though. So I continued. "Is Crow here?" I asked.

The circle opened up a bit and a well built, sleeved out (arms covered with ink), brown-skinned middle-aged Mexican looked me up and down.

"Yeah that's me, and I already know who you are, white boy. You got a lot of guts coming up in here like this! " he said as he casually looked around the big yard.

I said, "Look, bro, you gotta understand that your dude lost his mind. I was just giving him a ride and it turned into a hostage situation. He took this other girl hostage from Idaho and…"

"Look, Rojo," he cut me off. "That's what they call you ,right? I know what happened. I know that you called 9-1-1 and Grizz shot himself before they could get to him."

The circle started to get a little tighter and I knew it was coming. "I know you told on our homeboy and caught a charge for it," he laughed "Ain't that some shit, Dreamer?" Crow nodded to his partner. "Yeah, homes, that's some funny shit. Only in Benton county," he replied.

"I don't know what else I could have done," I managed to say.

"We know Grizz was losing it and he shouldn't have killed those people in Kennewick. He made the whole scene hot and we can't afford those types of missed moves on our team," Crow said. He knelt down and two of his soldiers stood on either side of him. "This is what I'm going to do, Rojo. I'm going to give you a pass. Grizz cost us a lot of dope and money. He was getting to be a liability and now we don't have to take him out." He paused. "He took himself out!" he said with a grin.

I was a bit taken aback and relieved that I wasn't going to get "taken off mainline" (beaten up and put in protective custody).

"Alright, so we're cool?" I asked, making sure they were being serious. The circle dispersed and Crow just gave me a nod.

"Holy shit" I said to myself as I walked away. Some other inmates were watching the scene and looking at me wondering what that was all about. My heart was still racing, my hands were shaking and it was difficult to slow my breathing down.

I made it back to my cell and fell onto my bed with a huge sigh of relief. My biggest fear was now gone. I could do my time knowing that they were not seeking revenge for that incident.

On March 28, 2007, Judge Swisher refused to shorten my five-year sentence. I had filed my motion February 12, 2007, asking to change my sentence. The judge said I could pursue the matter further in an appeal if I wanted. I did appeal the length of my conviction, but not the conviction itself.

Swisher did cut my attorney's fees to $600, from $3,261, but I was still left with a legal bill that included more than $37,000 in expert-witness fees and investigators. The bill originally totaled more than $41,000.

On May 1, 2008, the Washington Court of Appeals rejected my appeal of my 60-month sentence. In a six-page ruling, it said I had presented no evidence my offender score -- my criminal history -- was incorrect. It said Judge Swisher had acted perfectly reasonably and within the law when he sentenced me to the extended period of 60 months.

Six months after my encounter with Crow, I was transferred to a camp where I was put on a fire crew for the Department of Natural Resources. I did another 18 months there and was shipped to Tacoma work release (Progress house). I finished my time there and was eventually released to a clean and sober house on Hilltop, in Tacoma, WA.

Carrie

Carrie pled guilty to first-degree rendering criminal assistance and, in a plea bargain not offered to me, was sentenced to six months. I never got a chance to talk to her about what had happened. She's been imprisoned at least once since then for possession of meth. We're not in touch. I sometimes think about her and wonder how she's doing.

A Message of Hope

I hit the street with a new-found ambition to succeed. It took me a while to re-acclimate to society. After being locked up for five years, it takes more than a minute to get used to cars, trees, people in plain clothes and freedom. I remember going into Safeway to buy a toothbrush. I ended up having a panic attack from all the choices. Red ones, green ones, square head, round head. It was too much. I just left the store. In prison you get one toothbrush. I was feeling a bit more relaxed after a month or so.

I had several goals and was well on my way to achieving them. I had already landed a good job while I was in work release, painting ships and ship parts down at the tide flats.

I was saving money and staying off heroin. But I was drinking every chance I got and did not have a plan or goal for recovery. I was on community custody (parole) and had to take urinalyses (UA) randomly several times a month. I didn't have a lot of room for error.

After I had been out for about two months I got my license back, bought a car with insurance and received a raise at my work. I was doing OK but heading for disaster. Too much money and no life skills equals calamity for me. I had no defense against old friends, old playgrounds and the only lifestyle I knew: drugs, alcohol and desperation. I was relying on self-will. Even though I hadn't shot any dope since I had been out, I was unconsciously looking for a window of opportunity to do it, just one last time.

That day came and within a month after saying "I'll just do it once," I had lost my job, my car got repossessed, I got kicked out of the clean-and-sober house and got arrested for a dirty UA.

Back to the streets I went. I had made it about nine months before I was arrested for another possession of heroin. A piece of heroin, maybe ten dollars worth, had somehow got stuck on a $20 bill in my pocket. As DOC was searching me for a failure to report, they took my money and started counting it and two of the bills were stuck together. The sticky substance field-tested positive and off I went. I was sentenced to 24 months in prison.

This whole time, the book you are reading was stowed away in a back pack. I always tried to keep it in a safe place, but when you're living a lifestyle like mine, you never know where you're going to end up. During this time it fell into the hands of an angry girlfriend, who tore it up into hundreds of little pieces. It took me two weeks to tape it all back together. It had been lost in a storage unit and accidently thrown away. After each mishap it would somehow find its way back to me.

I ended up going back to prison three more times after the James Moran case, each time for drugs. I was hopeless, strung out and could not quit, no matter what the consequences were.

I remember sitting in my car one morning in front of a gated community. I was trying to "kick" (quit heroin) and I was in my third day of withdrawal. The worst day. A girl I knew had given me the code for the gate and had been wanting me to score for her for the past two days. My stereo was cranked with Rancid singing "Dope-sick Girl." I was on my second Four Loko malt-liquor drink, with tears dripping from my face, wallowing in a sea of self-pity. My willpower was fleeting as I struggled against putting the code in.

If I go in there, I'm going to score for her and get another dirty UA and lose my car, my house, my job and everyone's trust, I thought. A half hour went by before I made the decision to once again give my life away. I put the code in and went in. Three days later I was on my way back to prison.

What is wrong with me? I would ask myself. I was in a pitiful state of incomprehensible demoralization. Every time I would get out of prison I would set all these goals. Car, house, career, girlfriend and social status. Recovery was never on the top of my list. I felt that I had enough sense not to do the same thing again, but every time I would start doing well, I would sabotage myself and get high. Many times I put a gun in my mouth wanting to die, wanting to be free from the bondage of myself.

My thinking was the problem. Lack of power was my downfall. I had no control. I ended up in the psychiatric ward my last time to prison and saw no hope in sight.

Forty-two misdemeanor convictions and 11 felonies later, I was given the gift of desperation. I was in the R-units for my fourth time, literally two months after just leaving there. I hit my knees and begged my Creator, whom I choose to call God, for an exit strategy. I had exhausted all other paths and the only one left for me was a god of my understanding.

I dove into personal-development books, spiritual books, as well as health and fitness books. The one book that I really started to study was Alcoholics Anonymous. It was my autobiography. I started going to meetings. I started to build up accountability in my life. One thing I never thought I could do was quit drinking. I was willing to let go of the drugs but alcohol was my crutch.

I was learning about myself more and more each day. It is said that one who tries to understand the universe usually understands nothing; but one who understands himself will understand the universe.

One thing I knew about myself was that I could not be left to my own devices. I could not trust myself. Every time I would get out of prison with my forty dollars "gate money" (money the state gives you to get home) I would go to the first store I saw, buy two or four Lokos and drink them in the bathroom, hop back on the bus and head to Tacoma.

By that time, my judgment was impaired and I would end up getting high to suppress the anxiety of freedom. I knew that I had to report within 24 hours upon release to take a UA, so I just wouldn't report, or I would wait till I took a UA, then get high. I never took the time to design a better way to live.

My intentions were to just do it once, but obviously that never worked. A couple months later, I would be right back where I was before I went to prison the last time: strung out and hopelessly miserable in my skin. My ego had me hostage and I became complacent, even addicted, to suffering. That's all I knew. My life was driven by guilt and shame. It was time to make a change or die at my own hand.

What it all boiled down to for me was that I wasn't willing to let go of my old ideas. I wasn't willing to do whatever it took to build a life around recovery. I honestly didn't even think recovery was possible.

I had three months before I was to be released and I was determined to make a change. So my exit strategy came in the form of several men who were bringing the message of hope into the prison twice a week. Their message was conveyed from a blue book called Alcoholics Anonymous. Their stories were similar to mine and the common discomfort that we shared seemed to be the key element that bound us together.

I got every phone number I could from the volunteers who were bringing the meetings into the prison and started to build the accountability I needed. I had to bridge the gap between prison and society. I knew that I could not fight my addiction alone.

On April 1, 2013, eight years after the Juan incident, I was being released from prison for the fourth time. I had taken all the precautionary steps to defend me from myself. My older brother Allen was meeting me in the parking lot of the prison. I had several phone numbers of volunteers I was going to call as soon as I got to Olympia, Washington.

Some had offered to take me to my first outside meeting. I left no grey areas for me to wonder off into.

I asked a woman standing out front if I could use her phone to call my brother and let him know I was out. He said he was on his way. I went into a 12-step meeting that was already in progress and took a seat with a sigh of relief. I was safe from myself in here.

Twenty five minutes later my brother showed up, and we left Tacoma in the rear-view mirror. That night I called one of the volunteers who had given me his number and he came and picked me up from my brother's. He took me to a men's meeting and told me to get a sponsor.

I was far outside my comfort zone. I felt like it was the first day of high school. Awkward and intimidated, I took my seat and scanned the room. "I don't fit in here. But this is my new life," I told myself.

I shook off my fear and approached a large guy with tattoos and steel-toed boots.

I asked him to be my sponsor and he agreed. This would the beginning of my trip into willingness, open mindedness and the elusive virtue of honesty. It brought me to the first step of twelve that would launch me into a journey into self.

In order for the miracle of recovery to take place, I had to have the willingness to change every facet of my life and the way I thought it should be run. I had to let go of my past and all my old ideas absolutely. I had to acquire the proper guidance from people that had gone into recovery before me. I had to remain teachable and open minded.

I didn't focus on the results; I focused on the actions. I started to master the mundane things in my life. Making the bed, exercising, and living in the now. I began to silence the mind (ego) and open my heart (spirit).

I started to realize that I had been suffering from a spiritual malady and I needed spiritual chemotherapy. I needed to stay connected to like-minded people --other people who were in the trenches fighting for a better quality of life and freedom from addiction.

The constant battle against ego was in full swing. I worked through those feelings of indifference and self-centeredness. I surrounded myself with positive people doing positive things.

My life was still full of adversity but I was learning to deal with them without the crutch of drugs and alcohol. I had to go to outpatient twice a week, report to DOC weekly and take random UAs. I had a pending court date for a DUI and had fines that total more than $200,000.

Instead of getting stuck in self-pity I started a gratitude list.

I started writing down all the things I was grateful for. I even took it a step further and started to write down the things that were causing difficulty in my life. It seems crazy to write down that I was grateful for the officer that gave me a DUI, grateful for the Department of Corrections, grateful for the DMV for taking my license and grateful for 18 weeks of outpatient treatment.

One month after I started my gratitude list, things started to get strange. I went to court for a DUI in downtown Tacoma, where I used to run and had accumulated 30 of my 40-plus misdemeanors and seven of my felony convictions. I was armed with letters from my DOC officer, my outpatient counselor and a few people who were in recovery and had reached some worthy social status.

The judge called me to the stand and I made my way through gang members, thugs, prostitutes and dope fiends -- that is, a normal Tacoma courtroom audience. I took my seat at the all-too- familiar defense table and waited for the court to address me.

The judge was studying the computer, looking over my file for a full minute, which is a long time in the courtroom. This is never good.

“Well, Mr. Tucker I have to be honest with you. I was expecting to see someone in his late fifties, maybe even early sixties," the judge said. "Considering your criminal history it’s hard for me to comprehend that you're only 39 years old."

He continued, "What’s even more astonishing is what you’ve done with your life today. I have read you’re DOC file and the report your current officer has filed. Most people with your kind of past never recover. They end up in the system, and then their kids end up in the system and it’s just a revolving door.”

My mind went from, “Oh man, he’s going to really break me off a hefty sentence” to “Man, what’s this guy trying to say. Is this good?”

“Mr. Tucker!” he said. “Could you please tell the court how you, of all people, managed to turn your life around?”

I was taken aback and it took me a second to recover.

“Well, your honor, I was given the gift of desperation. I was tired of waking up every morning in complete bondage and walking around thinking the world was going to cave in and swallow me. I have been shot at, stabbed, held hostage and witnessed the human mind melt down to the point of suicide. But in the end, it was surrender that got me here today. I ceased fighting everyone and everything. I gave myself to a simple program and followed direction from people in the rooms of Alcoholics Anonymous."

I could have gone on but I felt like I had said enough.

The judge sat back up and started typing on his computer.

"OK, Mr. Tucker, this is exactly what the court system tries to accomplish. Very seldom does it happen, but you are proof that people can change. I am dropping the DUI and it looks like you have a few tickets holding up your license up." he paused and looked at me for a second and went back to the computer. "I'm going to take these tickets off your record as well so you can go get your license back today if you'd like. Good luck to you, Mr. Tucker."

I got up in disbelief and noticed all the open mouths in the court room. I wasn't the only one in shock. I immediately went to the DMV and got my license back and rejoiced.

The next day I went to outpatient treatment , and my counselor pulled me into her office before our group started.

"Mr. Tucker, I don't think we can do anything for you here. You're beyond this class and we are going to graduate you -- today."

Again I was in disbelief. I still had 13 weeks to go to finish my treatment. "I've already run this by your DOC officer, and she is fine with you graduating."

Conclusion

Every day, I nurture my recovery like a mother and protect it like a father. I believe all these miracles that have happened to me were through faith in the process followed by unceasing action. Action is what completes the miracle process.

Addiction is an over whelming foe and has cleverly disguised itself in my thoughts and talks to me in my own voice. I continued to feed the parasite whose only goal was to destroy its host -- me -- while the people who loved me were forced to suffer as well. They had to take front-row seats and watch helplessly as I destroyed myself. There were no words or amounts of love that could have saved me. I was the only one who could make the choice to surrender. I was the one who had to believe in something greater than myself, for I had gone beyond the reach of human aid.

For all the helpless onlookers and all the addicts that still suffer I have this message of hope for you: **Recovery is possible**, no matter how far down the scale you have gone. As long as an addict can still draw a breath, there is hope. Never give up this fight, for it takes each of us working together if we want to grow beyond addiction.

For me, the first step toward personal freedom was awareness. I discovered that my suffering was the effect of wrong thought in some direction. This is a clear indication that I was out of harmony with self and my creator. I had to find harmony which I built on respect of self, others and honesty.

By the right choice and true application of my thoughts I began to experience a divine paradox. As always, but not always knowing, I was attracting the equivalent of what I expressed. All along I had been attracting not what I wanted, but what I was. I attracted dishonest people because I was dishonest, I attracted drug addicts and trouble because I was a troubled drug addict.

But now I sit at the opposite end of the spectrum. I am honest in all my affairs, I help others improve their quality of life and I live with humility and gratitude. Therefore the quality of my relationships has grown beyond my expectations and each one of those qualities is given back to me every single day.

My collaboration with other addicts is essential to improving my quality of life in recovery. As I continue to seek the will of my Creator, His presence in my life becomes more profound. The evidence of His work in my life shows up every day I don't use or take a drink. It seems to me that when we addicts harness the power of faith, we exude enough light to illuminate the world.

The End

Slang glossary

The Blade -- the area of a city where drugs, gangbangers and prostitutes can most easily be found

The Block -- the area where the blade is located

carnal -- brother

chonies -- underwear

dope -- usually refers to heroin, but can also refer to other drugs offered for sale

esé -- dude

hella -- very

get well -- get high

hina -- girl

homes, homie -- homeboy

kibble -- heroin

mija -- little sister or female friend; a woman with whom the speaker has no sexual relationship

novia -- girlfriend

rig -- syringe

Rojo -- Red (nickname)

órale -- Hey

tar -- heroin

teener -- 1-3/4 grams of meth or heroin

ten-piece -- $10 worth of heroin, usually 1/10 of a gram. a common amount to buy

twenty-piece -- $20 worth of heroin

vato -- homeboy

well (adj.) -- high

wife-beater: a tank-top t-shirt

About the Authors

Mark E. Tucker is a graduate of the National Academy Of Sports Medicine as a Certified Personal Trainer. He owns Reach For It Fitness (reachforitfitness.com) and owns and operates Whidbey South Construction, which builds and remodels homes. In Mark's spare time, he helps other addicts achieve sobriety and speaks his message of recovery in jails, detox centers, prisons and fellowship halls around the Northwest.

Dan Richman has written for trade journals in the computer and healthcare industry, for newsletters and analysts, and for the late, great *Seattle Post-Intelligencer*, where he covered business and technology for a decade until the paper's demise. He has written two books and ghost-written a third. He lives on Whidbey Island, Washington.

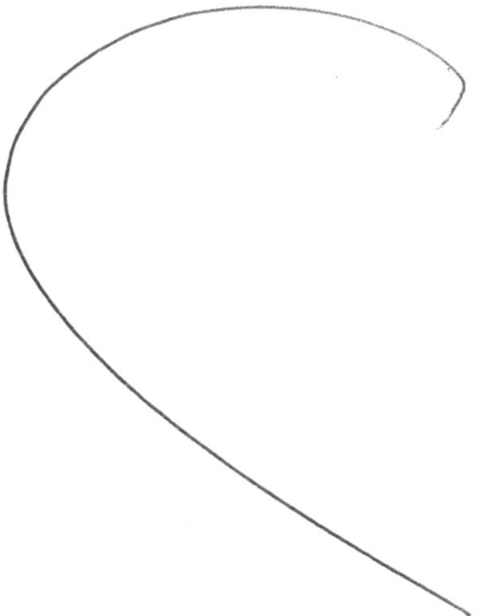

52802787R00128

Made in the USA
Charleston, SC
27 February 2016